A POLITICAL CAMPAIGN:
ECSTASY AND AGONY

DOUG MCFARLAND

A POLITICAL CAMPAIGN:
ECSTASY AND AGONY

iUniverse books may be ordered through booksellers or by contacting:

iUniverse
1663 Liberty Drive
Bloomington, IN 47403
www.iuniverse.com
1-800-Authors (1-800-288-4677)

First published as *Few Are Chosen: A Campaign Memoir*

ISBN: 978-1-5320-8286-3 (sc)
ISBN: 978-1-5320-8308-2 (e)

Print information available on the last page.

iUniverse rev. date: 09/20/2019

PROLOGUE

The apt analogy to a campaign for public office is a ride on an amusement park roller coaster. The candidate, giddy with anticipation, climbs aboard and begins a slow, agonizing grind up a seemingly endless hill. The car pauses at the top of the hill, then gathers speed as it swoops down, up, and around, seemingly ready at any second to leave the tracks. The rider bounces up and down, side to side, forward and backward, again and again thrilled, apprehensive, exhilarated, half-sick, laughing, terrified. At the end, the rubbery-legged passenger rises from the seat physically and mentally exhausted.

This is the story of my marvelous ride campaigning for a seat in the United States Senate. It happened years ago, in the state of Minnesota, but the experiences are true to a candidate and a political campaign today in any of our 50 states.

As with any story of politics, this story is about people. A candidate who can't connect with people might as well not buy a ticket for the ride. Many of the people in these pages remain bright in memory, and others have faded into the mists of time. I describe, as honestly and truthfully as possible, the people who came and went in the campaign. Some will appear wise, or hardworking, or savvy, or loyal, or committed. Others will appear foolish, or cunning, or simpleminded, or devious, or shortsighted.

Truth-telling applies to my actions and thoughts also. I'll tell of my triumphs, and my disasters, honestly. While politics is about people and building coalitions and gathering support, it is also about the candidate. The candidate must have enough self-confidence, ambition, ego, hunger, fire in the belly, or whatever you call it to step forward. Any budding candidate who sits at home waiting for the telephone to ring is soon going to conclude the telephone doesn't work. A political campaign is about stepping forward, not being dragged kicking and screaming into the fray.

This story is not told to advocate a political philosophy or to promote partisan political positions. It happens to be about a Republican, but it could just as well be about a Democrat. This is a story of American politics and American campaigning great and small. It's also about having fun while pursuing a serious purpose. I still laugh at the things wild and wonderful that happened along the campaign trail and hope you will, too.

Along that trail, I picked up a lot of knowledge—ranging from tidbits to wisdom—about people in politics and candidates in campaigns. People say they want honest answers from a politician. Well, they're in here. Some of the answers may produce a knowing nod. More of the answers, I believe, will produce a "wow." I'm not trying to polish my future political reputation or ready a run for the next office. Time has moved onward. So, here's the straight scoop on what a candidate running for office really experiences and really thinks.

I step back from the story occasionally to make an observation or to state a lesson learned. As a professor, I can't seem to help myself. This is not a how-to-do-it book, but it does have some practical tips about politics and campaigning. These observations, lessons, and tips are sprinkled into the story in italics, and many are collected in the final chapter.

I answer the following questions, and many more, while describing my days and months on the campaign trail.

- What don't people know about politicians?
  What's the first question everyone asks a candidate for office? What's the second? What does a candidate first look for upon arriving at a political event? What do incumbent U. S. Senators and aspiring candidates talk about in unguarded

moments? Do politicians have tough skin, or do they bruise easily? How does a person transform from a low-key, ordinary common man or woman into an energetic, high-octane political candidate in a small-town gas station rest room?

- What is life on the campaign trail?

    What's a typical day in the life of a candidate on the trail? Is driving through pitch black midnight with the temperature at 25 below zero to the Icebox of the Nation as much fun as it sounds? Which is more important to a candidate: raising political support or raising money? Why does a politician always seem to be looking for the next hand to shake? How does a candidate work a room? A convention? A parade? When does a candidate need a chaperone? Why do candidates take seriously signs, portents, and omens? Why are politicians always late? Is a campaign harder on the candidate or the candidate's family? Why do so many politicians have bad backs? How does a candidate make daily decisions based on half-truths, guesswork, and rumor while trying desperately to avoid the big mistake? What does a candidate do while traveling in a car between campaign stops? What's a stall warning on a small plane sound like?

- What are some truths about the American political system?

    Why do political parties nominate candidates near the conservative or liberal ends of the political spectrum instead of a centrist who can appeal to both sides? Why do all politicians seem to be liars? What's the practical effect of campaign finance reform laws? Why is Social Security the third rail of American politics? Does a person have to be an extrovert to succeed in politics? Is the statement "money is the mother's milk of politics" true? Why is the national political debate becoming more hostile? How does a political candidate get attention in a sea of public apathy?

- Want a few how-to-do-it tips?

  How can a speaker get up close and personal with an audience? Why shouldn't a candidate eat before speaking? Is memorizing a speech a good idea? Where should a candidate sit at a table full of supporters? What's the best answer to a question about a hot-button issue? When is the better response to a question about an obscure issue to confess ignorance than to open your mouth and remove all doubt? Finally, what's the most important word in the statement "I want to win the right way?"

★ ★ ★ ★ ★

This story begins two years before the general election. The timing was right for me professionally. I was in my eighteenth year of teaching at Hamline University School of Law in St. Paul. With these years of service, teaching awards, and many publications, I could slice time from my familiar Hamline duties to run a campaign.

As much as such a statement is ever possible, the time was right in our family. Mary and I had been married 19 years. She worked part-time and volunteered at church. Our four children—Amy, Stuart, Katie, and Wesley—were all old enough to be in school, ranging from a high school junior down to a third grader.

Mary had always supported my past big ideas, from leaving law practice to try law teaching, to running unsuccessfully for the state legislature, to uprooting our family and moving to Washington, D.C., for two years so I could work for the Chief Justice at the Supreme Court of the U.S. Now comfortably ensconced back in Arden Hills, a northern St. Paul suburb, our life was good.

Then I told Mary I wanted to run for the Senate. From her reaction, I could as well have proposed moving our family to Afghanistan. A private person, she did not at all like the idea of entering public life. Still, she was supportive of this idea too. Later, when we told the kids, they were enthused about the coming adventure. The ride was about to begin.

CHAPTER ONE

Why Are You Running?

The first question anyone asks a political candidate is "Why are you running?" The response "I thirst for power" is obviously no good. Neither is "I like to bask in applause." "I'm committed to public service" is bland. Only a little better would be "I can do better than the folks there." *The first task of any candidate is to craft a suitable answer to the first question. The answer must have both the substance to grab the voter and the patina of truth. It must mix a popular issue or two with a call to action.* "My children and yours will soon be taxpayers, and I want to eliminate the federal budget deficit instead of placing it on their backs" is good, for example. Good, but not the simple, whole truth.

No politician answers the question "Why are you running?" with the simple, whole truth. The unvarnished truth probably is "I really don't know. Something inside I can't explain is driving me to run. I want to do some good, and just feel it's the right thing to do." That's the truth. The decision to run for office is more a subconscious calling than a conscious decision. Abraham Lincoln said his ambition was to achieve the esteem of his fellow citizens; he also said the drive for public office was like a little engine constantly running inside him.

What I can do is identify the exact date of my decision, and what conscious thoughts were kicking around in my head at the time. The date was April 12, two-and-one-half years before the election. The thoughts involved ethics, ambition, the Civil War, and baseball.

Thoughts of ethics involved fellow Republican David Durenberger, at that time the senior Senator from Minnesota. Durenberger had been elected to the Senate three times and was popular enough to have continued for as long as he liked—until he caught himself in a financial ethics scandal and he was publicly reprimanded by the Senate. I liked Durenberger. Most people in Minnesota did. Yet I was upset that he had embarrassed our state and our party. As a Republican concerned with morality and ethics in government, I knew we as a party just plain could not have Durenberger running for us again. The question became who was going to deny him a free ride to re-nomination? No Republican had even given a hint of taking on the sitting Senator. Someone had to do it.

At 46 years old, I still wanted to make a public mark in life and politics was the opportunity. The time to make a mark passes quickly. Campaigning and politics are for the young. An incumbent can hold onto office into old age, yet almost no one past a certain age can realistically make a first run for high office. The campaign is too draining physically and mentally. Voters do not want to vote for a newcomer already showing signs of age. The time was right.

The Civil War worked into my thinking, too. I loved to visit the battlefields, look at the terrain, picture the troop movements, and evaluate the command decisions. The grandeur of the grassy vistas overwhelmed me. At the same time, battlefield visits with thoughts of brave men acting on the stage of history, doing heroic things with their lives, drove me into a sense of insignificance. The days of my life were rolling seamlessly by, class after class, semester after semester. Nothing heroic. Nothing historic. No public mark. Not even an attempt.

All these thoughts came together on April 12. My mother Joy's sudden death four years earlier had started my father Doug Sr. on a slow, four-year decline. When a nurse at the retirement home called to say dad had declined again and couldn't talk, I drove from the Twin Cities to my boyhood home, Sioux Falls, South Dakota, for a weekend visit.

All day Saturday I sat by his bedside, mostly in silence. Sometimes I talked to him about our family, my classes, people he knew, old stories he'd told me, sports teams, the weather. He couldn't respond, but he did seem to understand. Sunday morning again I sat with him.

During these hours, I recalled a conversation the two of us had repeated many times. Dad would tell me that in his youth he had been an outstanding athlete, playing basketball and baseball. I can picture him even now, nodding and smiling as he told his stories. In one, he pitched for a town baseball team. He threw so hard no batter on the other team could even hit a foul ball. "You can't hit what you can't see," said one. Dad would usually end by saying "I could have been in the major leagues."

I would usually respond "Well, why weren't you then?"

"The scouts didn't come here. We never had any opportunities."

"Why didn't you make an opportunity for yourself? If you were that good, why didn't you write to a baseball team and ask for a tryout, or even just buy yourself a train ticket to Florida one spring?"

"People just didn't do that," he always answered. "And I had to go to work to make money."

My dad possessed many wonderful qualities, but I had years earlier realized he could have been endowed with more ambition. His lifetime dream was to be a professional baseball player. He was of the age that he could have pitched to Babe Ruth. Now his dream was reduced to memories of what could have been. All was missed opportunity. He had not tried, even if the result would have been failure.

Sunday morning at his bedside, the decision crystalized. I'm going to run for the Senate. I might get one vote. People might laugh at me and chortle about Don Quixote tilting at windmills. I didn't care. In my old age, I would know I went for my dream.

I took dad's hand and said "I want you to know something. I'm going to run for the U. S. Senate." His eyes grew wide. We looked at each other. He couldn't speak or he probably would have said "People just don't do that."

An hour later, shortly before the time I would need to leave him to drive home to the Twin Cities, dad's hand squeezed my hand tighter and then slowly relaxed. Before I fully realized what was happening, he was gone.

Days and months later, I was thankful to have been with dad at his passing and glad I had told him of my fantastic dream. One vote or thousands, I would follow through on it. Ironically, the modest inheritance from my folks made the dream possible.

Why run for the Senate? Because of a sense of ethical conduct, because ambition and opportunity coincided, because of the Civil War, because my dad never took a train to Florida, and because I felt called. Of course, I never said any of these things to people who asked. I told them I was running because Dave Durenberger couldn't run for us again and I wanted to fight for conservative principles. Those two were true enough, but they were the public answer, not the answer from deep inside.

* * * * *

Like most political spouses, Mary was supportive when I told her, but that's a long way from happy. The dream was mine, not hers. The months that followed did not help. We both learned that politics is harder on the spouse than on the candidate. The political spouse is akin to a parent watching a child at a piano recital or on a ball field. The child is concentrating and warming to the task; the parent's guts are churning with hope and apprehension.

We told no one else. No one would want to hear this impossible dream of a political nobody more than two years before the election. Life went on. Teaching classes. Coaching Little League baseball. A canoe trip chaperoning a church youth group. A family vacation trip. Working for local candidates in that year's election.

Late that summer, I had lunch with a good friend who practiced law in Minneapolis. As usual at one of our lunches, we talked politics. Once again as usual, he expressed his opinion that hidden powers-that-be in the state secretly pull the strings in elections. I didn't tell him that soon I intended to find out.

CHAPTER TWO

Getting To Know You . . . Getting To Hope You Like Me

For the next few months, Mary and I were the only two people who knew of my plan. I was about ready to burst. Outside of a few people in the local Republican Party where we had lived in the Minneapolis suburbs of Golden Valley and Minnetonka, and a few more locals where we now resided in the St. Paul suburb of Arden Hills, I didn't know any party leaders across the state; I'd never even met the state party chair. How does a political unknown start a campaign for any office, let alone a state-wide campaign for the Senate, from scratch?

One person I did know was my district's state senator, Fritz Knaak. A lawyer, a fast-talker, a go-getter, a party activist, a state senate assistant minority leader, and a party spokesman, Knaak was always ready to take on the Democrats—a feisty bantam rooster type of guy. He had a sharp mind and sharp elbows. Knaak owed me for my volunteer work in his latest campaign, and he was not running for re-election, so I figured he would give me the straight story. I asked Fritz to have lunch with me.

When we eventually got down to business, I hesitantly told him of my plan to run for the U.S. Senate and waited for his reaction. I was worried he would erupt with guffaws, and after he'd finally caught his breath choke out "That's the funniest thing I've heard in a long time." Realistically, I expected him to say something along the lines of "Great, Doug. If that's what you want. More power to you. Good luck. Keep me informed."

Knaak's actual reaction surprised and delighted me. His face lit up. He became excited. "Great, Doug," he said. "I can help you a lot."

"Really, Fritz? You can? You think this is realistic?"

"Of course, it's realistic. In fact, I can talk to people for you." He was getting more enthused about my campaign than I was. I was thrilled with this unexpected reaction. Knaak peppered me with questions; one was "Do you know how to pull together a press conference?"

"Well, no."

"I do," he said. "I can get you the room at the state capitol office building where the press likes to go for press conferences. You need to start getting the word out. I can really get this thing off the ground for you."

"Wow. This is great, Fritz. Thank you. Thank you. What should I do next?"

"Wait to hear from me. I'll talk to a few people I know at the legislature and get back to you."

I floated out of the room. This was far beyond my wildest hopes. Maybe I would get more than my own vote after all! Maybe I wouldn't be laughed at as the modern-day Don Quixote of Minnesota.

For the next few days, I spent plenty of time staring at the telephone and willing it to ring. Thursday. Friday. Saturday. Sunday. By Monday, I couldn't wait any longer. I called him.

"Fritz, this is Doug. At our lunch you said you were going to talk with some people about my running for the Senate and get back to me. Have you heard anything?"

"Yeah, I did talk to some people about you running for the Senate."

"And?"

"They all asked me why I'm not running. You know, I'll have to think about it."

Back to the original plan. Call a party leader or activist I had met. Invite the person to have lunch—or just coffee—together. Make a favorable impression. Ask for advice. Ask for names of others to call. Write the advice and names on index cards. Pick up the tab. Go home and call those new names. Campaign by lunch. Politics by retail.

One of the early meetings was with Evie Axdahl, the Minnesota Republican National Committeewoman, and kindly grandmother to just about everyone in the party. We met for midmorning coffee in an ice cream parlor. I gave Evie my usual pitch. I'm running to make sure our party upholds high ethical standards, and to promote conservative issues and values. I'm selling common sense, a good background, a supportive family, and hard work. Having taught at Hamline for nearly 20 years, I can negotiate my teaching schedule to have plenty of time to campaign. I can articulate the Republican message.

All of that may look like pretty thin gruel, but people serious about party politics really want to know four things: are you conservative or liberal, can you carry the party message, are you personally trustworthy, and can you raise money? Two years before the election, the right answers to the first three questions open the door; the fourth answer comes later.

Evie gave me 44 names of party people across the state. I wrote on the note cards furiously. She also told me to spend $500 to join the state party Elephant Club so I could attend their luncheon meetings and meet party donors who had big money. We had hit it off—of course Evie hit it off with everyone. Word filtered back to me within an hour that Evie had called people and told them "We may have found our candidate."

★ ★ ★ ★ ★

Through these days, I was campaigning on the side. My regular job was teaching law at Hamline. Part of the job that year was serving on the faculty hiring committee. The big event of the annual hiring season was the November hiring conference in Washington, D.C.

A conference in Washington was happy serendipity. I flew in early to do a little political business on the trip. When I worked at the Supreme Court, I had met Chuck Heatherly, Director of the White House Fellows, who had since moved to the Heritage Foundation, the influential conservative thinktank. He gave me enough advice to fill three index cards: announce early so the press starts calling for comment, say I don't expect Durenberger to run again, get on the mashed potatoes circuit with a standard speech that requires only the first and last paragraphs to change, and find a couple of issues to ride.

Heatherly also told me to call a man named Morton Blackwell for professional advice on campaign organization and polling. I couldn't wait to get back to the hotel to call, so I decided to dial Blackwell from a pay telephone in Union Station. When Blackwell came on the phone, I said "Hello. I'm Doug McFarland. I'm running for the Senate from Minnesota, and Chuck Heatherly gave me your name and telephone number."

"What was that again?" He could hardly hear me above the background clatter of train announcements, shoeshine stand wisecracks, shopkeepers, and passing tourists.

Louder, I said "My name is Doug McFarland. Chuck Heatherly at Heritage told me to call you. I want to run for the Senate from Minnesota."

"What was that name again?"

"Doug McFarland."

"You want to work in the Senate?"

"No, I'm running for the Senate," I shouted into the telephone.

"From where?"

"Minnesota. It's the Dave Durenberger seat. I don't think he's going to be able to run for us again."

The conversation improved a little from that point. Blackwell told me the run was a real long shot, but he could still remember a young, unknown lawyer named Orrin Hatch sitting across from his desk and telling him he wanted to run for the Senate from Utah. Hatch had become a leader in the Senate. Blackwell said if I wanted to run, I should run. Anything is possible in politics.

★ ★ ★ ★ ★

The day after returning from Washington, I recommenced the campaign by lunch. Steve Knuth and I met at Applebee's. Knuth was young, ruddy-faced, energetic, and politically savvy—an up-and-coming political operative on the make. I tried to sell myself to him. Turned out he was trying even harder to sell himself to me. Knuth was a political consultant looking for his next candidate. He said he wanted to formulate a detailed plan for my early campaign.

Two days later, Knuth presented his plan. The key elements for the early days were to publish opinion pieces in newspapers around the state, mail an introductory letter to party leaders and delegates, attend party meetings, and cultivate the four most important political media people in the state. As the months passed, we would create a campaign structure. He took a pen and sketched out a campaign organization chart that included a kitchen cabinet, a campaign manager, a political director, a finance director, a press secretary, a treasurer, a steering committee, and field staff. He also presented a timeline. All of it sounded great. I was sold. Knuth and I began to meet regularly to discuss strategy.

A major topic of discussion for the two of us, and indeed at all my lunch meetings with others, was other potential candidates. Names continued to float onto and off the list. People knew former Senator Rudy Boschwitz wanted to run to reclaim his seat four years hence, but would he move his timetable up two years for what was expected to be an open seat? Would state House leader Steve Sviggum give it a try? Would Congressman Jim Ramstad step out from his safe U.S. House district to go for the Senate? Who would add a female presence to the race? Word was that state representative Gil Gutknecht wanted to run for first district Congress, but he knew he couldn't beat the incumbent Democrat, so might he try the Senate? One name that kept surfacing was Cary Humphries, a retired Cargill executive. Humphries was like me a political unknown, but he had advantages: he had business contacts to raise money, and he was active in Christian organizations, which would give him a leg up with social conservatives. Knuth told me I needed to call Humphries about lunch.

★ ★ ★ ★ ★

Steve Knuth also told me to attend the semi-annual Republican Party state central committee meeting in December. I was so naive in party politics that I'd never heard of the state central committee. Knuth explained the annual state party convention had over 2000 delegates and another 3000 alternate delegates. The state central committee had fewer than 300 members. State central committee members were the activists of the activists. These were the people I had already started meeting one-on-one for coffee or lunch. This would be my coming out event as a candidate.

The meeting began at 9:30 Saturday morning at a suburban community center. I arrived early to meet as many of the members as possible before the meeting started, and later also roamed the back hallway during breaks. After three hours, I had wrung the good from the meeting.

As the meeting droned on, I found myself standing in the back of the auditorium near Bill Salisbury, the political reporter for the St. Paul *Pioneer Press*. Salisbury was one of the media people Knuth had told me to cultivate, but that was planned for later. Salisbury introduced himself, asked my name, and said "Looks like you're trying to work the room."

"Well, I guess I am."

His interest perked up a little. "What are you running for?"

"I'm thinking of running for the Senate."

"State senate? What district?"

"U.S. Senate."

Salisbury's interest jumped to a whole new level. He asked why I was running, and I repeated my standard answer of ethics and conservative principles. We chatted a while longer. He gave me his card. We agreed to have lunch.

★　★　★　★　★

Soon after the state central committee meeting, Bob Weinholzer, the state party chair, finally agreed to have lunch. We met at state party headquarters in Bloomington and drove to a nearby hotel for a buffet. Since Bob was rotund, the fact that he opted for a buffet and liked to eat was not a surprise. The surprise was Bob's openness and breadth of knowledge of party people. We had a great talk over lunch. Bob knew everybody in the party, and he was willing to tell me frankly what he knew. I asked him who else might run. He asked me about issues. I asked him for more names of people to see. He asked me about fundraising.

At some point, the talk turned to the issue of abortion. This continued to be a major issue for every candidate, Republican and Democrat, in every election. A prolife Democrat, or a prochoice Republican, might as well try to preserve a snowball in hell as try to get party endorsement in Minnesota. Bob and I both knew that abortion, and other social issues, continued to be at the top of the priority list for many Republican and Democratic activists.

One typical activist that Bob told me to call was Reuben Lundquist, who Bob said was the party boss of the fifth district (Minneapolis and suburbs). I called and suggested lunch. Lundquist said no need for lunch. We'll just meet. I found Lundquist to be a big bear of a man with a full wave of silver hair. He was wearing a fine suit and proudly displayed his stars and stripes tie that he had worn for our meeting. He liked to laugh, and he did so as he handed me his business card: "Professional loafer. Inventor. Traveler." Lundquist, as expected, was a social conservative and a man of strong religious convictions. He quizzed me. Why are you running? What about the issues? How about abortion? Can we rely on you? Can you raise money? Who else is supporting you? No, it's too early to give you my support. Here are the names of some other people you should see. He seemed to be primarily interested in finding out if I shared his conservative views.

My lunch with Tony Sutton, political director of the state party, was quite different. Tony was a protégé of Bob Weinholzer. He was built like Bob, and like Bob, he was an honest, realistic political operative. We talked strategy, not issues. Tony ticked off a different strategy for every one of the eight congressional districts [a Minnesota map showing the eight districts, and several cities, can be found in the Appendix]. He suggested I start with my home district, the fourth, encompassing St. Paul and northern suburbs: see Ron Carey, Gail Sutton (Tony's wife was a party activist and experienced political operative in her own right), Judie Fotsch, Joan

Garvey, and others. Next, he said, the conservative second district was a key: see Allen and Julie Quist, farmers near St. Peter—Julie believed we lose elections because of mechanics, not policy. Next, the first and seventh districts were important. Tony added names. The third would split, he said. Tony told me who to see in the third, but quickly added about one leader "He's shifty. Don't trust him." The eighth would be solid. Use this person to get to this person. The fifth was fractionalized; Reuben Lundquist was the best person to see. The sixth was controlled by Ed and Eileen Fiore, so see them. Tony was a treasure trove of political and party information, and I knew instinctively I could trust him.

During the month of December, I met personally with as many big names in the party hierarchy as possible. As word spread, I increased the pace. The danger was that someone who considered himself or herself a big name would not receive one of these early calls and would line up behind someone else out of wounded pride. By the end of the year, still nearly two years prior to the election, I had talked at length with 59 party leaders, and had calls in to another like number. Some, like Evie Axdahl, offered encouragement and advice. Some, like Reuben Lundquist, wanted to advance their political philosophy. Some, like party officials Bob Weinholzer and Tony Sutton, were doing their job. Some, like Steve Knuth, hoped to land a job.

Knuth came to my office at Hamline at 11:30 on December 23. After talking strategy, we went downstairs for the law school holiday lunch. I introduced him around as my political consultant. Knuth got a free lunch, and I got a chance to show my colleagues that my campaign was serious.

★ ★ ★ ★ ★

Another person who hoped to land a job was Cary Humphries, the only other potential Senate candidate who had been calling and meeting with party insiders. The two of us were finally able to schedule a breakfast meeting on Christmas eve morning.

Humphries wanted to meet at seven a.m., and he was waiting for me with a bright eye and a firm handshake. Score one for him. Humphries was in his sixties, possessing only a thin band of hair around a bald head;

he had an almost ascetic appearance. Score one for me. After exchanging Christmas greetings, we slid in on opposite sides of a booth. He had retired from a successful business career at Cargill, a Twin Cities agricultural giant, with both personal money and business contacts. Score another one for him. He had no political experience and seemed a little unaware about the rigors of the campaign to come. Score another one for me. He was transparently honest and above-board, and a genuinely nice person. Score another one for him. Humphries seemed almost too nice for politics, and he didn't seem to be the type willing to get down and dirty fighting for the nomination or a political position. Score another one for me.

When the food arrived, I raised my fork poised over the plate, ready to dig into my favorite meal of the day, when he said "Should we pray before eating?"

"Oh, uh, yeah, certainly," I stammered.

Soon we were talking about the upcoming Minnesota prayer breakfast, as well as the national prayer breakfast in Washington, both of which he attended every year. I had never been to either one. I have always been a privately religious person—a typically reserved Scandinavian Lutheran. Humphries' tradition was public expression of faith and evangelism. Still, these prayer breakfasts genuinely interested me.

I suggested "Maybe I should attend the Minnesota prayer breakfast."

Humphries peered at me over his reading glasses. "Do you think it would be appropriate to attend now for the first time? People might think you are there only because of the campaign."

"Uh, yeah, you're probably right." I wasn't interested in the prayer breakfast as a campaign appearance, but because I had never attended previously, that would be the obvious assumption. I didn't go.

We spent the rest of our hour together subtly trying to talk each other out of running. Neither of us succeeded. Humphries would run. I would have to beat him.

★　★　★　★　★

By the end of the year, my initial fear of being ridiculed was gone. I now knew scores of party leaders around the state who were taking me seriously, and Steve Knuth was my professional campaign consultant. On his advice, I had written a political commentary, "Republicans in the Long Run." It described how our party had taken a beating in the previous election, but we would come roaring back in two years because we were truly the party of common sense and the common people. We mailed it to about 50 newspapers around the state, and a third of them printed it.

Even so, I remained an unknown to the general public and to the media. The St. Paul *Pioneer Press* published a cartoon on December 15 showing Senator Dave Durenberger imprisoned in stocks with the Republican elephant scanning the distance. Durenberger was saying "Of course—if you know someone who's in better shape to run than I am..." I knew somebody. Out of a state population of four million, only a couple of hundred Republican party activists knew who I was, but that was just fine for two months of politics by retail.

CHAPTER THREE

You Need Professional Help

After a brief lull for the holiday season, the campaign began again in earnest the first week of January. Hours committed increased dramatically. Steve Knuth and I talked strategy on the telephone daily. I continued campaign by lunch, meeting with another dozen party leaders. I wrote and mailed to newspapers around the state another political commentary, this one called "Conservatives Care." The theme was conservatives care for common people by respecting them enough to allow them to make decisions for their own lives. Party activists for months to come proudly showed me copies they had clipped from their local papers.

A professional photographer took my official campaign photo. The pose he induced Steve Knuth, Mary, and me to select looked soft and gauzy; the photographer said it made me look accessible. I thought it made me look like a dweeb.

★ ★ ★ ★ ★

State party political director Tony Sutton had recommended I start my appearances at party meetings in my home congressional district, the fourth, so on the evening of January 5, I showed up at the monthly meeting of the fourth district executive committee in St. Paul. Many who I would come to know, and who would become stalwarts of my campaign, were there. Bob Weinholzer, state party chair, was also there.

After I made my brief pitch and answered a few questions, Bob motioned me into a small storage room cluttered with furniture. He asked how the campaign was going, and hardly waited for a response before unloading "Doug, you need professional help." Two months earlier I would have thought he meant my idea of running for the Senate showed I needed to have my head examined. Now, I knew he meant a political professional. I reminded Bob that Steve Knuth was advising me. Bob was not a Knuth fan, but I was. The campaign by lunch was proceeding nicely. Newspapers around the state had published the commentaries I had written at Knuth's prompting. We had formed a kitchen cabinet that was scheduled to meet later in the week. Here I was at a district meeting. The word was spreading. All of this was happening with minimal out-of-pocket expense, and that was important since the campaign was running out of my pocket. I was not inclined to listen to Bob.

The kitchen cabinet ideally is a handful of the candidate's long-term political allies. These are the committed and trusted few who are committed from the humble beginning. The beginning usually is at the largest table in the candidate's home, hence the name kitchen cabinet. The name is said to go all the way back to Andrew Jackson. Since I had no long-term political allies, Steve Knuth and I had put together a small group of my friends and new allies who would attend the first kitchen cabinet meeting.

Knuth arrived early. He handed me an eight-page campaign proposal. It began with an overview of the different phases of the campaign, featured an organization chart, proposed the message, identified short-term tasks, and concluded with a six-month budget for January through June, which was still nearly a year-and-one-half before the election. Everything looked great until I reached the budget. It called for raising increasing amounts of money, totaling $29,000. This was a major problem, since my donations to date added up to $17. Along with the donations, total expenses for the period were estimated to be $17,200. That was a nice surplus, but my eye was drawn to a line for consultation fees adding up to $5750. Today I would look at that number and think "dirt cheap." Back then I looked at it and blanched. Knuth had been advising me for free, and now he expected to be paid? I tried to keep my expression neutral, but my dismay must have been obvious. Looking back, I realize that of course Steve Knuth, as a political professional, expected to be paid. I was the babe-in-the-woods. That was the beginning of the end for Steve Knuth and me, and it was caused by my own naivete.

The kitchen cabinet meeting later in the evening amounted to little. Knuth presented his campaign proposals to the group. We decided to mail an introductory letter to Republican activists statewide. Knuth would write it, and we all would meet again in a week to stuff and stamp the mailing envelopes.

A week later, the letter introduced me to party activists as a pragmatic fiscal conservative, announced my commitment to the Republican grassroots endorsement process, and promised "In the coming months, I'll be on the phone and on the road meeting and talking with as many of you as possible." The back of the letter reprinted one of my commentaries. It was a fine opening mailing. Knuth had done excellent work. He was hanging in there.

I was hanging in there, too, balancing a full-time campaign with family activities, a full-time teaching job, and other activities. All day Tuesday and Wednesday, I had chaired an arbitration panel in a securities dispute because I needed the extra income to fund the campaign. The previous weekend I had worked seven games as a basketball referee because I needed the physical exertion and release.

What kept me going was the thought that I had a realistic chance of winning. These early long days were the stuff of stories of success. Of course, my mind kept reminding me that a victory was a long shot. A note on my daily calendar from that time said "What if spend 60 hours/wk for 2 years + lose? Then you're a fool."

Not long after the letter hit the streets, Bob Weinholzer called. He announced "I thought you should know a rumor is floating around that Steve Knuth is working with Cary Humphries."

"He is?"

"Doug, you know that Humphries has a lot of personal money to finance his own campaign," Weinholzer continued. "Knuth will go where the money is."

"Bob, you know Knuth has been working for me. How good is your information?"

"It's good. I wouldn't trust Knuth for a minute."

"Why not?"

"Just believe me on this. If I were you, I'd be looking for a campaign manager."

The news was surprising, but not shocking. As the days had passed after my unfortunate balking at his proposed campaign budget, Knuth had not been calling as often, and he was no longer Johnny-on-the-spot returning my calls. I realized Bob was probably right. "Who would you recommend as a manager?" I asked.

Weinholzer gave me four names: Chris Georgacas, director of the Republican state House caucus; Gail Sutton, the wife of Tony Sutton, Bob's state party political director; Dwight Tostenson, former campaign manager for Congressman Vin Weber; and Jeff Larson, an up-and-coming politico. "The trouble is," Bob continued, "Georgacas probably won't leave his job with the House caucus, and you probably can't afford Tostenson or Larson."

That didn't leave me much choice, which was likely exactly what Bob had in mind. I asked "Is Gail Sutton any good?"

"Oh, absolutely. She's never managed a campaign before, but she's ready. She's a tremendously hard worker, and she'll be loyal to you. Of course, you understand that with Tony's position in the party, he has to remain neutral, but I wouldn't be surprised to see the two of them consult a little."

I liked that idea. This was sounding good. "How much would I have to pay her?"

"That would be up to the two of you." Bob threw out a number.

"Oof. I don't know if I can pay anyone that kind of money yet."

"Talk to Gail about being a combined campaign manager and

fundraiser. I think she could make it work. She could pay herself with what she brings in."

I really liked that idea. Bob made sense. Gail Sutton was one of the party activists I had met with over breakfast a few weeks earlier, and I already knew from our meeting that she was a hard driver. I called her. She wasn't surprised to hear from me. We agreed to meet over lunch to talk about the job.

Campaign Manager Gail Sutton

Gail Sutton showed up at O'Gara's Bar in St. Paul at noon fired up and ready for action. She wanted the job. Her resume showed she had a lot going for her: Hamline honors graduate, campaign positions, party positions culminating in state party finance director. She sat across from me in a booth. Short-cut brown hair, round-frame glasses, fast-paced speech, total intensity. She talked about making a big impression on party delegates without spending a lot of money. We went over the important people to work on for early commitments in all eight congressional districts.

How about salary? Gail said she would be half campaign manager and half finance director for the early months of the campaign. She would raise enough money to pay herself and run the campaign. How could I go wrong with that? One of the top political professionals in the state was willing to sign on to my campaign, which was thrilling.

I was sold, but the saying was that to get loyalty you have to give loyalty; I believed then and now in its truth. Steve Knuth was still my campaign consultant. He had done a lot for me. The idea that he was jumping to Cary Humphries may have been just another typical political rumor. I told Gail I would get back to her.

That same afternoon Knuth called me with the sad news that he was leaving to go to work for Humphries. I tried to sound appropriately surprised and hurt. The next morning, I called Gail to offer her the job.

I was a little sorry to see Knuth go. He had started calling me "Senator." It sounded good. A couple of days later, Gail and I ran into Humphries and Knuth at a district meeting. I heard Knuth call Humphries "Senator." It didn't sound nearly as good, although Humphries seemed to like it.

★ ★ ★ ★ ★

The following weekend, I learned what I call the law of political chains. The law of political chains has positive consequences. Sunday evening Gail and I were scheduled to meet to talk strategy. She asked if instead I could come to the home of her friend and party activist Ron Carey. I walked in the door to find his living room filled with campaign workers—my campaign workers—all bubbling over with the possibilities and excitement of a new and fresh campaign. By hiring Gail Sutton, I gained an unanticipated bonus: the support of a whole chain of her political allies. In addition to activist Ron Carey, who himself would become state party chair a decade later, the chain included Gail's husband Tony, the state party political director, and almost certainly also included Bob Weinholzer, the state party chair.

The law of political chains turned out to have negative consequences also. The next day, Monday, I had lunch with Zondra Wolcott. She was one of the most respected and experienced Republican fundraisers in the state, and she would have been the perfect complement to Gail Sutton for the financial side of the campaign. Wolcott was interested, but no sale. Yes, she thought I was a viable candidate. Yes, she thought she could raise money for me. Yes, Gail was my new campaign manager. No, no particular reason, just no sale. By hiring Gail Sutton, I had lost the support of a chain of her political enemies.

★   ★   ★   ★   ★

Tuesday evening only a day later was my first political bloodletting. Gail sent me to the meeting room of an apartment house in the Minneapolis suburb of Edina for the monthly meeting of the senate district 42 organization. Since Edina was the most Republican city in the state, I thought this would be friendly territory. The folks from Edina were having a potluck supper. That was good, too. I love potlucks. After we all ate, I gave a nice little talk. Everything was hunky dory until the question and answer session. Before long, someone asked "Are you prolife or prochoice?"

A decade earlier, in my only previous venture into public life, I had run for the state legislature. For various reasons, I had allowed myself to be identified as prochoice, even though the position never felt right to me. I'll return to that story and that issue a few months down the campaign trail.

A politician always likes to be asked a question in front of a friendly audience to which the "right" answer is obvious. This evening, I said confidently "I'm prolife."

I answered with confidence because my personal position matched the obvious "right" answer for 98 percent of Republican party districts. In senate district 42, it was the "wrong" answer. In the years since abortion had become a hot button issue, pro-lifers had swept pro-choicers from virtually all Republican party positions from state chair down to local convention delegate. Of course, the same in opposite was true of Democratic party positions, but that was not relevant here. Senate district 42 was one of perhaps two or three districts in the whole state party with a prochoice majority of delegates. They either had political memories stretching way back to my prior campaign, or more likely they assumed I was with them—why else would I show up at their potluck? They were hot. One after another peppered me with follow-up questions designed to soften my position. I tried to smile and respond thoughtfully, but they weren't buying. You'd have thought I had come out in favor of higher taxes and spending.

The delegates didn't make any progress with me, and I didn't make any progress with them. I left licking my wounds. The evening appeared to have been a bust.

One can never tell, however, who is listening. Months later, Walter Klaus, the venerable and respected chairman of the sixth congressional district that covered the northern Twin Cities suburbs, decided to support me. Klaus was fiercely prolife, and he revealed he had been another guest at the senate district 42 meeting. Had I wavered on my prolife position that evening, Klaus would have spread the word through the state and my campaign would have been stone cold dead within a week. Instead, Klaus spread the word that I would hold fast on the issue of most importance to most of the Republican party activists in the state. That was worth incalculably more than twenty votes in Edina.

Another person who was listening was of course my campaign manager Gail Sutton. As usual, she had chosen the event and accompanied me. Occasionally, later, I thought why would Gail send me into what she knew would be a hornet's nest? Only today, years later, has the realization dawned that maybe she also wanted to hear my answers on this issue and learn how I would respond when the pressure increased.

★ ★ ★ ★ ★

So, I had dodged a killing campaign disaster, but gaffes were not so easy to avoid. Faye Hatch, chairwoman of the sixth congressional district, and I met. I worked hard for her support all through lunch. When the moment was right, I tried to close the sale—even though I didn't really expect her commitment nearly two years prior to the election. I looked into her eyes and murmured "I want to have you."

We each looked at the other quizzically. After a pause, she replied "I think you're going to have me, but not today." A few months later, Hatch did commit to support me. Not all campaign gaffes are damaging.

★　★　★　★　★

The big news of January arrived in a frantic telephone call from my manager. When I picked up the receiver, without any preliminaries Gail blurted "I just heard that Cary Humphries had a heart attack over the weekend! He's going to drop out of the Senate race!"

"Whoa. Wait a minute. We'd better check this out, Gail," I cautioned. "You know how political rumors are."

She was not to be deterred. "Yeah, I know, but this one's good. He told Bob this morning."

Schadenfreude is the right word, but it is too strong. I wished only the best to the good man but couldn't help smiling at the elimination of a competitor. I wandered down the hallway to share the news with Mike Scherschligt, a close friend on the Hamline faculty. I told him "I need to confirm this. I'd like to call Humphries myself and ask, but that doesn't seem right."

"I'll call Humphries' secretary at Cargill," Mike volunteered with a sly grin. He was the most unusual combination of a Lutheran pastor and a law professor—with a mischievous streak. "I'll tell her I'm one of his old friends and ask about him."

"Do you really think you could pull it off?" I asked hopefully. Today, caller ID would likely deter us from this stunt, but at the time, we were not so concerned.

"Sure. Just listen," Mike said. As I listened, he dialed Cargill and reached Humphries' secretary. He was an old friend who had heard Cary had a health scare. Just calling to check in on him. Yes, there was a health scare over the weekend. A heart palpitation. No, not a heart attack. Cary was resting and seemed fine. Yes, he had decided to drop his campaign for Senate. He was taking his heart scare as a sign from God that he should not run.

Mike and I grinned at each other. Humphries was fine, and he was out of the Senate race. Good news all the way around.

I couldn't help grinning a little, too, when I thought of Steve Knuth. He had abandoned me to go to work for Humphries. He had picked the wrong horse. Within a week, Knuth's new horse never made it to the starting gate.

Over the following months, other candidates and rumors of other candidates appeared, but Knuth never was able to latch onto one. I saw him at several party meetings until eventually he drifted out of sight. Last I heard he moved to Montana.

I truly did not hold ill will against Steve Knuth, since he had helped me get started and now Gail Sutton had my campaign rolling smoothly. My children weren't so charitable. For months, every time I returned from a political meeting, Amy or Stuart, or both, would ask "Was traitor there?"

CHAPTER FOUR

Politics By Retail

Minnesota is a caucus state. Early in each election year, citizens across the state attend their party's precinct caucus, which usually consists of a handful of people in a local schoolroom. While caucuses are touted as town meeting citizenship in action, the primary business of the caucus is to elect delegates to the Basic Party Organizational Unit convention. That convention elects delegates to the state convention. The state convention endorses party candidates for statewide office. With only a few notable exceptions then and now, the endorsed party candidate wins the primary election. Party endorsement at the state convention was our goal.

The experiences and lessons learned in a caucus state may not all transfer directly to a state with a different electoral system. Mostly, they do. Years after the events here, today we can see that also in other state systems that bypass the party endorsement process in favor of a primary election, those primary elections are being won by candidates who appeal to hard-core party activists.

Gail Sutton knew how to campaign in a caucus state. She handed me pages of telephone numbers. Call members of the state party executive committee, then call congressional district party officers and selected key people in the eight congressional districts, and then work down to party legislative district officers. The theory was that at least two-thirds of these activists from the previous election cycle would remain active and be elected delegates a year hence.

My typical weekday evening was eat dinner at six, trudge down the stairs to the basement at 6:30, pick up the cordless telephone and the calling list for the evening, and begin dialing. Around nine or 9:30, put down the phone. So began the campaign. Telephoning hour after hour. Night after night. Week after week. No glamorous television appearances. No roar of the crowd. Politics by retail.

The conversations were all standard. The recipient, who was a party activist, knew of me. We got acquainted. We talked Durenberger. We talked issues. We talked other potential candidates. We talked potential Democratic candidates. We talked chances of winning the general election. We talked fundraising prospects. I jotted notes of the person's issues and concerns for future reference.

A few weeks later, Gail gave me a list of the same people to call again.

"Why would I want to call them again?" I balked. "We just talked two weeks ago."

"Because these people see themselves as party leaders," Gail explained. "They expect it. They want to be cultivated."

Indeed, they did. Most were pleased to receive even my fourth or fifth call. The repeat calls showed we valued the person's party status and in turn that he or she could get behind such a hard-working candidate.

When the timing seemed right, near the end of each call, I asked for the person's commitment, a promise to vote for me on the first ballot at the state convention, which was still well over a year away. Tony Sutton, Gail's husband and the state party political director, had said "These people like to get behind someone early. And when they commit, they keep their word. Commitments are crucial. They're also a good way to discourage other candidates from getting into the race. If someone starts calling around and finds a lot of delegates already committed to you, he might not run."

So, at the end of every call, I asked for a commitment. And wonder of wonders, many of these folks–even those who knew me only as a voice over the telephone–did give their commitment.

The popular image of a political candidate giving speech after speech in front of cheering crowds is not reality. It's not efficient. The reality is the candidate, alone, with a telephone stuck to the ear, courting delegates or asking for money. Evening after evening of campaign by telephone was drudgery, and the daily anticipation of another evening in the basement was worse, but it worked. The commitments accumulated quickly.

*   *   *   *   *

When Gail said the two of us were attending an evening district party meeting, I rejoiced at the respite from the basement and the telephone. Gail and I drove north to the eighth congressional district committee monthly meeting in McGregor, west to the second district meeting in Olivia, or south to the first district meeting in Mantorville. We arrived at six when the delegates gathered for dinner. My mouth watered, but I never ate. I needed to move around from table to table, and I couldn't do that with mouth full and hands covered with barbeque sauce. Also, I remembered reading that Richard Nixon had never eaten before a speech. He worried he would belch while speaking. Shortly after seven, the program usually began.

The first of the district meetings we attended was the eighth. District chair Vern Gruhn, who had committed to me on the telephone, introduced me right away. In all the districts, party people understood that the visiting candidate needed to appear and be off. After my talk and a few questions, we were on the road home.

These early party meetings were a breeze. The speech was repeatable, and the questions were standard. Since I was not expected to know anyone there, I could confidently stick my hand forward to introduce myself with no chance of embarrassment that my booming "Good to meet you" would be met with the response "Yes, Doug, we met last month."

Return visits to the monthly district meetings weren't bad either, as in the car on the way to the meetings, Gail Sutton and I went over the names of people who likely would attend, with their quirks or issues. Gail was worth her weight in gold for this knowledge alone. Recently refreshed, I could remember all their names.

People respond to a candidate who remembers their names. Hubert Humphrey was said to be able meet a person one time and years later call that person by name even when bumping into him or her in a totally different context. For years, I thought that was an interesting if peripheral talent. I now believe that recalling names is a primary ingredient of political success. It was a large part of what made the ordinary politician into the icon Hubert Humphrey.

This talent largely eluded me. One of Gail's primary jobs at party meetings and conventions was to stay near my side. When, for example, Sue Jirele approached, Gail would call out "Hello, Sue." Then I smiled and said "Great to see you again, Sue. How are things in Waseca?" Sue beamed. That sounded better than my lame coverup "How you doing?" And it sounded a whole lot better than my unaided attempt, which was just as likely to come out "Hello, Dorothy. How are things in Bagley?"

★ ★ ★ ★ ★

The rest of February our campaign tallied growing political support, success after success. I added commitments daily. Others didn't want to commit so early, but they weren't hostile; I hadn't bumbled or alienated anyone enough to create active opposition. People might not be for me, but no one was against me.

Competition melted away. Over sandwiches at his office, former Senator Rudy Boschwitz told me he did plan to run again for the Senate, but not until the following election, as everyone expected. Fine with me. I run this time, and Rudy runs the next time. I went directly from Boschwitz's office to see Steve Sviggum, the leader of the state House Republican caucus. Without any prompting, Sviggum said "I want you to know that I'm not a candidate for Senate." More good news.

Our reconstituted kitchen cabinet met for the first time. Gail Sutton had put together a new group of her political allies who were now my political allies. Most lived in the Twin Cities: Ron Carey, Judie Fotsch,

Joan Garvey, and Reuben Lundquist (now wearing a red, white, and blue tie with an American bald eagle). Jack and Therese Vaughn came from Duluth, Andy and Margie Kessler came from Wadena, and Gary Carlson came from Willmar. I was excited people cared enough to drive great distances to join us. Chewing bagels and drinking coffee, we sat in a large circle of chairs in our family room.

We all talked strategy, although mostly the meeting was Gail announcing our strategy. I was a little embarrassed that people had come so far for little more than to listen to a pep talk. The group did have a meaningful say on choosing our campaign colors and logo; they decided on bright red with white lettering for the signs and an outline of the state of Minnesota with my name inside for the logo.

We opened a campaign office. Gail had looked for weeks for an inexpensive, easy-to-locate place with room for a couple of desks, quick access to a freeway, and parking for volunteers. She found a second-floor, one-room office near Rice Street and highway 36 in Roseville, a St. Paul suburb. I walked in for the first time to find Tony Sutton flat on his back, screwing together a prefabricated desk. Gail was glowing. Her campaign nest was taking shape. We eventually had two desks, a large table for preparing mailings, a donated copying machine, and wall artwork consisting of political district maps.

The only negative was the telephone company demanded a $1000 deposit. It had been stiffed by political campaigns before. We had far better things to do with a precious $1000 than to put it on ice with the telephone company, but we had to have the lifeline of the campaign.

Within a few days, we had an office, an address, letterhead paper, business cards, and a telephone number. We were a campaign!

Steve Clark showed up about this time. He was a small man with a big political thirst. With a mop of brown hair and glasses, Clark looked like a backroom accountant. In fact, he did know accounting from two years as an actuary. Good. Steve also knew some foreign policy because he had studied for a State Department exam. Better. Steve was willing to work for the time being as an unpaid volunteer. Best. Gail said she had told Clark she would pay him from time to time when the campaign treasury allowed; in the short run, if we had no money, no pay. He could agree because his wife Leslie was working. Of course, when I was elected, Clark would expect some sort of position. What did I think? Welcome aboard, Steve.

Whenever I stopped by the office over the next few months, Gail was at her desk, pulling hard on the straw into her huge cup of Pepsi-Cola. Steve Clark was usually at the other desk, working the telephone, attempting to line up appearances or fundraising visits.

Ken Morris, my former law student at Hamline, was a successful businessman and consultant. He was also a committed Republican who would himself run for the state legislature a few years later. I asked Ken to be my treasurer and he accepted. I never had to worry about keeping track of the money or the required reports again.

The political side did have an occasional disaster. By the middle of February, Gail Sutton and I had made the rounds to seven of the eight congressional districts for their monthly committee meetings. The tough one was the distant seventh. Their February district meeting was scheduled in the upstairs room at the airport in Fergus Falls, three hours northwest on interstate highway 94 from home. Despite a forecast of snow, Gail and I started off under a threatening sky in the late afternoon. Bob Weinholzer rode along with us so he could greet the party people as state chair. Soon the snowflakes started, and before long we were driving in conditions approaching whiteout. We talked about turning back, but Gail decided I needed to be seen at the seventh. The three of us arrived at the airport access road about a half-hour late. A single set of tire tracks through the fresh snow marked the road. Bad sign. Sure enough, the meeting had been cancelled due to the snowstorm. We could do nothing other than turn around and drive back home through the blowing snow. This story may seem hard to believe today when cell phones are ubiquitous. Not then.

Two nights later was a far more successful evening. The party state executive committee, composed of twenty of the most active and influential party leaders from the entire state, held its regular monthly meeting at party headquarters in Bloomington, a Minneapolis suburb. Gail Sutton invited the executive committee members to a reception at a nearby hotel following the meeting. They all came to eat free food, to chat more informally, and to feel out the new guy. Gail's idea and execution were flawless. The reception was a huge success. As some began to drift into the night, I found myself sitting at a table alone with Julie Quist, chairwoman of the second district.

She asked "Now assume, Doug, that you've cut a lot of federal spending and it turns out the budget deficit can be eliminated with a small tax increase. You'd vote for that, wouldn't you?"

"No, I wouldn't. The answer is cutting more spending. I'm not voting for a tax increase." She smiled. The right answer. Most candidates have long voting records. As a relative unknown, my political views were suspect; the party people wanted to be sure I wasn't a closet liberal.

★ ★ ★ ★ ★

If only the financial support side of the campaign would have been half as successful as the political side. Granted I started as a political unknown, but our campaign had progressed so well that I expected people to recognize our success and the contributions to start flowing.

Like everyone else, I'd received plenty of solicitations on the telephone at home. I wanted to hire my own political telemarketer. My assumption was a telemarketer raised the money, kept a percentage, and forwarded the largesse to the candidate.

Wrong, explained Gail Sutton. A telemarketer did keep a percentage of the funds raised, but also charged a fee for each call answered. Even if the total call consisted of the recipient telling the telemarketer to jump into one of Minnesota's 10,000 lakes, we were still charged the fee. I wasn't yet well known, even among Republicans, across the state. In other words, we were more likely to lose money than to make money. Telemarketing was a no go.

The best early way to raise money, she said, was to comb through the lists of major donors to the past two Republican Senate campaigns and the past two Republican gubernatorial campaigns. She and Steve Clark worked the telephones to reach these donors and ask them to meet with me. Before long, we had a series of appointments. Gail prepared a folder containing a slick array of materials to hand to each potential donor.

The federal contribution limit for one person for the Senate campaign was $1000 per election. The max contribution for both a primary and a general election added to $2000. Even for a couple, the sum for the election cycle was only $4000. To the people on these major donor lists, $1000 was no more than the change that would fall between the cushions of their sofas. I thought any reasonable, sensible Republican candidate who came calling should be able to walk away with $1000. I didn't mind at all if the donor also gave to other competitors for the same office. That too turned out to be wrong.

One typical early fundraising call was on Wheelock Whitney at his office in downtown Minneapolis. Just making the appointment was something of a triumph since Whitney was a mover and shaker in both the party and the business community. If my lawyer friend had been correct about a shadow group controlling Minnesota politics, then Whitney certainly was in the group. I needed his contribution, but even more importantly, I needed his acceptance and goodwill as a leader of the financial community.

Whitney had years earlier been the Republican candidate for Senate and another time for governor. Each time, instead of seeking the party endorsement by courting party activists, he had spent large sums of his own money to win the primary election. Due in part to the resulting lack of commitment from the party regulars, he had been beaten soundly in both general elections.

Bill Salisbury of the St. Paul *Pioneer Press* had told me a great story about Whitney's campaign for governor. Soon after winning the Republican primary, big city financier Whitney started flying around the state. He landed in Thief River Falls and pronounced himself ready to take questions. The first question was "What is your position on leg-hold traps?" Bill and I had both chuckled as we imagined the urban businessman struggling to understand, much less come up with an answer to, a question about cruelty in animal trapping.

Whitney showed me to the couch and coffee. We talked for an hour about taxes, education, term limits, health care, and campaign strategy. Eventually, Whitney mentioned he was chairing the re-election campaign of Republican Governor Arne Carlson. He said "The number one priority I have this year is re-electing Arne Carlson."

"I have no problem with that" I responded. "Even though I worked for others for governor, when Carlson became the Republican candidate, I sent him money and campaigned for him."

"Good."

"In fact," I said, "I've been trying to get in touch with the governor, but so far he hasn't agreed to meet with me."

Whitney said "Well, keep trying."

"I will. I would be glad to run with him. I'm staying out of the governor's race. It's not my race."

"Fair enough."

I asked Whitney to be on my finance committee. He declined. I had expected that. I asked for a contribution. He declined again. "Too early" he said. I had not expected that. My plan was to leave his office with a nice check.

As our conversation wound down, I mentioned his run for governor. He sighed and said "And now I can't even get elected delegate in my precinct."

"Pro-lifers?" I asked.

Whitney nodded ruefully. Even though I was a prolife candidate, I didn't believe in denying delegate slots to people on the other side of the issue who had carried a lot of water for the elephant—people like Wheelock Whitney.

As I rose to leave, I could see Whitney was having a little trouble rising from the plushy couch. As I had done many times for my dad, I extended both arms, and Whitney grasped both of my forearms as I pulled him to his feet.

"I like you, Doug" he pronounced. I liked him, too. But no money.

Over the months to come, the scenario repeated itself often with big donors. Glad to meet you. Like what you are saying and doing. No, too early for a contribution. Their reluctance to contribute to a viable candidate puzzled, and truth be told irritated, me. Months later, one of them shared a likely reason, which I will at that time pass along.

The people who did contribute to my campaign were not the party fat cats. They were people who had personal ties to me: people from our neighborhood, people from our church, people from our Little League, people from Hamline University.

At that time, George Latimer was Dean of the Hamline law school. Latimer was a well-known and well-respected Democrat. While mayor of St. Paul for twelve years, he himself had run for governor, only to find out—as had Wheelock Whitney—the issues that matter to people outside the Twin Cities are not the same issues that matter to people inside the Twin Cities. Latimer had moved directly from big city mayor to law school dean, and his garrulousness, sense of humor, and sharp political instincts produced continued success.

Naturally, Latimer and I talked a few times about my own political efforts. Despite being on opposite sides of the political fence, we liked and respected each other. Latimer enthusiastically supported my efforts. One example of that support—and of his puckish sense of humor—was his whimsical memorandum to the faculty titled "Liberals for McFarland:"

> To the dismay of many Democrats, I accepted a huge donation from a prominent Republican in support of my candidacy for governor. Wheelock Whitney made the contribution, not because he wanted me to be governor but because he loathed the prospect of my opponent, Rudy Perpich, being elected once more.
>
> What Wheelock and I understood is that even evil has its gradations. It is with that understanding, and in that spirit, that I begin this "Liberals for McFarland" campaign. I am going to make a contribution to our colleague's efforts for nomination to the United States Senate and I encourage those of similarly perverse views to do the same.
>
> I am contributing to Doug's campaign first because of my sure knowledge that he is the least evil of the Republican possibilities. Secondly, I want our esteemed colleague to

know that our friendship is with him even if our ideology
is not.

Several checks arrived, even though the Hamline law faculty was almost entirely liberal Democrats. I did better with them than with big money Republicans.

My next chance to solicit big money Republicans was at the February luncheon of the Elephant Club. As national committeewoman Evie Axdahl had urged, Mary and I had sent in the minimum $500 contribution to join. I vigorously worked the room, talking up my campaign and asking people for the opportunity to call on them. In contrast to party activists, the Elephant Club members were not eager to hear from me. They were used to candidates trying to get into their pockets.

Truth be told, these early campaign financial failures, particularly in being unable to convince big donors to write checks, didn't bother me much. They said the time was too early, and the time was early. I expected the money to come rolling in months down the line as the party coalesced around my candidacy. Both Gail Sutton and Steve Clark were working hard and not being paid what they deserved, but that would change down the line too. What seemed more important at the time was our lengthening string of political successes.

CHAPTER FIVE

Thirty Days Hath Convention Season

While the personal campaign by telephone calls, lunches, party meetings, and appointments had proceeded apace through January and February, we were all—Gail Sutton, Steve Clark, the kitchen cabinet, committed supporters, and of course the candidate—eager to break into broader public awareness. The first opportunity came in March.

Elections at the precinct caucuses across the state a month earlier had advanced delegates the next step up the party ladder to conventions of Basic Political Organizational Units. The BPOU was typically the same as the state legislative district in the Twin Cities or the same as the county in the rest of the state. BPOU conventions were important: the people who cared enough about the party to attend these off-year conventions 20 months prior to the general election would remember the candidates who cared enough to come to see them that early.

The problem was that more than 120 BPOU conventions spread over the 31 days of March averaged to four conventions a day. In fact, most met on Saturdays, so any given Saturday had more than 20 conventions, often hundreds of miles apart. We had to pick and choose where to attend.

Our first choice was easy. Carleton County was the only BPOU meeting on Monday evening, the first day of March. Gail Sutton, Steve Clark, and I piled into the official campaign car—my family minivan—and drove a hundred miles due north. We pulled into the town of Cloquet shortly before the seven-p.m. start and found 40 convention delegates crammed into a small classroom at the local school. Steve passed out the modest two-sided cardstock literature piece Gail had prepared for the BPOU conventions, and Gail and I worked the room.

When the convention began, we all sat quietly in the rear, listening to the boilerplate business of any political convention: call to order, pledge of allegiance, reading of the convention call, credentials report, and the like. Soon enough, the chair introduced me. Gail and Steve ignited a loud welcome. I dodged through the student desks to the front of the room.

For the first of 46 times that month, I delivered my memorized BPOU convention speech. It ran six minutes. I told them about my family and noted my mother's maiden name was Johnson (couldn't hurt in a Scandinavian state). I told them I was a lifelong Republican and a pragmatic conservative; my degree was from Macalester, but that didn't make me a liberal; my job was law teaching, but that didn't make me an ivory tower professor; and my intent was to help people, but that didn't make me a Democrat. I mentioned fiscal conservatism, foreign policy, agriculture, education, and campaign reform.

At the end, I answered a few questions and thanked the delegates for attending. The applause was generous, although Gail and Steve once again were the loudest. All three of us left the school building in a jovial mood.

The time was around eight p.m., and we faced a two-hour return drive. As usual, I had not wanted to eat dinner before the speech, so the three of us stopped at the local McDonald's for the perfect on-the-road meal. Their small cheeseburgers and fries fit one hand with the other hand free for the wheel.

The parking area of the McDonald's in Cloquet was covered with ice from a recent storm. Cars approaching the drive-thru window had worn two ruts deep into the ice, and each was filled with dirty, icy water. The three of us stepped carefully across the ice and ruts on our way into the restaurant. On the way back to the car, I stepped onto the narrow area between the two parallel grooves in the ice. By now, this area had become crowned and worn smooth by people entering and exiting the restaurant. Next thing I knew, my feet were as high as my head.

I landed lengthwise in one of the ruts. There the dignified U. S. Senate candidate lay after giving his maiden convention campaign speech—flat on his back in slushy ice water in the parking lot of a fast food restaurant. One thought raced through my mind: I had not spilled a single fry or a drop of my drink. The drive home was both soggy and satisfied.

★ ★ ★ ★ ★

The next evening was the Crow Wing County BPOU convention. Gail Sutton and I drove the three hours northwest from the Twin Cities to Brainerd by ourselves. After the speech and the usual following questions and answers, the two of us lingered in the outer hallway to see whether any delegates would want to ask me a personal question or two.

One did. After a little small talk, he got to the point. "Did the two of you drive up here?"

"Yes."

"Did anyone else come with you?"

"No."

"I'm just mentioning that it might look bad for a married man and a married woman to be traveling alone together. Maybe you should think about having someone else ride along."

Immediately, I knew he was right. Nothing was going on between Gail Sutton and me, but she was a young, attractive woman. Tongues would wag if given any opportunity to wag. Some delegate could think that the two of us seemed chummy when we arrived in the car, or even that he saw the two of us gazing at each other across the convention room, and rumors would spread like wildfire. We didn't need that.

"You're right," I said. "I hadn't thought of it."

"Just trying to be helpful."

"You are. Thanks very much. From now on, someone will ride with us." For the rest of the campaign, Gail and I never again traveled alone to a party convention or event. My wife Mary, Steve Clark, or another volunteer always rode along; most often, the chaperone would be one of my own children. No rumors allowed here.

★ ★ ★ ★ ★

Saturday, March 6, was the first major road trip of the campaign. Choosing which conventions to attend was tough for two reasons. First, since nonelection year conventions had little business other than to elect BPOU officers and to listen to visiting speakers, they seldom lasted three hours. Second, *everyone had the schedule of conventions. State and local party bigwigs wanted to greet the delegates. Candidates for every level of office—U.S. Senate, governor, U.S. House, state auditor, state attorney general, state senate, state house, county offices, local offices—wanted to give their pitches. Speakers were called in the order they arrived. That meant if a candidate arrived at a popular convention a little late, the whole day's schedule could be destroyed.*

Differing start times—morning, afternoon, and evening—made appearing at several conventions in one day possible, but Gail still had to plan our itinerary carefully. She decided on a swing through the friendly, conservative, solidly Republican second congressional district, the southwest quarter of the state.

The plum convention of the day was populous Dakota County, at the southern edge of the Twin Cities metro area. Two hundred delegates were meeting at nine a.m.

My daughter Katie and I picked up Gail at her home in Woodbury, an eastern St. Paul suburb, around seven a.m. to drive 40 miles south to Farmington High School in the middle of Dakota County. I had decided to take the chance of driving my red BMW sports car for the day so as not to put too many campaign miles on the blue family minivan. That meant we wanted to be careful not to be seen in the car by any of the delegates. We parked near the far end of the school parking lot a little before eight a.m.

Red and white McFarland for Senate signs lined the sidewalk leading to the entrance doors. My signs also covered the doors and hallway. Gail's advance team had done a great job. As we walked into the school building, Gail whispered into my ear "Time to grip and grin." I gripped and grinned for more than an hour until the convention came to order. Several other candidates and officials also schmoozed delegates. Bert McKasy, the other active candidate for Senate, was also gripping and grinning. Gail sidled up to me and said "You're first up on the speaker's list. Bert is right behind you."

"Good. We'll get out right away." We wanted to listen to McKasy's speech to size up his speaking abilities, but we decided that getting to the next convention was more important. We would have scores of times in the weeks ahead to listen to him speak.

Gail whispered again "When you finish speaking, hang around the front a little. When Bert walks toward the microphone, step up and shake his hand. Let everyone see the two of you side by side."

I had to chuckle at her deviousness. Bert McKasy was a small man, standing perhaps five feet eight inches tall. He had wispy brown hair and large glasses. He looked like a stereotypical university professor. I was six feet eight inches tall with a full head of silver hair. People said I looked like a Senator. Well, fine, let's use whatever advantage we have.

The plan worked perfectly. When McKasy walked to the front of the room to deliver his speech, I intercepted him and stuck out my hand. He was taken slightly aback and extended his hand tentatively. I shook it vigorously and edged closer to him to give the delegates plenty of time to size us up together. Gail and I laughed all the way to the car at the far end of the parking lot.

We left Farmington around 10:15 to drive 115 miles due west to Olivia for the Renville County BPOU convention. *Every convention was the same and every convention was different. Arrive. Grip and grin. Wait to be introduced. Listen to speeches of other candidates who had arrived earlier. Speak. Shake more hands. Hang around in the back a few minutes for anyone who wanted to have a personal word. Leave as soon as possible for the next stop.* This convention was a little different as we arrived just in time to share a potluck lunch with the 35 delegates.

On westward to Benson in Swift County. Next, Ortonville in Big Stone County. We were now hard at the western border of Minnesota. Katie and Gail ate dinner with the delegates. I worked the tables. That was always touchy; some people wanted to talk; others wanted to eat. The convention began around seven, and by 7:45 we were back in the car.

Thirty-six miles due north in Wheaton, Traverse County, 25 delegates were convening in an empty store on main street. No one was outside, so we risked parking directly across the street. The light shining through the front window of the storefront glowed brightly into the dark night. I didn't anticipate this small convention would produce one of the most memorable moments of the campaign.

Delegates filled the room. Some sat at desks, some sat on folding chairs, some stood. They invited me to speak almost immediately; no other candidates had favored them with a trip so far west.

After my standard talk, they asked if I would take questions. Of course. They had a lot of questions. Eventually, a man rose and in a slow, measured voice asked "Are you a lawyer?"

"Yes, I am." Where was he going? Lawyer bashing? Lawyer joke?

"Are you a member of the American Bar Association?"

Now I saw his direction. "I was a member of the ABA when it was a professional group, but when they stuck their noses into politics and took a prochoice position, I resigned."

I expected murmurs of approval. What I got was a throaty roar. In that small room, 25 people sounded like a stadium full of thousands. I almost staggered backward as their collective voice rolled over me. Here was the power of the abortion issue writ large.

Walking back into the inky night, the three of us were more than 200 miles from home. Even high on the Wheaton roar, that's a mighty long drive late on a dark night after a full day of campaigning. The day totaled 18 hours, 300 delegates, and 500 miles.

Well past midnight, Katie and I dropped Gail off at her home and headed along I-694 toward our own home when red lights flashed in the rearview mirror. The state trooper who looked into our window saw an exhausted man in the driver's seat and a frightened teenage girl in the back seat. Political literature was strewn about the interior of the car.

"Where are you going?"

"We were just going home a few miles ahead to Arden Hills. We've been out all day campaigning in southwestern Minnesota."

He let us go with a warning.

★　★　★　★　★

Months earlier, Steve Knuth had said that newspapers would occasionally run speculative articles peering into the political future, and an early goal would be to have my name included on any list of potential Senate candidates. Since then, I started every day early by hustling across the front lawn to collect both Twin Cities newspapers, spreading them out on the kitchen table, and eagerly scanning them for a political article. Finally, on Sunday morning, I found one.

The *Pioneer Press* gave a brief report on my southwest swing and early successes in lining up party leaders. Bill Salisbury noted "Bert McKasy is getting ready to jump on the train," and went on to speculate that five others, including state representative Gil Gutknecht, might decide to run. The article featured quick profiles of strengths and weaknesses of each potential candidate. Salisbury listed my strengths: "First candidate out of the chute, he's running hard. Tall and distinguished, looks like central casting's idea of a senator. Impressive academic and [party] resume. Staunch conservative with a moderate style." For weaknesses, he wrote these: "Unproven commodity. Novice candidate. Least known in the field. Not flashy. Opponents can portray him as a big-city lawyer-professor." That all seemed fair enough. Finally, we no longer seemed to be running a stealth campaign.

★　★　★　★　★

The week between the first two Saturdays in March passed in a quick blur. I taught classes at Hamline, chaired a securities arbitration panel, and attended single BPOU conventions on Monday and Tuesday evenings. Friday, I turned back to fundraising. George Pillsbury, a member of the wealthy family and a former Republican state senator, was on the list of people to call. Pillsbury was one of the party leaders who had been mostly shut out of party activities by the abortion issue. He didn't like that one bit. Pillsbury said the time was too early to contribute. Besides, he wanted a prochoice candidate. "Doug, just send me a one-page statement on choice," he said.

He knew I'd been campaigning as prolife. Apparently, he expected I might switch to prochoice to get his money. Pillsbury hadn't heard the roar of the Wheaton crowd.

★ ★ ★ ★ ★

The second Saturday of March was another long day on the road through rural and small-town Minnesota. This time Gail decided the best bang for the buck would be in the first congressional district in the southeast corner of the state. The day was brilliantly sunny and crisp. What a perfect day for campaigning. Everyone was in a good mood.

After driving 90 miles south to start the day with breakfast and a speech in the elementary school cafeteria where the Waseca County BPOU was convening, Gail, my daughter Amy, and I drove east 60 miles to Rochester. The Olmstead County convention was the plum of the day. Other candidates knew it, too. We arrived in time to listen to speeches for nearly two hours, and since the delegates were in session, I couldn't even work the room. By noon I was the last speaker standing between the delegates and their lunch. That's a dangerous place to be, so I pushed through the speech quickly.

Later, stops in Goodhue County, in suburban Bloomington for the College Republicans, and in Meeker County added up to a day of 15 hours, 285 delegates, and 325 miles. Mary and I arrived home exhausted, yet I was also exhilarated. The feeling was the same one that often comes on Friday afternoons. Satisfaction of completion of hard work glowed inside. During convention season, the expression should have been "Thank God It's Saturday."

★ ★ ★ ★ ★

The routine of conventions was Gail sent one or more of her young crew ahead to slime the convention room walls and entryways with our signs (slime seems such a nasty word, but that was the vernacular passed down to us by

*earlier campaigns). Gail, our chaperone for the day, and I arrived hours later
to find a sea of red and white McFarland for Senate signs. This meant some
early morning departures for our people so they could claim the choice sign
spots at distant conventions.*

About five one morning, Ron Carey—a true stalwart of the
campaign—arrived at our house to collect two of our children, Stuart
and Katie. They were to ride with him to a distant convention, assist in
sliming all the walls with signs, and wait there for Mary and me to arrive
hours later for the speech and then a ride home with us. Both Stuart and
Katie thought that the long ride in Ron Carey's car would be a great time
to complete their short night's sleep. It wasn't. All Mary and I heard on the
later ride home was how mean old Ron had made them work the entire
trip sorting literature, pre-taping signs, and blowing up balloons.

When I couldn't attend a convention personally, Gail sent a surrogate
speaker, or sometimes to small, remote counties, only a letter. She had a
list of thirteen speakers to choose from, including my wife Mary, daughter
Amy, Rich Villela, Steve Clark, and Ron Carey.

★ ★ ★ ★ ★

On Tuesday evening, BPOU senate district 34 convened at the high
school in west suburban Orono. Convention chair Gary Carlson, an
active supporter, placed my name first on the speakers' list. Bert McKasy
and his wife Carolyn arrived soon after we did; he made second on the
list. In contrast with the small rooms of county BPOU conventions,
this large suburban district was meeting in a spacious open hall with an
elevated stage at one end. On stage was a single table with three chairs
for convention leaders. In front of the table was a bare metal stand with a
microphone attached at the top.

During graduate studies in speech-communication ten years earlier,
I learned many things theoretical and practical that were useful in the
campaign. One idea was that a speaker who wants to persuade people
should get as close to the audience as possible; any barrier, such as a raised
stage, a rostrum, or even a microphone stand, creates distance and makes
the speaker less persuasive. For this speech, when I was introduced, I

bounded up onto the stage, removed the microphone from its stand, jumped back down from the stage, and spoke from a position on the floor of the hall in the center aisle close to the first row of seats. Convention after convention I always stood as close as possible to the audience to speak. I was always amazed that not one other candidate for any office did the same. Every one of them marched up to the designated spot, usually on an elevated stage, and stood stiffly behind the microphone, or worse yet behind a massive rostrum, to deliver the speech.

After I finished speaking, we lingered in the hall to hear Bert McKasy speak. When his name was called, McKasy strode up the steps onto the stage and took his place behind the metal stand and microphone. He grabbed the stand and shuffled nervously. He pulled three or four letter-size pages from his jacket pocket and proceeded to read his speech. Two weeks of conventions, and he was still reading his five-minute speech! Classical rhetoricians taught that an important speech must be delivered from memory. That is why I worked so hard to memorize all my speeches, including this first one.

Yet I don't want to single out Bert for his speech-making. My own delivery had improved greatly after four weeks of BPOU conventions.

Everyone has the image of a polished politician effortlessly delivering a flowing speech at the drop of a hat. That is not the reality. Practice works.

★ ★ ★ ★ ★

Around four the following Friday afternoon, Gail, Mary, and I embarked on the longest road trip of the year. North and west of the Twin Cities lay the seventh and eighth congressional districts, encompassing two-thirds of the land area of the state. The time had come to take it on. We began with an easy 120-mile drive due north to Duluth. The good news was that both Duluth BPOUs, with a combined number of 80 delegates, were meeting together. The bad news was that the Duluth conventions were the only game in the state that evening, so every party official, every candidate, and every hanger-on was there.

We arrived around 6:15 to begin three solid, uninterrupted hours of grip and grin, speak, and more grip and grin. Make an impression. Remember names—kitchen cabinet members Jack and Therese Vaughn, Congressional candidate Phil Herwig, friend Jerry Arnold, party VIPs Andy Larson and Pat Carlson, scores of others. Stay on message. Answer friendly questions—or was that a trick question? The expenditure of mental energy for those three intense hours was huge, and the physical toll on the body—especially the back—was surprisingly large.

The last half hour, Gail and I engaged in a running negotiation. I wanted to get on the road. Ahead lay five hours of middle-of-the-night driving across 255 miles of mostly two-lane highway from Duluth to Moorhead on the other side of the state. She wanted me to shake more hands. Finally, we walked out around 9:15. We picked up a McDonald's road dinner and started west.

Gail took the wheel so Mary and I could rest, but neither of us could rest with Gail driving. She liked to go fast—she had purchased a new, fire-red sports car with her first earnings from the campaign. The problem was not driving fast. The problem was she didn't like to slow down for cars ahead of her. When we came roaring up behind another car, Gail maintained speed until the last second, then mashed on the brake to avoid a rear-end collision. After we backed off a few car lengths, she would again roar up to close the gap until she had to mash on the brake again. This cycle might repeat four or five times until a clear spot to pass opened.

The effect was like sitting in a rocket sled. Resting was not an option when every minute or two our heads snapped forward with the braking, then back with the sudden acceleration, then forward again, then back again. Our evening of intense concentration was not yet over. Now Mary and I were concentrating not on remembering names and answering questions but instead on keeping our feet from stomping on imaginary brake pedals and gritting our teeth from saying anything.

After about the first half-hour, every so often I said, "You know, Gail, we don't really have to make it to Moorhead tonight. We can stop somewhere and start earlier tomorrow."

"No," she muttered without taking her eyes from the road, "we'll make it."

"Now that I've eaten something, I feel better," I ventured. "I could drive."

"I'm fine."

A few minutes later, Mary would say, "I'm not really tired at all. I can drive."

"No, this is my job. You two should rest for our big day tomorrow."

We continued our restful drive westward on highway 210 through the blackness interrupted only briefly by a few small towns. Finally, in response to another one of my offers, Gail admitted she was spent, so I took the wheel. She had put in 90 minutes and knocked off 85 miles. I drove another 90 minutes, punctuated only by a few more towns, and covered another 80 miles. That left us 90 miles short of Moorhead, and none of us were in any shape to drive.

We stopped at a motel in Wadena. I was glad Mary was along on this trip. She felt warm and comfortable as we drifted off to sleep in that small motel room far from home.

At six the next morning, we continued our discovery of the size of the seventh congressional district. Its vast, mostly empty area covers far more than the northwest quarter of the state of Minnesota. Candidates with money flew around the seventh district. We drove. Ninety miles to Moorhead for the Clay County BPOU convention. Concentrate on

Georgiann and Bob Stenerson, key players in both Clay County and the seventh district. Seventy-five miles north to Crookston and lunch at the Polk County convention. BBQ hamburgers were delicious. Sixty miles east to Bagley where BPOU chair LeRoy Sundbom had fulfilled his promise to keep the Clearwater County convention in session until we arrived. Delegates receptive and enthusiastic. Race 50 miles south to Park Rapids for the Hubbard County convention to find they had already adjourned. At least that put us back on schedule for 35 miles south to Wadena—where we had stayed overnight and started the day—for the Wadena County convention chaired by kitchen cabinet member Andy Kessler. Forty-five miles south to Alexandria in Douglas County. Potluck dinner. Warm welcome. One hundred forty-five miles southeast to home. Drag into our driveway around eleven p.m. Saturday night.

Summary of two-day trip: 875 miles, 270 delegates, 31 hours. New places and new faces. Everything first-time fresh. Tremendous feeling of progress. This two-day swing was the most satisfying road trip of the entire campaign.

★ ★ ★ ★ ★

The BPOU convention season ended a few days later, on Tuesday evening, March 30, with three large Twin Cities districts. We started in a Minneapolis senate district, moved on to south-suburban Bloomington, and finished in the southwest suburb of Chaska. Bert McKasy was already at the community center waiting to speak. Bert and I exchanged some friendly banter as we stood at the back of the room and waited the expected few minutes until the convention chair introduced him and then me.

This chair didn't seem to understand the unwritten rule that candidates need to speak and leave early. The convention droned onward. We listened for over an hour to reports on credentials, awards for local fundraisers, and debates on resolutions. Bert and I both sat down.

Finally, the chair announced that candidates were waiting to address the delegates. He peered down at his list and said "The first candidate we have here tonight for the U.S. Senate is Bert Mick-CASEY." Bert leaped from his chair, stomped forward to the stage, grabbed the microphone, glared out at the room, and practically shouted "I'm Bert MACK-asee, and I'm running for Senate." I don't know that I've seen him more worked up before or since. Apparently, this was the end of a long day and a long BPOU convention season for both of us.

CHAPTER SIX

Was That A Stall Warning?

The end of the successful BPOU convention season brought all of us on the campaign a high of satisfaction from hard work rewarded with accomplishment. Then, from a completely unexpected direction, I got kicked in the stomach. Ray McCoy, the dean of students, called me in my law school office to say "A female student wants to file a complaint of harassment against you."

I laughed out loud. "What? Who is it? What did I do?"

When he gave me her name, I said "I don't have a clue who that is." Not remembering students' names may at first seem unusual, but after teaching two classes each of 70 or more students every semester year after year, I remembered few names.

"Well," he continued, "she wants to file a complaint and we have to deal with it. But don't worry, it doesn't involve touching or language or anything like that."

"Well, what kind of a complaint is it then?" I demanded.

"She says for one thing you came down too hard on other students in your evidence class last fall for coming in late—singled them out."

"I came down on someone else too hard, and she didn't like it?"

"Yeah, that's it. The second is she was working at the library desk one day and you came in and talked to her. I asked her if it was library business or something else, and she said it was library business."

"You've got to be kidding me."

"And the other thing she mentions is that a few days later she was talking to another professor at the front of the room after class and you came into the room for your class and stood behind her as you erased the board."

Now I was part dumbfounded, part outraged, and thoroughly sick to my stomach. A student wanted to accuse me of harassment. Since the student was female, people would immediately think sexual harassment. She was raising nothings that happened six months earlier. She either had personal issues of her own or political motivations; if the latter, I could be sure the story would reach the media.

"Ray, do you have any idea how silly those things sound? Can't you just tell her to get lost or dismiss this thing summarily?"

"Doug, I tried to talk with her about whether she really wanted to go through with this thing. If she files, we have to do something about it."

"You're the dean of students. Tell her it's ridiculous."

"I did talk her into meeting with you and me to talk about it."

"Ray, the whole thing is asinine. What makes you think I would dignify this by meeting with her?"

"I think you'd better do it. Maybe she'll listen to reason."

Even though the chances that she would listen to reason seemed remote, I showed up, fresh off the campaign trail, at the dean of students' office the morning of April 2 to meet my accuser. The first thing she said when I walked into the office was "I don't know if you remember me." I didn't.

McCoy and I spent the next 20 minutes trying to reason with her. She wouldn't budge. She had an agenda.

I left the meeting with my guts still churning. She obviously had nothing, yet just as obviously she had something. The simple headline of a harassment complaint against me would likely be a front-page story, and all our months of effort would wash out just like that. Few would bother to read the actual allegations, if they were even reported. The two words "sexual harassment" would be all that registered. No one would see the page 33 story a couple of months later that the complaint had been summarily dismissed. The mere allegation would be devastating.

Still, the political schedule would not wait. Within a half hour of leaving the meeting, I returned to the state office building in downtown St. Paul for another full afternoon of meetings with more Republican state legislators. Gail wanted me to convince them they wouldn't be running with an anchor at the top of the ticket. How about a harasser?

★ ★ ★ ★ ★

Another Republican I wanted to meet with was Vin Weber. Weber had been the Republican Congressman from the second district, and now was a high-powered lobbyist in Washington. He was also the Republican king maker in Minnesota. Gail and I had tried to get to Weber directly through letters and telephone messages. We had tried to get to him indirectly through his right-hand man in the state, national committeeman Jack Meeks. Now the rumor was floating that Weber was lining up behind Gil Gutknecht for Senate. Gail and I became even more frantic in trying to reach him.

To that end, I attended a program of the Center for the American Experiment, a Minnesota conservative think tank, when Weber was scheduled to talk. After the program, I made my way through the milling crowd to Weber's side. We both gripped and grinned, but this was not the time or place for substantive talk. I'd find out later whether this little personal touch would produce a meeting.

★ ★ ★ ★ ★

My primary job in early April was writing a speech for the eight congressional district conventions that were scheduled later in the month. Even with our frenetic schedule attending as many BPOU conventions as possible, I had been at fewer than half. That meant most congressional district delegates had never laid eyes on me. The district conventions would be another crucial introduction. Each of them would allow me— and every other candidate for state-wide office—a strictly enforced six minutes to speak. That's not much time to introduce myself, tell a joke, talk issues, invoke Republican heroes, blast Democrats, exhort the troops, and exude optimism about the coming election.

Gail and I worked through many drafts of the speech. We agreed on almost all the content. It again introduced my family and party history. It repeated my campaign theme of honesty, common sense, and hard work. It highlighted six major issues in bullet-point fashion; time did not allow any depth. On taxes and spending, I tried to be both pithy and memorable by saying "The federal budget is worse than a zucchini plant; we need spending control, not higher taxes." The speech wound up with an exhortation to work together to win the election.

The one area Gail and I didn't agree was how to turn some of the phrases. I wanted subtlety. Gail wanted bold strokes. This especially showed in our argument over how to handle the issue of abortion.

Gail said flatly "You have to tell the delegates you're prolife."

"They already know I'm prolife. Our literature says so."

"You have to tell them. It's a red meat line."

"I have plenty of other red meat lines."

"Maybe so, but they expect and want to hear you're prolife from your own mouth," Gail countered. "These people have been betrayed time and time again in the past. They need to hear you say it."

Whether the delegates wanted that red meat or not, I wasn't about to throw it to them. At that time, I still hoped to bring people together as a prolife candidate who spoke reasonably and didn't rub the issue in the faces of prochoice people. The line finally came out as "I'm a pragmatic, fiscal conservative, much in the tradition of Jack Kemp and Vin Weber. While I don't wear my religious views on my sleeve, I am certainly in agreement with the social issues of our party."

After writing and memorizing the speech, I needed to hone the delivery, so on Wednesday evening before the first Saturday convention, Gail scheduled a practice session in a law classroom at Hamline. She brought in a half dozen of our loyal supporters to listen and deliver their critiques. They thought the content of the speech was all right. Their primary criticism was I didn't show enough fire and passion in the delivery.

They were right. Perhaps because of years of teaching, my natural speaking style was a conversational delivery. Translating that to politics, I pictured myself in the Senator Bob Dole mode. Dole was bright, conservative, and witty, and he'd gone a long way in politics. The trouble was that he was too witty for his own good. At the nationally televised debate, Dole was asked why he wanted the job of Vice President. He answered the pay was good and it involved no heavy lifting. I thought he was hilarious. The people I talked to thought he was just plain mean. So conversational and witty was out. I would try again and go for passion.

We also videotaped the repeated performances. Like other speakers, I had carried a vision of myself holding an audience spellbound. Then I watched the videotape. Instead of a powerful orator dominating the room, I saw a tall goof tilting from side to side like a drunk. Instead of a leader calmly surveying all parts of the vast hall, I saw a bobble head doll jerking his head back and forth aimlessly. Instead of a booming voice commanding the crowd, I heard a slow, lugubrious, boring monotone— except when I tried harder to show passion and sounded hurried and screechy. I could only shake my head and run through the speech yet again.

★ ★ ★ ★ ★

Delegates didn't expect a candidate to do the impossible and appear at more than 130 BPOU conventions. Delegates did expect to see the candidate at all eight congressional district conventions. To miss a district convention would be a disastrous sign: the candidate didn't care enough, wasn't organized enough, didn't have enough money, or didn't have enough guts.

The problem again was even though four Saturdays were designated for the congressional district conventions, three districts, hundreds of miles apart, all chose to convene at 9 a.m. on April 17. The sixth district was meeting in the Minneapolis suburb of Maple Grove; the seventh district was meeting in Moorhead, on the North Dakota border; and the eighth district was meeting in Hibbing, in the heart of the iron range in northeastern Minnesota. We worked on all possible driving combinations. All were impossible. Too many miles, too little time. Driving was out. We had to fly.

Gail Sutton worked more of her magic, and she found a private pilot willing to fly us around the state on Saturday for the cost of gasoline for the airplane. He's a good conservative trying to build up his flying hours to work toward a job as a commercial pilot, Gail said.

Small plane safety was a topic of interest to any political candidate. Several political candidates, and sitting members of Congress, had been killed in small plane crashes on the campaign trail. Consequently, some candidates refused to travel in single-engine planes; some Washington political consultants demanded their clients use a dual-engine plane with two pilots. We didn't have a consultant, a dual-engine plane, or a second pilot. Our choice was dictated by what we could afford: one engine and one pilot in a four-seater.

Who would fill the four seats? Seats one and two were easy: the pilot and the candidate. Gail as the campaign manager was certainly the logical choice for a seat. That left seat four. Mary was willing and even eager to go, but I told her I didn't want our four young children to become orphans. As a person who believed in God's will, I did not truly fret about the airplane crashing. At the same time, I also believed God helped those who helped themselves: I saw no need voluntarily to create a potential disaster. With reluctance, I gave in to our daughter Amy's entreaties to fly along. At least in the event of disaster, our other children would still have their mother.

The final plan took shape. Friday night we would start in Moorhead with a hospitality suite. Gail would rent a room in the convention hotel, move out all the furniture, and arrange for appetizers and soft drinks. Along with a few volunteers, Gail and I would station ourselves in the hospitality suite in the hopes of meeting and greeting delegates arriving the evening before the convention. When the scheduled three hours for the hospitality suite ended around ten p.m., Gail would drive to

Hibbing, Steve Clark and I would drive home to the Twin Cities, and our volunteers would spend the night in the room to await the morning convention. Saturday morning, Mary and I would drive the ten miles from home to the sixth district convention in Maple Grove, then Mary would drive Amy and me to the nearby Crystal airport. Amy and I would fly to Hibbing, then on to Moorhead. If plans went awry, we had a loyalist in Moorhead with a surrogate speech in his pocket.

Early Friday afternoon, I joined Steve Clark and four boisterous young volunteers in our family minivan for the four-hour drive northwest on I-94 to Moorhead. Steve drove. Gail Sutton was already in Moorhead, ready to take command.

The one instruction I personally gave the volunteers was to use plenty of tape on the campaign posters; the absolute last thing I wanted to was to see was one of my posters slide off the wall to the floor. I didn't give the volunteers a reason, but Gail and Mary knew. Over the years, I had seen many posters of many candidates slide to many convention floors. Every time I saw a poster on the floor, the candidate soon lost. I regarded seeing a poster on the floor as a sign. Cary Humphries had dropped out of the Senate race because he thought his health scare was a sign. I thought a falling campaign poster was a sign. Gail humored me on this. Mary thought it was ridiculous. No matter. I believed it. I didn't want to see any of my posters on the floor.

When we arrived at the convention motel in Moorhead, the volunteers hustled to the large meeting room and began to slime it with McFarland for Senate posters. Later, I checked their work and was gratified to see they had nabbed most of the good locations and that the posters were securely fastened.

Gail and I changed into delegate-meeting clothes and waited in the hospitality suite. We probably would have had a more productive evening by joining the sliming work. Along the motel hallway of half a dozen hospitality suites, the most common sight was a candidate or personal aide wandering into another candidate's suite to pass a little time. Delegates were scarce. A little before nine, we closed the hospitality suite early and scattered. As planned, the volunteers stayed in the room to await the morning convention. Steve Clark and I started the four-hour drive home with an estimated arrival time of 1:30 a.m. Gail left for Hibbing to oversee morning preparations there. The last thing I told her was to make sure all the campaign posters had plenty of tape.

★ ★ ★ ★ ★

Bright and early Saturday morning, Mary, Amy, and I drove along I-694, the Twin Cities' northern beltway, to Maple Grove, where the sixth congressional district delegates were meeting at the junior high school. We arrived in plenty of time to meet and greet, and to place high on the speakers' list, but we were not the earliest birds. Bert McKasy and his wife Carolyn were already there working the early arrivals.

I listened closely to McKasy's speech. He had improved. His delivery was still not smooth and forceful, but he was not reading the speech either. Then the convention chair called my name, and for the first of eight times, I delivered the congressional district speech. It wasn't my best effort, but the practice with volunteers a few days earlier had helped.

We hustled to the Crystal airport. Three of us—the pilot, Amy, and I—would fly to Hibbing. Gail would be waiting for us at the airport. After the Hibbing convention, Gail would take the fourth seat in the plane for Hibbing to Moorhead. The day was sunny and clear with little wind—perfect flying weather. We spotted our plane and pilot right away. As the pilot and I extended our right hands towards each other, I saw the pilot had a thumb and parts of two fingers missing. Amy saw it too; she seemed about to panic.

"I notice you had an accident with your hand," I tried to say casually. "Does that affect your flying?"

"Nah. It's no problem at all. I can still hold the stick fine."

"Will it affect your ability to get a job with a commercial airline later?"

"Nah. I'm OK."

The pilot's assurances hadn't helped Amy, but we had no choice. We kissed Mary goodbye and squeezed into the plane. This was my first time in a small airplane, and I immediately discovered that small planes were not designed for big people. I scrunched into a seat designed for passengers about 5'8" tall, instead of 6'8" tall.

The small plane bounced along the taxiway to the runway, turned into the light breeze, and gathered speed as we jostled along the runway. It seemed to object to leaving the ground, but eventually, it rose a little, then more and more, and we were off to Hibbing.

Amy and I had been looking forward to our first low-level flight, and we enjoyed the sights as we flew north. Huge Lake Mille Lacs lay in the western distance. The farther north we flew, pine forests increasingly covered the ground. I also enjoyed listening in on the pilot's communications with ground stations on the radio headset he had given me. Too soon, we circled over the pine forest and descended into the Hibbing airport.

Gail was waiting, toe tapping, at the airport. She spoke even more rapidly than usual. "The delegates are at lunch. I've arranged for you to address them while they eat. Let's go." We sped to the convention motel. I had the lunch crowd to myself, as other candidates and party officials had started in Hibbing and were long gone, or they had started in Moorhead and were still on the way. The eighth congressional district delegates were in a good mood over their food, and they shouted their approval of the speech. We were back at the airport by 1:30.

I remembered the small plane had seemed reluctant to lift off from Crystal with three people on board, and now Gail made four. We jounced along the Hibbing runway, gathering speed, coming closer and closer to the tall pine trees looming beyond the end of the runway, as the plane labored to take to the air. Finally, we lifted off and floated above the tree line. When the pilot banked right to aim the nose of the plane west, a high-pitched alarm started whooping. I tried to keep my face turned straight ahead as my eyes darted left to the pilot. He appeared calm, but he was a whirl of motion at the controls. We lost a little altitude, our course straightened, the whooping stopped, and we began ascending again. I didn't turn to look at Amy or Gail or ask the pilot whether we had heard a stall warning; I didn't want to know.

Since we had no time for lunch with the delegates in Hibbing, Gail had obtained box lunches. Not long into the flight we began eating our sandwiches. Soon after, from the backseat Gail moaned, "I don't feel so good."

"What's the problem?"

"I've never been very good with motion sickness."

"Oh, great. Should you be eating anything?"

"Maybe not. Ohhhh."

I tried to focus on my own lunch and on the scenery. That worked for a while until the unmistakable sound of retching came from the back seat. Gail had found a use for the bag in which she had carried the lunches.

A volunteer met us at the Moorhead airport. We arrived around four p.m. at the convention motel I had left only 17 hours earlier. The convention was clearly in its final stages and the delegates were growing weary. Our surrogate speaker heaved a great sigh of relief when he saw us arrive; he would not be needed. I delivered the speech for the third time that day; it flowed even better, and I made sure to throw in a reference to being back in town after the previous evening's hospitality suite. Afterwards, I shook just about every hand in the place. We had nowhere else to go.

Gail remained in Moorhead to collect the posters and the volunteers. Amy and I happily climbed into the plane for the third and last time. The plane, again lighter, seemed more eager to return to the air. We tracked I-94 southeast from Moorhead back to Crystal uneventfully as afternoon faded into evening.

Mary was waiting for us at the airport. We rolled to a stop, and I crawled out of the plane. Three two-hour flights jammed awkwardly into the front seat of the small plane had been sandwiched around frantic, high-stakes, high-tension activity. I could hardly stand.

That day was the first of many, varied physical ailments of the campaign. That the back went first was typical. News stories at the end of the year reported that both Senator Paul Wellstone and John Marty, the Democratic candidate for governor, were to undergo back surgeries. The combination of sustained high tension and pressure of a campaign together with travel requiring long hours sitting in the cramped spaces of small planes or cars was a sure-fire recipe for back agony.

Sure-fire back pain

On this evening at the Crystal airport, I was not thinking about my aching back. I was rejoicing about making all three conventions in one day. I had seen the other Senate candidates Bert McKasy and Gil Gutknecht, and candidates for other offices, at the convention halls and at the airports. Flying did not place me one-up on the others, but failure to fly would have put me one-down. I was tremendously grateful to our pilot. Gail and her people had done the best job of any of the campaigns in sliming the convention halls with posters. My speech, improved each time, had been received enthusiastically. I went home walking tall, even if I couldn't straighten up.

★ ★ ★ ★ ★

About this time, an event happened that a year later would have a deciding effect on my campaign, but that could not be foreseen. Allen Quist, a former state legislator, a farmer near St. Peter, and a solid social conservative, entered the race for party endorsement against incumbent Republican Governor Arne Carlson.

Carlson had been elected governor in a bizarre series of events. Holding the office of state auditor, he had directed his efforts toward the governorship for years. When party state convention delegates chose a political newcomer over him for endorsement, he ran in the primary anyway. He lost. Then a few weeks before the general election, the newcomer was hit with a scandal. The party turned to Carlson, and he won the general election.

This history meant Governor Carlson and party activists eyed each other warily. The relationship did not warm over the first three years of his term. Activists were prolife; he was prochoice. They were conservative on other issues; he was liberal. They liked to be cultivated; he preferred to ignore them. Still, by early spring of this year prior to the general election, nearly every one of the activists I talked to was willing to swallow hard and endorse the sitting governor for another term. All he had to do was ask.

Instead of reaching out to activists, Carlson did not attend any party meetings. Instead of simply keeping his peace, he signed a full-page newspaper ad for Planned Parenthood and worked hard to push a gay rights bill through the state legislature. He seemed to be going out of his way to thumb his nose at party regulars.

A dump Carlson movement, with Allen Quist as its candidate, sprang to life. Quist played the party activist game, appearing everywhere, speaking at conventions, cultivating the delegates. Carlson refused to play the game. His strategy obviously was to bypass party endorsement at the state convention and go directly to the Republican primary without it. This offended party people even more.

Quist's entry into the governor's race had no initial effect on my campaign for the Senate. I kept repeating the same thing I had been saying all along when rumors of his challenge began: that's not my race and I take no position on it. Over the coming months, I probably repeated that phrase more than a thousand times. That was the only sensible position for me to take, and it had the added benefit of being true.

★ ★ ★ ★ ★

The next Saturday schedule showed conventions in the contiguous first, second, and third congressional districts—much more compact. The weekend began with a 90-mile drive from home to New Ulm for Friday evening dinner with second district delegates. Gail, Mary, and I sat down to dine with about 200 congenial companions. Of course, we didn't do much sitting or much dining. I had to work the room. So did Mary and Gail. The goal was to press the flesh and have a meaningful minute or two of conversation with every delegate and every spouse in the room. That's a lot more difficult than it sounds.

Working a dinner involves balancing. Balance spending time chatting with the people at your own table against appearing timid and afraid to get up and work the room. Balance looking energetic moving about the room against looking desperately frenetic. Balance reaching every person in the room against taking time for an intelligent conversation at each table. Balance visiting every table against letting people eat when dinner arrives. Balance the need to appear relaxed and confident against the need to appear serious and senatorial. Balance the warmth of openness against an aura of mystery. Balance getting up close and personal against invading personal space: squatting next to a person who is sitting at a table works nicely, except for the aching back and knees at the end of the dinner.

Another critical balance was concentrating on the person in front of me against watching my back for someone approaching. People say they like a politician who really talks to them and isn't always looking for the next hand to shake. The problem was my eyes did wander. I was not so much looking for the next hand to shake as trying to make sure I didn't get an unexpected hand from someone whose name I could not call to my tongue in a split-second. A quick look around usually gave me the necessary few seconds for the next person's name to emerge from my memory bank.

By the time our little group of three started the 90-mile drive back home, my shirt was soaked with sweat. But the dinner wasn't over. Now was the time for second guesses. Did I make every table? I don't remember talking to Neal Breitbarth. Why didn't I remember Gerald Woodley's name? What a stupid answer I gave to Maureen Krumrey's question. Linda Pettman must have felt slighted when I cut her short to turn to Ron Frauenshuh. Most of all, where was I looking while shaking hands or answering questions?

I knew a sincere, warm person—a good politician—looked into the other person's eyes when shaking hands or conversing. The problem was that when concentrating, as to remember a name or answer a question, I have always found myself looking blankly toward the ceiling as if the answer were printed up there. So at the end of this dinner, or any dinner or reception through the campaign, I could later remember many times when I had been talking to someone and hadn't any idea where I'd been looking—except I knew it wasn't into the eyes of the other person. Looking into another's eyes wasn't that hard. Why couldn't I remember it?

Who knew a dinner with like-minded friends could be so draining? Coaches in baseball keep their players loose by reminding them they are playing a game. At the beginning, the umpire calls out "Play ball!" Well, an umpire for a politician attending a dinner or reception would call out "Work room!"

The dinner had taken its toll. Mary and I, and Gail, were all completely worn out when we reached home Friday night, so we agreed to get a decent night's sleep and push back our Saturday morning departure time. That meant when we traversed the 90 miles back to New Ulm for the 9 a.m. convention, we were at the tail end of the speakers' list and had to listen to more than a dozen speeches: state party chair Bob Weinholzer, national committeeman Jack Meeks, national committeewoman Evie Axdahl, Senator Dave Durenberger, former Senator Rudy Boschwitz, Senate candidate Bert McKasy, Senate candidate Gil Gutknecht, Governor candidate Allen Quist, Attorney General candidate Tad Jude, and others.

When my turn finally came, the second congressional district delegates packed into the hall were still in a good mood even after a long morning of political speeches. The second district was the home of farming, small towns, and solid Republican majorities—my kind of place. They cheered and clapped at all my expected applause lines, and even also at a few others. Their reception gave me a rush of adrenaline to carry forward to the next convention in the first district.

In the car on the two-hour drive to Rochester, Gail reported she had slid up behind Vin Weber, the former second district Congressman, to try to get his reaction to my speech. Her report was that Weber had whispered to Jack Meeks "He's really good." Another boost of adrenaline. Bring on the first district!

The first congressional district in Rochester was also fertile Republican soil, although the delegates were not as single-mindedly conservative as in the second. The delegates in the first had also heard a lot of speeches, as the same speakers from New Ulm had arrived and spoken in Rochester in roughly the same order. While the Rochester delegates did not greet my speech with the powerful hunger of the New Ulm delegates, they did greet it with enthusiasm and several applause breaks.

We drove hard the next hour-and-a-half to reach the community center in the Minneapolis suburb of Edina before the third congressional district convention adjourned, only to find we had arrived early enough to listen to several of the speeches for the third time. Seemingly every other candidate and office holder in the state had followed the same plan as ours for the day: second district to first district to third district.

The third district delegates responded to my speech positively, but without the uproarious response of the first two conventions. Part of the reason for their more subdued response was the end of a long day. Another part of the reason highlighted a major tension of the campaign. We had concentrated on portraying me as a rock-solid, dependable conservative. That was essential to survive as a Republican candidate outside the Twin Cities, but problematical inside the Twin Cities—especially in the third congressional district. The third district in suburban Minneapolis had the largest concentration of Republican moderates in the state; Edina was the place I had been beat over the head at the potluck dinner for announcing I was prolife. Our campaign had largely been ignoring the third district, not only in time and attention but also in failing to throw them some bones in the speech.

The last day of congressional district conventions was the following Saturday, May 1. The fourth district of St. Paul and suburbs was my home, and the fifth district of Minneapolis and suburbs was the home of kitchen cabinet member Reuben Lundquist and district chairman Jack Gausman, who was firmly in my camp. Both districts felt comfortable.

Delivering the same speech for the seventh and eighth times, I was feeling comfortable too. The same could be said for the other candidates. The hardships of the campaign trail were producing a weary sort of camaraderie. By this point, each of us thought that we had heard the others' speeches often enough to remember them. As we waited our turns, we joked that when one was introduced, another should just step forward and deliver that other person's speech.

CHAPTER SEVEN

A Month Of Disasters

★ ★ ★ ★ ★

Convention season was a two-month rush of anticipation, suspense, exhilaration, tension, and all-out physical and mental effort. With its end, the time returned, as it always does, for politics by retail. Time to come down from the excitement of the crowds. Time to go back to the basement to spend long evenings on the telephone. Time to meet one-on-one with potential contributors. Time to try to earn free media from reporters. Time to make appearances at more party meetings. Finally, at the end of the month, time to stretch beyond party insiders to the general public. Some months are longer than others in politics. May was one of them.

Gail Sutton and I had been pursuing Dane Smith, the political reporter for the Twin Cities' newspaper, the *StarTribune*, but he had been putting us off. The big city paper wouldn't give me—or other aspiring politicians—the time of day until I made some sort of mark to show I was a serious contender. Now the three of us were sitting down together for lunch.

Smith insisted on bringing a photographer with him even though Gail told him we had a professional head shot photo to give to him. The photographer took a few photos and left us to our lunch. Later, whenever a story about me appeared in the *StarTribune*, it ran with their photo, not ours. In the low light of the restaurant, their photo had come out a little dark. My hair could have used a quick comb. My expression was a bit surprised. Instead of looking approachable, as in our photo, I looked as if I'd just been hit with a cattle prod.

Gail and I talked up our growing list of committed delegates and successes at the conventions. "We're beating Bert McKasy badly in the count of committed delegates," she said, "and Gil Gutknecht hasn't done much yet. We like our chances."

Smith countered, "How about Vin Weber being behind Gutknecht? Won't that make him the man to beat?"

"I've heard the rumor that Vin's behind Gutknecht too, but he claims he's not," I said.

"But what if Weber does come in behind Gutknecht? Won't that make things pretty tough on you?"

Here was the spot where my manager Gail Sutton put her foot into my mouth. She said "We're not worried about that. The last candidate Vin gave the party was Jon Grunseth, and we all know what happened to him." Three years earlier, Grunseth had won party endorsement for governor, only to be forced off the ticket by scandal two weeks prior to the general election. That was when the party turned to Arne Carlson, and he had been elected governor.

I should have recognized I needed to pull Gail's foot from my mouth. Maybe with more experience with political reporters and politicians, I would have known enough to do it. At the time, I thought it was an amusing little witticism, a throw-away line that would quickly vanish into the political ether.

After lunch, Gail and I compared notes. "Do you think we'll get anything out of them?" I asked her.

"Nah, you know the *StarTribune*. They won't run a puff piece about a conservative Republican. About the best we'll get is a mention the next time they decide to write about the Senate race in general."

We did get a mention the next time Smith wrote about the Senate race. Only a day or two later, an article mentioned the candidates, speculated that Vin Weber was behind Gutknecht, and reported that McFarland's manager didn't fear Weber because, she said, the last candidate he had given the Republican party was Jon Grunseth.

Uh, oh, that was bad. I should have called Weber immediately to apologize and to tell him the line was supposed to be a private joke that we never intended to be printed. The reason I didn't call was that Vin Weber was a former Congressman, a successful Washington lobbyist, a brilliant political strategist, and the leader of the Minnesota Republican party. I thought the crack would roll off his back like water off a duck. It didn't.

About two weeks later, my former law student Duncan McCampbell set up a lunch for journalist Barry Casselman and me. Casselman was reputed to be close to Weber, so I thought this might be another way to reach the man. Near the end of our discussion, Casselman said "You remember a while back the *StarTribune* reported that your manager said you weren't worried about Vin Weber being behind Gutknecht since the last candidate he gave the party was Grunseth?"

"Yeah," I chuckled a little. "That was a pretty good line."

"Well, Vin is upset about it."

"He is?"

"And he would like some assurance that is not your attitude toward him."

Another self-inflicted wound! A throw-away line may have soured the state Republican kingmaker on me? You bet I will assure him. I like and admire Vin. I want and need his support. Be sure to tell Vin that Gail said it, I didn't, and neither of us expected it would see the light of day. I've been trying to meet with Vin for a long time and am available any time at his convenience. If we ever do get together, just have him bend over and tell me which cheek to kiss. Well, all right, I didn't say the last line, but I did say all the others, and I meant them.

This was an object lesson in political ego. A politician—even a superpower in the state—bruises easily. I shouldn't have been surprised since I bruise easily too. In a business with little hard information or solid feedback, the primary sources of information are rumor, guesswork, half-truths, and perceived slights. Grudges are easily formed on good information and bad. Both Gail and I would have to be more careful in the future with our witticisms.

★ ★ ★ ★ ★

With the daily pressure of travel and conventions over, we also re-doubled our fundraising efforts. I was ready to go hunting for big money. Both Gail Sutton and Steve Clark spent hours on the telephone in our small office calling the lists of past major Republican contributors. Only one in ten agreed to meet with me. Still, we thought, if we could pop the maximum $1000, or even $500, from each of them, we would be in great shape. Gail updated the folder we would hand to the prospects. It contained a few pieces of literature, a biography, my two newspaper opinion pieces, and a campaign plan.

We had lunch or coffee during the month with a retired insurance company CEO, the president of a suburban technology company, the president of a securities firm, an executive with the grain exchange, the president of a memorabilia company, the president of a suburban bank, the head of an accounting firm, a physician, the manager of a suburban mall, the political man for the president of a construction company, and many others.

After a few of these meetings, a check arrived in the mail. Upon opening one envelope, Gail cried out "Thank God." She had already missed a payday or two.

Much more often, our visits followed the same pattern. Gail and I arrived at the business office. The potential contributor gave us a personal tour of the business. We talked politics for a while and eventually worked our way into my campaign. He—at that time, nearly all the potential major contributors were male—said he liked what he heard. I asked for money. He said sorry; the time was too early in the political cycle–seven months until election year and eighteen months to the election. A few were also afraid of alienating Senator Dave Durenberger, who still had 20 months to go as the incumbent.

I was puzzled. The contributor had taken time to meet me. He thought I was a good candidate. He liked my message. A contribution would be pocket change to him. Still no money. Did he think Gail and I had come to get his personal views on the issues? What was the problem? Maybe I just plain couldn't close the sale. Maybe I wasn't crass enough and should have said "Let's be frank. I'm here today to collect your contribution for my campaign. I want your check for at least $500 before I leave."

One person eventually volunteered a reason that made sense. *He said that contributing to a political candidate was much like investing in a stock or picking a horse at the track. Everyone wanted to pick the winning horse or a stock going up; no one wanted any losing stocks in the portfolio even though overall the portfolio was a winner. Therefore, people would not place their bets until they had a pretty good idea of which stock was going up or which horse would win.* As the horse, I would much rather they just backed the field to have a sure winner.

A few contributors were reluctant to contribute because they saw themselves as party moderates and didn't like my prolife position. They wanted to give money to a prochoice candidate. Why did they agree to the meeting then? The contributor must have known my position on the issue before agreeing to meet. The desire to give only to a prochoice candidate also made little sense because it ran directly contrary to the desire to back the winning horse. The political reality in Minnesota was that the Republican candidate would be prolife.

Here's my conclusion on how the dynamic plays out. [The dynamic is the same for a Democratic candidate. Just replace "conservative" with "liberal" or "progressive."] A Republican candidate needs and seeks both political and financial support. Political support is firmly in the hands of conservatives, mostly social conservatives, and is available only to a candidate who takes solidly conservative positions on every issue of any importance. How about a moderating influence on the positions of that candidate from the moderates of the party? Since moderates have little political support to contribute, and moderate ideas do not stir deep passions, the best chance for moderates to influence candidates is through financial support. Yet they won't contribute because the candidate is too conservative. As the campaign continues, the candidate keeps gaining political support from conservatives, and keeps getting the financial door shut in his face by moderates. How is this going to affect candidates' positions on issues? It certainly is not going to moderate them. In the end, moderates complain their influence continues to wane and outsiders wonder why parties don't nominate more centrist candidates.

★   ★   ★   ★   ★

The law student who wanted to accuse me of harassment had not gone away. Instead, she filed a complaint, but not until after she had told her story to several other professors (and undoubtedly many students). The only good news was that the media had not picked up on it. My response remained the same: the complaint didn't even deserve a response, and the school should dismiss it summarily. The law school dean of students didn't think that was possible. In the meantime, the process churned forward. It wasn't just the process. Every time I thought about the subject, my stomach churned.

★   ★   ★   ★   ★

Another form of trouble was approaching sooner rather than later. The state party elected its officials every odd-numbered year at the summer state central committee meeting. That meeting was in June, only a month away. Bob Weinholzer was running for reelection as state party chair. Chris Georgacas, one of the party people Bob had recommended to me as a potential campaign manager, was challenging him. Weinholzer was popular with the delegates and had done a creditable job in his four years as state chairman, but the vagaries of electoral politics had dumped a few Republican election losses into his lap. That created an opening. Even so, most people wondered why Georgacas would leave a solid party job as chief staff aide to the state Republican House caucus to take a run at Weinholzer.

Gail Sutton had her theory. "Vin Weber wants Gutknecht for Senate, and he knows Bob will help you, so he needs to get rid of Bob. He told Chris to run." Maybe that was true, and maybe it was just another wild political theory.

Officially, I had no horse in the race. Unofficially, I really liked Bob and hardly knew Chris. Also, Bob was willing to help me. He had said "Doug, as party chair, you know I have to remain neutral in your race. I can't do anything openly for you. One of the few things I can do is to appoint you to the task force of your choice." Weinholzer had created several task forces to study issues for the next election: a task force on small business, a task force on taxes and spending, a task force on agriculture, a task force on social issues, and others. Since I'd been trying to position myself in a rural state as a champion of the farmer, I said "I'm weak in agriculture. Give me that one. It will be a good chance to learn." Bob granted the small favor, although six months later, at the next state central committee meeting, it would blow up in my face.

State party chair Bob Weinholzer

★ ★ ★ ★ ★

The topper for the month of disasters came at a noon luncheon. Senator Dave Durenberger had been scheduled to address the Edina Rotary at the Edina Country Club. At the last minute, he cancelled. A member of the club asked me to take his place.

Wealthy suburban Edina! Probably nearly all Republicans! Potential contributors! A chance to spread my wings by speaking to a real live citizens group, instead of dependable party activists. I leaped at the invitation.

The speech went well. Afterwards, I opened the floor for questions. That's when things fell apart. These people of the Edina Rotary didn't ask the standard questions, such as "What are you going to do about crime," which I by now could have answered in my sleep. They asked pointed questions about issues of import to business and specific bills before Congress.

I've been in political audiences myself and have always thought an incumbent has a tremendous advantage in this situation. The candidate already in office can speak to specific, even esoteric, matters with at least the appearance of familiarity and understanding. "What do you think of Senator X's proposal for eliminating the tax on manufacturing of widgets?" "Well, just last week Senator X and I were discussing that at the hearing on the bill. Blah, blah." "What is your position on S.R. 573?" "My legislative assistant is hard at work on that. Senator Z and I plan to introduce an amendment to that bill next month, and here's what it will do . . .."

Contrast the ability to make confident, knowledgeable replies with the situation of a person running for office. An audience member asks "What do you think of Senator X's proposal for eliminating the tax on manufacturing of widgets?"

Here's what happens for a non-incumbent, even one who has studied many issues for many hours. You stare at the questioner with a smile frozen tightly to your lips to give the impression that's exactly the question you hoped would be asked. The sweat begins to trickle down your sides. Your brain races through the options for your answer.

Option one. "Who cares? Ask me about something of general relevance to the American people, not some obscure tax loophole. Why don't you just pay your fair share?" That answer might be truthful, but for obvious reasons will not do.

Option two. "What the hell is a widget?" That answer would also be an honest, truthful response, but it too is no good.

Option three. "Tax on widgets? Here is my general position on taxes. Blah, blah." A possibility, but a transparent dodge of the question.

Option four. Start with a lie. "I'm glad you asked me about that." Show confidence. "The proposal is to eliminate the tax on widgets." An easy guess. "Since my general position on taxes is the American people are overtaxed at all levels and by nearly all kinds of taxes, I support eliminating the tax." Flash the questioner a hard smile and a quick nod. Quickly turn to the other side of the room to find another questioner. Another transparent dodge.

That leaves only option five. "I'm sorry not to be completely familiar with that proposal right now. My aide here is jotting down your question and I will look into it in the next day or two and get back to you." This response exudes sincerity, honesty, and openness (assuming the listeners overlook the lie about bothering to look into a question that no one will likely ever ask again). I like it. The question is so obscure I can't even fake an answer. So, there it is. That's my answer. Next question.

"What is your position on S.R. 573?" Again, the frozen smile and the trickling sweat. Since I just used up the honest answer about looking into an issue not familiar to me, that response seems to be out. These folks will not be too impressed with a candidate who answers everything "I don't know." Let's try option four.

Lloyd Cherne, the head of his own engineering company and a long-time Republican donor, asked about legislation dealing with technology and patent protection. Maybe because I recognized his name and thought he might be sympathetic to a Republican candidate, I tried to stumble my way through an answer. Big mistake. Worse, I guessed wrong about his position on the issue. His response to my answer was to announce in a loud voice "I don't think you know much about patent protection." How could I respond to this hammer blow between my eyes? The retort "Of course not. What person of sane mind does?" came immediately to mind, but I suppressed it. I smiled generously and announced to all "I seem to have hit a nerve," probably succeeding only in compounding the mistake by appearing to be smug and not to care.

Other questions went better. I left the meeting with my head still attached to my shoulders. Or so I thought. Looking back, I can picture Lloyd Cherne and others from the luncheon spreading the word all over town to other Republicans, business colleagues, and worst of all, potential donors about the aloof, know-nothing, smart aleck professor who had the chutzpah to think he could fill in for Senator Durenberger and speak to the Rotary. Half his answers amounted to he didn't know, and the other half were B.S. He'd better go back to his ivory tower because he doesn't belong in the real world. The wonderful opportunity resulted in a campaign disaster, and in the hindsight of years passed, this one might have been the worst of all.

The obvious advice on how to respond to obscure, unanticipated questions is to prepare better on the issues, but that's too glib. No human can anticipate everything another human will find important. A candidate will always be hit with odd-ball questions about leg-hold traps or patent protection or the gold standard. A friendly questioner will approach after the event to offer guidance on the unfamiliar issue; that also happened to me. A hostile questioner, or one offended by the cluelessness of the answer, will simply conclude the candidate is an ignoramus or worse yet announce the conclusion to the others assembled. The safe course likely is to dodge every odd-ball question or to admit being uninformed no matter how many times at one event. As the saying goes, better to be thought a fool than to open your mouth and remove all doubt.

CHAPTER EIGHT

Remind Me Again Of My Profoundly Held Beliefs

Every candidate for every office in every campaign must take positions on the issues of the day. Some issue positions are fundamental and therefore immutable. Others are peripheral and therefore open to creative mutation.

I received a telephone call in early summer urging me to oppose any law requiring helmets for motorcycle riders. While the issue is state and not federal, I happily agreed. You got it, and my position is mature and solid. The call reminded me of my first—and only prior—campaign for public office—a seat in the state house of representatives—more than a decade earlier. A few weeks into that campaign, as I was knocking on doors, a man asked "What do you think of mandating helmets for motorcycle riders?"

Standing on that man's porch and thinking about the issue of mandatory motorcyclist helmets for the first time, I knew why I had never thought about it. I didn't give a rip. Off the top of my head, I responded

"Seems to me a modest enough requirement to save some lives and prevent injuries." His face darkened, he muttered "OK," and he closed the door. He had my number and it was the wrong number.

A little subsequent research on my part showed that proposals were floating around the state legislature to require motorcycle riders to wear helmets. The proposals were opposed by many riders who insisted on their God-given right to feel wind blowing freely through their hair. All right, let's reconsider. Proponents thought that helmets were a good social policy to reduce injuries. Opponents thought their basic rights were at risk. An intellectual, do-good argument against a visceral, fundamental response. Who would feel strongly enough to ask about the issue?

A few weeks later, at another door, a woman asked me about motorcycle helmets. I announced "I'm against them. We don't need more restrictions on our freedoms." She gave me a broad smile and said "That's what I wanted to hear." I smiled too because I knew that's what she wanted to hear.

A person might accuse me of being intellectually dishonest, of lying to the voters, of telling people what they want to hear, or of flip-flopping on the issue. I don't think so. After looking into the issue, I firmly committed to a side. My answers were consistent from that point forward. More importantly, this was a minor issue of no salience to me.

Early in the Senate campaign, I taped two cartoons to a shelf in my law school office. One showed a politician sitting behind a massive desk; he was asking an aide "Remind me again of my profoundly held beliefs." The other was a six-panel strip in which a voter was watching a politician on television. The title in the first panel was "The story of American politics." In the five succeeding panels, the voter said "Hey, listen to this guy," "He's talking common sense," He's not tied in to politics as usual," "He's actually telling the truth," and "Too bad he's a nut who can never be elected." I never needed to be reminded of my profoundly held beliefs, but I didn't give a whit about changing my initial reactions to marginal issues.

★ ★ ★ ★ ★

On June tenth, Gail Sutton and I met Betty Wilson for breakfast. Wilson was a former political reporter for the *StarTribune* who more recently had written some political pieces for *City Pages*, a liberal, alternative, inner-city paper. The pieces fit her reputation of being tough on candidates, especially conservatives. We were taking a risk by meeting with her, but we couldn't pass up the chance for some free, unearned media.

Wilson asked many questions, some of which seemed to be designed to probe whether I was a right-wing zealot. I mentioned that her friend George Latimer, the Hamline law dean and state-wide Democratic leader, had told me that opponents would try to paint me into a right-wing corner. I repeated his reassuring advice that they would have a tough time with that paint job as I was a thoughtful, reasonable conservative. She seemed unimpressed.

Gail and I waited with both anticipation and trepidation to see what kind of free media we had earned this time. A week passed. Another week. No article ever appeared. We were disappointed. Apparently, I had not been nutty enough to write about.

★　★　★　★　★

The summer state central committee meeting we had been anticipating for weeks was Saturday, June 12, at a hotel in St. Louis Park, a Minneapolis suburb. As with the seventh congressional district convention two months earlier, the state central committee meeting really began the Friday evening before in the candidate hospitality suites.

Every campaign rented a hospitality suite for the major conventions and party meetings. At this meeting, a dozen hospitality suites lined one side of an open, second floor corridor overlooking the atrium. Each suite, stripped bare of furniture except for a couple of chairs and a table, offered delegates and other guests a chance to get up close and personal with a candidate. If the presence of the candidate were not enough attraction to stop by, the hospitality suite also offered goodies to eat and drink.

Gail Sutton, working as usual on a tight budget, arranged for several of our volunteers to bring dishes from home such as meatballs, veggies and dip, cheese and crackers, and cookies. Other candidates offered deli platters. Some offered desserts. One offered root beer floats. One candidate made a serious political error by offering beer to a group composed largely of social conservatives.

After three hours in the sweat lodge of the hospitality suite, Mary and I drove home for a short night's sleep. On Saturday morning we were back at the suite by eight a.m. to greet delegates as they walked along the hallway to the meeting. A few stopped to try our rolls and coffee. Most were more interested in getting to the meeting room.

Gail was wired. She was always hyper for a convention or meeting, but this day she was wound even tighter. She had a personal interest in the outcome. Bob Weinholzer faced a tough challenge in his effort to be re-elected state chair. If Bob lost, new state chair Chris Georgacas would clean house, sweeping Gail's husband Tony Sutton from his job as executive director of the state party.

Gail became even more agitated when she found out the St. Paul *Pioneer Press* had set up a ballot box just outside the meeting hall for a straw poll on senator and governor. A month earlier, she had decided we didn't want a straw poll.

"Why, Gail?" I argued. "I'd kind of like to know how we're doing."

"Because you'd lose to Gil Gutknecht, and probably to Bert McKasy too. It's too early. We're not ready for a straw poll yet."

Our people on the state executive committee had followed Gail's instructions and voted down an official party straw poll for the state central committee meeting. Now the newspaper had snatched defeat from the jaws of our victory by deciding to conduct its own straw poll. The poll was a nasty surprise, and we couldn't do a thing about it. Worse yet, the newspaper was making no effort to protect the integrity of the results. Anyone and everyone could vote. Not only could a delegate vote more than once, but also any campaign worker, political hanger on, or even an overnight guest of the hotel from Timbuktu could wander by and vote.

"Let's call in our people from all over town to get over here and vote," Gail exploded. "If they're going to pull this kind of crap, we'd better play the game."

"That doesn't seem right to me, Gail," I said. Naïve politician talking.

"You know damn well the other campaigns don't care what's right," she rasped. "I've already seen some of their workers voting."

"Well, OK, let's make sure we all vote and all of our people here vote, but I don't want to call in anyone. Don't play games. I don't want to win that way." Another mistake.

As the day went on, Gail became even more frenzied. She occasionally walked to the meeting hall and back, but more often stayed in the suite to receive reports. She undoubtedly wanted more than anything to work the floor at the meeting to scavenge some votes for Bob, but of course she could not. She was my manager, and thus the face of my campaign. State party chair Bob Weinholzer could not officially take sides in the Senate race because of party rules; we could not unofficially take sides in his race because of alienation of Georgacas supporters. After a few hours, we realized Bob was going to lose.

"Those sons of bitches," Gail erupted. "After all Bob's done for them, the bastards are going to throw him out."

"Take it easy, Gail. We don't have a horse in this race. We're not directly connected to Bob. If he loses, it's not like we lost."

"Damn right it is. That's what they're doing. They know we're out front in the Senate race, and if Bob is reelected, he'll probably be able to get us the endorsement. They have to beat Bob to beat us. Those bastards."

My primary concern was less Bob's re-election and more to keep Gail, Steve Clark, and the others in our room behind a closed door. The last thing I wanted was for one of them to charge off to the meeting hall and vent like this in front of the delegates or within hearing of the reporters covering the meeting.

Eventually, Bob did lose. Gail was beside herself. "Those ungrateful sons of bitches." "After all he's done for them." "The bastards."

I was not as upset. At the time, I thought Bob, bound by state party rules, could do little for me beyond offering advice and friendship. Looking back, however, I see Bob's loss blunted the rocket trajectory of my own campaign. Now, instead of our man as state party chair and his people as the field representatives, we would have to deal at arms' length with someone else's man and his people, all of whom were likely hostile to my campaign. Word filtered back to us that new state party chair Chris Georgacas had passed one of the party's field representatives in the hallway after the vote and said simply "You're fired." Georgacas's term as state party chair did not start for another two weeks, but the message was clear. Bob Weinholzer was out. Tony Sutton was out. All the field reps were out. Gail Sutton's chain of political allies, which meant my chain of political allies, had just grown much shorter.

To add insult to injury, the *Pioneer Press* announced the results of its straw poll for Senate: Gil Gutknecht 27 percent, Bert McKasy 24 percent, Doug McFarland 17 percent, undecided 10 percent, and others trailing. Gail was doubly furious. She had made a smart, successful political move defeating a vote in the state executive committee for a party straw ballot and been undercut by the newspaper. Then when the balloting was opened, the results were a sham; we received several reports of ballot box stuffing. *I wanted to win the right way, and I should have realized, the key word in politics is "win."*

As I sank into a chair in the hallway, absorbing the events of the day, Dane Smith of the *StarTribune* and another reporter walked past. Both were deep into their conversation and didn't notice me. They were enthused that they had a good story. Smith said cheerfully "Looks like a Weber sweep." The other reporter nodded. At that point in late afternoon, I didn't have the energy or will to announce my presence. I couldn't dispute them anyway. This had been one of those shouldn't-have-got-out-of-bed days that happen to politicians and people alike.

Mary and I left for home. By that time, Gail had cooled to a slow simmer, but I still extracted a promise that she would keep herself under control for the rest of the day.

That Saturday was a bad day on the campaign trail, but a candidate endures many bad days. The first option is to go home, disconnect the telephone, pop open a beer, turn on the television, and never be seen in public again. The other option is to get back on the campaign trail.

★ ★ ★ ★ ★

We started a series of day trips around the state. The first day was Duluth. Gail Sutton, Steve Clark, and I drove 120 miles up I-35 to arrive in midmorning. I talked to the political reporter for the newspaper and recorded an interview for a radio station. The three of us had lunch with a dozen activists who had been gathered by our strong supporters Therese and Jack Vaughn. In the afternoon, two television stations recorded interviews with me. A good day.

A few days later, the three of us left town at six in the morning to spend the day in St. Cloud. We began with breakfast at a pancake house downtown and were delighted when ten local activists turned out to hear what I had to say.

The highlight of this day trip was my appearance on the Paul Stacke show. Stacke was a popular morning talk show host on WJON radio in St. Cloud. Gail told me he was conservative and should be friendly. On the air, I made my standard pitch for fiscal conservatism and balancing the federal budget. Even this bedrock position was a little tricky. While everyone favored cutting government spending in the abstract, everyone had personal pet projects. Consequently, I had created a long list of "safe" cuts to cite as examples: scrap the space station, bring home one-half of our troops in Europe, eliminate the National Endowments, and slash federal civilian employment. I estimated the savings at $400 billion annually. I told the story that my nine-year-old son Wesley had looked over my shoulder at some of these figures and announced "We should get rid of these. Are we paying for them?"

Candidate meets the media

In the middle of the discussion about government spending, Stacke asked me "Do you think the holocaust actually happened?"

Startled, I hesitated before answering "Yes."

He didn't follow up, but during a later break he said that he had interviewed some conservatives who thought the holocaust was a fabrication of the liberal media. I hadn't thought I was coming across as a looney.

Eventually, Stacke opened the phone lines for listeners to call in with questions. I had a little worry that no one would call, but the phone kept ringing. Most callers asked standard questions. Just when I was starting to feel comfortable, one listener asked "You say you want to work to eliminate the federal budget deficit?"

"Yes, that's my number one priority."

"Well, then, since entitlement programs are such a large part of federal expenditures, that must mean you will look into cutting Social Security."

In my mind, red lights flashed, gongs sounded, and a gravelly voice intoned "Danger. Danger." The caller was not a friend; he was obviously trying to get me into trouble.

The truth is that entitlement programs, the primary one being Social Security, were then, and continue today, to be almost out of control. The only realistic way to balance the federal budget is to gain at least some small measure of control over entitlements. The honest answer would be yes, the caller is right, balancing the budget will require tough choices. Something must be done to rein in entitlements. We might have to do something such as raise the retirement age or increase the payroll tax. Anyone who has looked at the federal budget can see that.

The truth also is that no politician with an ounce of political savvy will say that. Social Security for decades has been known as the third rail of American politics. The third rail in subway systems carries the electrical current; anyone touching it is electrocuted. Any politician touching Social Security is electrocuted. Don't even go near the third rail.

Young people today say they can't count on Social Security still being around for their retirement. I tell them not to worry about it. Democrats and Republicans alike will never touch that third rail.

I answered "No, I will not touch Social Security. We can do the job of balancing the federal budget without doing it on the backs of our senior citizens." Just like a contestant on the popular game show Family Feud, I could imagine my teammates clapping and shouting "Good answer. Good answer."

The caller was not giving up so easily. He said "You may not want to go after Social Security, but you may have to. At least you have to look at the annual COLAs." In other words, would I at least consider reducing or holding down annual Cost of Living Adjustments based on inflation, which continued to raise benefits every year?

The cornerstones of my campaign, which I had trumpeted in the first part of the radio talk show, were honesty and common sense. While my initial answer was heavy on the latter, now I could no longer ignore the former. I said "I have looked into COLAs. Social Security benefits are a contract between our nation and its senior citizens. Seniors have earned and are entitled to their full benefits. We absolutely maintain full 100 percent Social Security benefits that are entitled on retirement, but full benefits do not necessarily include annual additions that are unearned and unentitled. Because we need so much help with the federal deficit, I do think that the annual increases don't have to be the full amount of inflation for the year. In other words, if inflation for the year is, say, 5 percent, then the COLA for the year might be 2.5 percent. That would save a lot of money, not cut a single cent from promised benefits, and have only a small impact on the money anyone receives." My mind flashed "Honest answer. Honest answer."

"So, you want to cut COLAs?" The listener sprung his trap. "Don't you know that many older people live off Social Security?" Oh, crap. I couldn't shake this guy loose. He clearly was out for political blood.

"Of course, as I said, I will protect Social Security fully. I'm not talking about slicing one thin dime from earned Social Security benefits. All I said was that we could hold down increases in benefits, and even that was holding down the increases by only a little. I am not talking at all about cutting Social Security."

"I don't think you know what you're talking about" was the caller's final retort. He was wrong. I knew exactly what both of us were talking about. He did, too.

The lesson was that next time I would not get anywhere near the third rail. I'd just praise the hell out of Social Security and talk about the nation's pact with its senior citizens. I'd promise to deliver the goods just as well as anyone. And people say they want honesty in their politicians.

★ ★ ★ ★ ★

Back in town, I turned once again to the never-ending attempt to place some money into the campaign chest that didn't come directly from my own pocket. One person we had discovered on a donors list worked for a large insurance company. He invited me to speak to the company's luncheon group. Gail and I arrived with great expectations. After the speech, he thanked me profusely, and said the time for a contribution was too early. I'd heard that one before.

I had set out hunting for a contribution and ended up as the quarry. Instead of sending a contribution my way, he had filled an open spot on his lunch program schedule. I didn't have to pay cash for my lunch, but I did have to speak for it. The famous saying "There's no such thing as a free lunch" held. Maybe it should read "There's no such thing as a free lunch, but there is a free lunch speech."

★ ★ ★ ★ ★

The next morning, I had a second breakfast with Leon Oistad, who was a seasoned political operative, and who had been the manager for several major statewide races. He was likely the best campaign manager in the state. We were both attorneys, so we had common ground. He had already given me some free, good advice. Leon was a superb strategist. I really wanted him to join our team. The basic problem was I already had a campaign manager, and he was not interested in a lesser position. Leon hinted that without Gail Sutton in the way he might be available.

Gail Sutton and Leon Oistad working together would have been a great team. Their talents meshed perfectly. Leon was tops at strategy and Gail was tops at execution. Leon was a calming voice and Gail was a driving force. The problem was I couldn't afford both, and both wanted to be number one.

Since Gail Sutton had committed to me early, I was committed to her even though she had some faults. Her primary fault was that every setback, big or small, was a calamity. Since every political campaign was full of setbacks, we operated in a continual state of crisis. I also knew that some party people were turned off by her hard-driving approach. On the other hand, Gail was a tireless worker. She was the best political organizer in the state. She was politically astute. She knew everyone. And she was loyal. That was worth a lot.

I told Leon that I really wanted him to join us, but that I was sticking with Gail as the manager. Leon was looking for a place to land. Shortly after our breakfast meeting, he went to work for Bert McKasy.

★ ★ ★ ★ ★

The month ended with another day trip. After teaching class from 8 until 9:30 on Tuesday morning, I drove with Steve Clark 160 miles due west to Montevideo. Scott Van Binsburgen, a young insurance agent, with great enthusiasm showed us around his town. Van Binsburgen had volunteered when Vin Weber represented the Republican-stronghold second district in Congress; he had also volunteered for the Republican who was upset by Democrat David Minge to succeed Weber in Congress.

The election of Minge in the second district was disheartening to me as a Republican, but it was also encouraging. To be elected to the Senate, I would likely have to win on something of a fluke. How many elections resulted in flukes? Over the years in both my home states of South Dakota and Minnesota, the answer was several. Democrat George McGovern had no business being elected, by the margin of a hundred votes, to the Senate from South Dakota, but the popular incumbent Republican had unexpectedly died in the spring of the election year and the emergency replacement candidate couldn't string a sentence together. Republican Arne Carlson had no business being elected governor of Minnesota after being smashed in the primary election, but scandal forced the Republican candidate off the ticket two weeks before the general election and Carlson stepped in. Democrat Paul Wellstone had no business being elected to the Senate from Minnesota when he was the only Democrat who would dare to take on popular and well-financed Republican incumbent Rudy Boschwitz, but Boschwitz went down by writing an ill-advised letter the weekend before the election. Why not another fluke in my favor?

For dinner at six o'clock at a downtown hotel in Montevideo, we had invited activists from six surrounding counties to join us. A wonderful crowd of 14 showed up. They were enthused; I was enthused. They told jokes; I told jokes. We had a great time. Steve Clark and I left around 8:30 for the three-hour drive home. It went fast.

CHAPTER NINE

No Martini For You

July began with a bang in Forest Lake, a town twenty miles north of the Twin Cities. Its Fourth of July parade was the biggest parade in the state. As a wannabe instead of an officeholder, I was not allowed to have an official entry in the parade, but Gail Sutton wangled permission for our team to march alongside the Republican float.

She also brought a dozen of our volunteers with us. Gail supplied them with rolls of McFarland for Senate lapel stickers and simple 3 ½ by 8 ½ card-stock literature pieces. *The plan was for five or six of our people to work each side of the street. Their job was to stay ahead of the float, papering the crowd with literature and stickers. When the Republican float and the candidate came along a minute or two later, the people lining the curbs would know who I was from the advance work of the volunteers. My job was to shake as many hands as possible on one side of the street for a couple of minutes, and then hustle over to work the other side of the street for a while. I could not ride on the float.* People didn't want to see a candidate sitting on his rear on a float, Gail said; the candidate would look aloof and lazy. She also said that when the candidate was working one side of the street, the people on the other side could still see who it was from the literature. The theory sounded right.

As with so many things, practice does not match theory. What does happen is for about the first two blocks, all is well. The volunteers distribute the cards and stickers. I shake hands here and hands there. Half the people grab my hand gladly, and the other half recoil as if I have leprosy. About the third block, the smooth flow of the parade begins to coil and uncoil the same as traffic on a freeway; the floats begin to move forward in fits, starts, and stops. When the parade coils or even slows to a stop, the volunteers leisurely pass out lapel stickers and campaign literature. I try to grab every hand. The people on one side of the street hear me say "Hi. I'm Doug McFarland" time after time. The people on the other side of the street wonder who the tall galoot with his hand out is. Realistically, even the people who shake my hand probably don't catch the name. They may put two and two together from the literature and decide it was McFarland. They may decide it was McKasy. They may decide it was the candidate for mayor. They don't likely care much. They're looking forward or backward along the parade route for the good stuff, just enduring the passage of yet another politician.

When the coil releases, the party float speeds up to maintain its position behind the float in front of it. The volunteers, who have been strolling along the avenue handing out literature, notice the float is ahead of them. They break into a run to get back into position in front of the float. This leaves a long swath of parade watchers on both sides of the street completely untouched. I look up to see the float moving fast and the volunteers receding into the distance. At this point, I am a couple of parade entries behind the party float, and the people are probably thinking I'm a local insurance agent or car dealer.

Since I need to keep in the general vicinity of the volunteers and the float, I also begin to jog. Not senatorial, but at least the hundreds of people who see the bozo jogging past and waving wildly have no clue who it is. After a block or two of jogging, I'm back in position. Of course, now I'm winded and can hardly get my name out. After I shake hands for a block or so, about the time I get my wind back, the cycle repeats itself. It keeps repeating to the end of the parade route.

After a few parades, I changed strategy. *While a walking candidate does get close to a few people to press a little flesh, at best the candidate is on the wrong side of the street for half the crowd and at worst is separated from the parade vehicle and jogging anonymously past the entire crowd. The new strategy was that volunteers would still pass out literature ahead of the parade entry, but I rode on the float or truck. The perfect vehicle was a pickup truck. I stood in the back of a pickup plastered with McFarland signs and waved to the people on both sides of the street. Some spectators may have thought I looked distant or lazy rolling past, but at least everyone along the route saw I'd been there.*

★ ★ ★ ★ ★

The daily calendar for the weeks following the June state central committee meeting through July and August showed fewer and fewer political events. This is the natural rhythm of the political year. Just as in winter farm fields lay fallow regenerating for the next growing season, summer is the fallow time for politics. Outside of some local parades and county fairs, nothing is happening.

Either the campaign can go dormant for three months, or the campaign can create its own events. That's what Gail decided to do. The summer provided both roads not covered with ice and few other time demands. It was perfect for travel to all parts of the state. We would have breakfast in one town, lunch in another, and dinner in a third. Party activists would be thrilled a candidate had come to them, and they could get up close and personal. In between, we would stop by local newspapers, television stations, and radio stations to earn a little free media. These would be full, tightly scheduled days. The theory seemed perfect.

Once again, practice did not live up to theory. The first problem is I'm a private person, a little shy. That may sound strange for a politician, but many successful politicians have been private and shy. The same can be said for other professions in the public eye. The key question is when the red light of the camera blinks on, can the private person throw a switch and become a public persona? The question is the same for a politician walking into a reception, an actor stepping onto the set, a minister ascending to the pulpit, and a teacher entering a classroom. It's showtime!

I could throw the switch, yet everything had its cost. Every time I threw the switch, it took mental energy. The switch flipped on, and afterwards off, for three meals plus several media stops each day. It's showtime! It's over. On and off. Up and down. High and low. It's showtime! It's over. On and off. Up and down. High and low. Nearly ten times a day. The effect of throwing the switch several times a day was cumulative. By the end of each day, I was usually reduced to a political zombie.

The second problem relieved some of the tension of the days, at least in retrospect. Every day was tightly scheduled, and we had to find cafes and radio stations in towns far distant from our own experience. Gail Sutton or Steve Clark obtained detailed directions to every stop, but seldom did the local activist supply good directions. No matter what part of the state, the activist would always, always, leave something out; usually, the error was not something easily discernible such as turn left instead of turn right. Instead, the error would usually be leaving out a step entirely.

Consider directions such as these. Enter town on highway 12 going west to the stop light. Turn right on First Street. After several blocks, turn left on Fifth Avenue. Follow Fifth around the edge of the lake. Turn left on Beacon to the radio station. Look for the broadcast tower. Had we kept on looking for the tower, we would still be circling that lake. The problem was that we couldn't turn left from Fifth Avenue onto Beacon because Beacon and Fifth didn't intersect. We first had to turn right from Fifth onto Twelfth Street before we reached Beacon. GPS was not widely available. Sometimes the city map helped. Sometimes we figured out the missing step. Sometimes we drove by dead reckoning. Sometimes we had to ask for directions. Sometimes we spotted the radio tower in the wrong direction. Most of the time we arrived late. People know politicians run late. People don't know the reason is often bad directions.

After running late, and in a consequent state of anxiety and irritation, most of the first trip, we came to allow for bad directions. Eventually, Gail built wandering-about-town time into the schedule. Bad directions became a running joke. Which set of directions for the day would be the worst?

* * * * *

The second Wednesday of July, Tony Sutton and I drove north in my minivan. Since the new party chair had, as expected, fired Tony as soon as possible, on July first, he was available. This was a boon to me. Tony Sutton was both a razor-sharp political strategist and a storehouse of state political history. He possessed both a brilliant tactical mind and a streak of stubborn doggedness. Tony was almost always in an up mood: the stereotypical jovial fat man. Tony also knew everyone from his travels for the state party. Not only could he tell me who I would see in each town, but he also was invariably on good terms with them; his credibility rubbed off on me. And as a final bonus, Tony was male. We didn't need to take three in the car. No tongues would wag upon seeing the two of us together.

Tony and I left home before six a.m. to drive 130 miles due north to Brainerd for breakfast. Ten activists, including Crow Wing County chair Cindy Moe and kitchen cabinet member Andy Kessler from Wadena, were waiting for us. A glorious start for the day! After breakfast, we made the rounds to the Brainerd newspaper and two radio stations.

The day got even better 83 miles northeast in Grand Rapids. Tony wanted to check in with Gail at the office, so we found a convenience store with an outdoor pay telephone. We still had no cell phone. I sat in the passenger's seat of the van; Tony walked across the small parking lot to the pay phone.

Tony's face lit up like a kid spotting a present on Christmas morning. "Gutknecht's out!" he shouted across the parking lot to me.

"What?!"

Tony yelled "Yeah, Gil Gutknecht dropped out of the Senate race. We knew all along he wanted to run for first district Congress but was afraid to take on Tim Penny. Penny announced this morning he's not running again, so Gutknecht switched races. He's running for first district."

I sat there in the parking lot of a convenience store in Grand Rapids with a silly grin. Our toughest competition eliminated! That left only Bert McKasy and me on the Republican side, and I could beat Bert. I might have an actual chance to win this thing!

"Tell Gail to try to get through to Vin Weber right away and see if we can get his support" I yelled back.

"Right" Tony agreed. "She can try to go through Jack Meeks." He talked some more to Gail and hung up the telephone.

As Tony climbed back into the driver's seat, I said "If we can get Vin, we can maybe lock this thing up early. Scare off anyone else from jumping in."

"You betcha" said Tony. His face took on a dreamy look, and he added "You know, if Vin gets behind you, you're going to win. And then you'll be Vin Weber."

I nodded. For reasons that remained unknown, however, I never did get the backing of Vin Weber. Maybe it was personal chemistry. I had the feeling he didn't like me. Or maybe Vin Weber wanted to remain Vin Weber, thank you.

Tony and I floated through our afternoon visits to the Grand Rapids *Herald-Review,* the Virginia *Mesabi Daily News,* and Hibbing radio station WKKQ. We even ran a little ahead of schedule, so Tony showed me around his hometown. Hibbing lay in the center of the Democratic stronghold of Minnesota, the Iron Range north and west of Duluth. Tony regaled me with stories of Republicans being shouted down at public meetings or having their cars vandalized after events. He didn't scare me—we weren't planning to park overnight.

Dinner at the Hibbing Holiday Inn was another huge success. Nine activists were there, including the most important prize in the area, Joanne Muller, and her number two, John Brandt. Everyone was high with the news about Gutknecht and my prospects for winning. Tony and I left the group with reluctance around 8:30 to drive the 190 miles home.

On a day like this one, I could have campaigned all day and all night. The energy was flowing. Of course, euphoria in a campaign never lasts long.

★ ★ ★ ★ ★

The euphoria ended first thing in the morning. When I walked into my office at 9:30 a.m. after teaching evidence class, the telephone was ringing.

"Doug, this is Gail. We've got a real problem."

My stomach sank. Was this to be the back breaker I'd been dreading all along? The possibility of a single event breaking my campaign always seemed realistic. I was both a wannabe who had never held public office and a relatively new campaigner, so everything took on added proportions. "What? What's the problem?" I asked.

"Noel Collis and Sue Turch and the St. Cloud people just found out you were prochoice when you ran for the state legislature. One of McKasy's people is traveling around the seventh district spreading the word."

I felt a little better. "Didn't they already know that?" I said. This was 17-year-old news. While I had not volunteered it to anyone, neither had I kept it a secret.

"No, the people in St. Cloud didn't know that" said Gail. "This is bad. We could lose all our support in Stearns County unless we can stop this right now. You have to go up there and talk to them today."

Today? Oh, hell. An unscheduled trip to St. Cloud wasn't in my plan for the day. "Gail, you know I'm prolife, and so should they. We've talked before that I can't run so far to the right to get the party endorsement that it makes me unelectable in the general election."

"You have to get the endorsement first."

"Yes, but it can't be that bad. You go talk to them."

"It is that bad. If you lose Noel Collis and Sue Turch, you'll lose all of Stearns County. And think about Joanne Muller who you just saw in Hibbing. You know what her issue is. You have to go see Turch and Collis—today, if possible."

"Oh, all right, see if you can make the arrangements."

Gail called back. "Sue Turch, Noel Collis, and Shirley Borgerding will meet you at the St. Cloud Holiday Inn at four. I'll go with you. You have to convince them you're reliably prolife or you can kiss the endorsement away."

"Yeah, yeah, I know."

"You have to take a hard line. You can't be squishy on this issue."

OK, no pressure. The entire campaign depended on this meeting. Gail prepped me all the way to St. Cloud. We walked into the motel coffee shop to find the three county leaders waiting for us. From the looks on their faces, I could tell Gail had not been exaggerating.

I told them that in my run for the state legislature, I was new to politics and didn't begin with a strong personal view on the abortion issue. Party leaders in the area told me I needed to be prochoice to have a chance of winning my district that included St. Louis Park, a Minneapolis suburb; the district was one-third Jewish, and all were prochoice, they said. I didn't feel comfortable and tried to duck the issue. The local suburban newspaper sent out a questionnaire that asked whether I was prolife; my nuanced, lengthy answer was printed as "No." Soon I saw my lawn signs disappear from the front yards of some of my best supporters. This caused me to think a lot more about the issue and realize I was on the wrong side personally, but I was stuck with the public position in that campaign. I'd been prolife for the seventeen years since.

Sue Turch asked "Did you campaign as prochoice?"

"No. I never campaigned on it."

She asked "Do you still have your campaign literature from that election? I'd like to see whether you mentioned it in your literature."

I quickly agreed to send her my old literature. I dug copies out of my basement storeroom and was relieved to see that none of the pieces even mentioned abortion. We shipped the literature to Turch, and a few days later Gail called to tell me the three were back with us. Another crisis averted.

★　★　★　★　★

That weekend our son Wesley's Boy Scout troop camped out in Wisconsin. I was scheduled to travel with them Thursday evening, but the unexpected trip to St. Cloud scrapped that plan. I joined the group on the second day. That was fine with me, since sleeping an extra night outside in a tent was not my idea of fun.

The campout again raised thoughts of how compartmentalized a person's life can be. One day I'm a public figure striding the state in search of votes; the next day I'm a dad sleeping in a tent with grade-school boys and mosquitoes.

Even though the troop stayed at the camp until Sunday, Wesley and I left Saturday morning. His Little League baseball team was in a weekend tournament and needed him. I enjoyed Sunday, my 47th birthday, sitting behind the backstop with the other team parents watching baseball.

★　★　★　★　★

Gail had decided that our one-day trips weren't reaching the far corners of the state, so I cancelled my summer-school class the following Tuesday for a two-day, 700-mile swing through southwestern and southern Minnesota. Tony Sutton was unavailable, and Gail decided she could not get away from the office, so she sent Steve Clark. Steve wasn't as much fun to travel with as Tony, but he was an enjoyable, eager travel companion. Also, he deserved the small reward: he had been working like a yeoman for the campaign and to date had received little compensation in return. The first day took the two of us to breakfast in New Ulm, lunch in Marshall, dinner in Worthington, two newspapers, and three radio stations.

Marshall was a small town in farming country. I wanted to represent a farm state, so I needed to know something about agriculture. That's why I had asked Bob Weinholzer to appoint me to the state party agriculture study group. That's also why I was here in Marshall, trying to tell farmers that I knew something about agriculture.

One of the activists who came to lunch, Rick Bot, asked me a specific question about an agriculture bill pending in Congress. I understood the general tenor of the question, but that was about it. To attempt an answer or to beg off? The disaster of the Edina Rotary lunch flashed through my mind. Even so, I decided to forge ahead and gave what must have seemed to him a pretty lame answer. After finally shutting my mouth, I noticed a wry smile on Bot's face. I decided to take a chance and said "Well, I can't say I'm completely up to speed on that issue, but I'm here trying to educate myself about agriculture and what matters to you. How'd I do?"

"Well," he allowed as he broke into a wide grin, "I asked the same question to Bert McKasy when he was here last week. You did better than he did."

After spending the night in a Worthington motel, Steve and I were off on a day-two schedule west to east across the southernmost counties of the state: breakfast in Albert Lea, lunch in Austin, and dinner in Owatonna, plus stops at three newspapers and four radio stations. Gail decided she could get away from the office, so she met us in Austin and switched places with Steve. The rest of the day Gail and I traveled together and hoped no one would get the wrong idea.

Gail and I pulled into Owatonna shortly after the scheduled time of seven p.m. The two of us were shown into a reserved, private room at a dinner club in the middle of downtown. We found a large table with a dozen place settings. But no one was there. Even more embarrassing was that the club had assigned a server for our expected large party. The club had a vision of a big tab and the server had a vision of a big tip. Poof!

Every few minutes, the server reappeared in the room and asked Gail and me, the two frustrated and moody people who had showed up, whether we wanted a drink. Did I ever! In front of party activists, my drink was always iced tea. Now, at the end of these two long days, I wanted a mighty dry martini in a mighty big glass. By about seven-fifteen, I was ready to assume no one would show and order my martini. The problem was that I might take a sip or two, and then an activist would show up, just in time to smell the gin on my breath. That wouldn't do, so again the two of us declined the drink offer. We couldn't even order dinner for ourselves. If activists showed up later, we wanted to talk to them, not stuff our faces. If no one showed up, we wanted to get home, not while away the evening in a dinner club in Owatonna. We were stuck.

Finally, about seven-thirty, the server came back for the fourth time to ask whether we wanted anything. Gail and I looked at each other and at our watches. "I'll have a martini" I said to her. Gail ordered a vodka gimlet.

Not more than one minute later, activists John and Cammie Kahnke, farmers from nearby Waseca, walked into the room. They were apologetic at being so late. That was the least of my worries.

"Gail," I whispered, "go find the server and confirm my order for an iced tea."

"Right." She was already halfway out the door.

The four of us had a nice dinner and a convivial discussion of Republican politics. I collected commitments from both Kahnkes, but I never did get that martini.

CHAPTER TEN

The District Where Politicians' Cars Go To Die

While 95 per cent of Minnesota lies outside the Twin Cities metropolitan area, the bulk of the population, plus the power and wealth of the state, is concentrated in the metro. People in the Twin Cities refer to the rest of Minnesota as "outstate." People outstate don't much like that. It does sound a little isolated and backwards. A politician might as well say "I'm glad to be here outstate with all of you hicks and rubes." After only one or two ventures "outstate," I became aware that I was campaigning in "greater Minnesota."

Having covered the southern part of greater Minnesota in July, we were going north in August. The schedule called for Tony Sutton and me to leave at seven Sunday morning and return around eleven Wednesday night. We were going to the seventh congressional district, which covers the northwest one-third of the state [see the map in the Appendix]. The seventh is miles and miles of miles. Most of them are flat and empty. The seventh is the district where politicians' cars go to die.

My BMW was on a restricted miles lease, and I didn't want to leave the best part of the life of our new family Dodge Grand Caravan minivan on the long roads of the seventh. So, Tony and I sallied forth in my old Chrysler LeBaron. The sedan had been my parents' pride and joy, but it had seen better days even before I inherited it. The car was showing its age and a lot of rust. The positive side was that they had not driven much, so it was still well short of 100,000 miles more than thirteen years after rolling off the assembly line. Also, we looked forward to being spotted: a man of the people, driving an American car more than a dozen years old. The Chrysler was no longer shiny, and it protested at higher speeds, but I knew in my heart that my parents' car wouldn't let us down.

A four-hour drive northwest brought us to our first event, a Republican party picnic lunch in a park in the small town of Bagley. This was friendly territory. I had been in town for the Clearwater County convention in March and already had several supporters, including both county chairman LeRoy Sundbom and chairwoman Dorothy Dick.

Since the Bagley picnic was the only political game in the state on Sunday, most of the other statewide candidates were there too. Senate competitor Bert McKasy had driven up for the day. Tad Jude, who had recently switched from Democrat to Republican and was running for attorney general, was there. Allen Quist, the challenger for the gubernatorial nomination, was there. Arne Carlson, the incumbent governor, was not.

Quist's message of social conservatism was starting to catch fire, especially in greater Minnesota. I watched the picnickers nod as he spoke and heard their roar of approval at the end. Over the months, I listened to Quist speak many times. His speeches never tossed out red meat. He spoke about education and taxes and spending, but the delegates knew and liked where he stood on the social issues.

People in the Twin Cities don't have a clue how conservative greater Minnesota is. Every time I left the Twin Cities on a trip to greater Minnesota, Gail whispered in my ear "Remember, Doug, you can't be too conservative." My experience proved her right. Over all the months of speeches and appearances I made in greater Minnesota, party activists told me things such as "I want you to know that I'm going to vote for the most conservative candidate for Senate."

What is a candidate supposed to reply? How about "Actually, I'm a moderate conservative." Or maybe "I'm with you on the conservative issues, but we may not see completely eye to eye on priorities; my number one priority is taxes and spending." Perhaps "Thanks, but I'm trying to win the general election as well as the party nomination, and I can't do that if I appear to be too far to the right." In fact, all boiled down to the single response "Thank you."

I spoke next after Al Quist. Because Quist was a Norwegian farmer, and the crowd in Bagley was friendly, I decided to risk a joke. A Norwegian joke, even though technically an ethnic joke, is safe in Minnesota. My favorite is the Norwegian who dropped a fifty-cent piece into the accumulation in the pit underneath an outdoor toilet. He promptly threw in his watch and wallet, saying "I'm not going down there after a fifty-cent piece." That one might have been a tad inappropriate for a picnic, so I announced to Quist and the crowd that I'd heard of a Norwegian who worked hard to eliminate his accent when he spoke English. To test himself out, he walked into a store, approached the clerk, and spoke slowly and distinctly: "I'll have a quart of milk and a loaf of bread." The clerk said "You must be a Norwegian." "Well, yahhh," the Norwegian's accent returned, "how did you know?" "This is a hardware store."

★ ★ ★ ★ ★

In mid-afternoon, at the end of the picnic in Bagley, Tony and I headed east on highway 2 for an hour to Bemidji and the office of the Bemidji *Pioneer*. Managing editor Brad Swenson had agreed to open on a Sunday afternoon for an interview; that worked for us and gave him some copy for the next day's paper.

The interview was unremarkable except for one potentially major gaffe. See if you can spot it. Swenson asked what the focus of my campaign was, and I replied cutting the federal deficit, promoting agriculture, and improving education. Swenson asked why I was taking on Dave

Durenberger, and I replied that I wouldn't be doing it except his ethical problems meant that I couldn't vote for him again, and we Republicans needed a clear voice. Swenson asked hadn't Durenberger been a good Republican vote, and I replied that 90 per cent of his votes were good but that he strayed off the reservation on some votes. Swenson asked about the social issues, and I replied that I was conservative but hoped to bring the people in the party together on the abortion issue. Swenson asked about agriculture, and I admitted not knowing enough about the subject except that both my mother and wife were farm girls. Swenson asked about health care, and I replied that the answer was managed care accounts to give people an incentive to hold down their expenses instead of a massive federal health care plan.

The gaffe didn't even register with me at the time. Back in the car, Tony, with his trademark grin, asked "Doug, do you realize we are right across the street from the White Earth Indian Reservation?"

A head-slapping moment! "Crap," I groaned. "Maybe he missed it."

"I don't think so. I saw him write it down."

"Maybe he won't print it."

"Not likely," Tony chuckled. "It's pretty good."

"Well, nothing we can do about it now. We'll find out in the morning."

The next morning, we picked up a copy of the Bemidji *Pioneer* before we left town. Sure enough, the article was on the front page. It was large: 15 paragraphs. It used our official campaign photo. It was friendly. The second paragraph, about why I was running to replace Dave Durenberger, read "'Generally, he's done well in Congress,' says McFarland, who seeks the endorsement for the seat held by fellow Republican Durenberger. 'I'd vote more along the lines of Rudy Boschwitz. Ninety percent of Dave's votes have been good, solid Republican votes, but he strays off the reservation on some votes.'" There it was: the sort of gaffe that can sink a campaign. Yet I never heard about it again. I probably wasn't a big enough name to be able to make a gaffe.

Our second day was crammed completely full. After driving nearly two hours, we started in Thief River Falls with a late breakfast that drew several activists, including county chairman Marv Kading. We followed with stops at the newspaper and two radio stations. Next was Crookston for lunch with activists, including supporters Russ Sylvester and Norm Vanderpan, followed by the newspaper and a radio station. Then we were on to a radio station in Grand Forks, North Dakota, that broadcast into Minnesota. The last media stop of the day was scheduled to be a television station in Fargo/Moorhead that had promised a live interview on the five o'clock news—if we arrived before five. Since the drive from Grand Forks to Fargo was 80 miles, we needed to be on the road by three-thirty. And who knew how good the directions to the television studio were? If they were the usual, we could drive around Fargo for a half-hour trying to figure out which step of the directions was missing.

Tony and I cleared Grand Forks at 3:45, which gave us about 70 minutes to drive 80 miles and find the television station in Fargo. The good news was that the drive was all interstate highway. The bad news was that we were driving my thirteen-year-old beater. Tony was driving. He pushed hard. The engine, which made a rapid tapping sound at higher speeds, sounded as if it would seize up at any moment.

"Sorry I can't take it a little easier on the car, Doug."

"That's OK. We'll have to chance it."

"Think it'll hold together?"

"I think so. I don't think my parents' car will fail us."

When we turned off the interstate highway onto the Fargo exit and slowed, the car shivered from its efforts, but it didn't fail us. And for once, the directions were good. We raced into the television station at 4:57.

The receptionist announced over an internal loudspeaker that we'd arrived, and she showed us immediately to the set. The anchorman had already prepared a substitute story, but gladly scrapped it for the live interview. It lasted three minutes and consisted of standard questions that allowed me to state the major themes of my campaign. Three minutes of free media live on a local television newscast was huge. Tony and I walked out of the television studio still revved up by our race across the North Dakota prairie and the triumph of arriving in time for a successful media stop.

Our engines slowed considerably within the hour. We hosted a dinner for activists in Moorhead and the three-county area. We thought as many as 15 might come. Three did. After dinner, Tony and I speculated the poor turnout was the work of seventh congressional district chairwoman, and Moorhead resident, Georgiann Stenerson. I had called her again and again on the telephone. She never warmed to me, and never told me why. Tony's theory was that Stenerson was a Vin Weber disciple, and she was waiting for word from him who the anointed candidate would be. In any event, Stenerson had a throttle hold on the Moorhead area. We were going to have to look for votes elsewhere.

Later in the evening, Tony and I drove the 60 miles to Fergus Falls to be ready for breakfast with activists there the next morning. Because of the poor turnout at dinner, I felt some satisfaction that we didn't stay at a motel in Moorhead and contribute to the local economy.

Boon companion Tony Sutton

In the morning, the state senator from the area, Cal Larson, did not appear at the breakfast. This was not a big surprise, since he was one of the few Republican legislators who had not found time to meet with me at the state capitol. After breakfast, I finished interviews at two radio stations ahead of schedule. Tony had an idea. He said "We know where Cal works. Let's stop by his office and surprise him."

The two of us breezed into the small insurance agency storefront office on the main street downtown and greeted Larson as he sat at his desk. He was not pleased to be cornered. Larson may have been a strong Durenberger man irritated that I was shoving him out. He may have been a closet moderate irritated that I was courting conservatives. He may have been a long-time party warhorse irritated that I was reaching too high, too fast without paying my dues. He may just plain not have liked me. For whatever reason, he was polite but distant.

Tony and I chortled to each other as we emerged onto the sidewalk. I said "At least we caught him."

"Yeah, he couldn't very well duck you this time."

"Hope we didn't ruin his day."

"Nah," said Tony. "Say, do you think he'll be committing to you anytime soon?"

"Sure. As soon as we see a pig flying down this street."

We had a successful lunch in Morris with half-a-dozen delegates, headlined by county chairwomen Laura Carrington and Dolores McClerndon, and later we stopped by the newspaper and radio station. Another hour's drive brought us to Alexandria, our last stop of the three-day trip. We reversed the usual order by making the rounds to the newspaper and radio station first, and then joining activists for dinner.

The Douglas County organization was having a potluck. I was delighted. Tony was disgusted. I tried many times to talk him into the merits of potlucks, but the most he would do was to take a polite, small scoop from a couple of the dishes.

This event produced one of my most pleasant memories of the campaign. I had worked the telephones hard to these delegates. I had been to the Douglas County convention in March. They had seen me again at the seventh congressional district convention in May. Several were already committed to me. Tony and I arrived just after most of them had been through the dinner line and taken their seats. As we walked in, I could hear several voices. "There's Doug." "McFarland is here." "Oh, look, Doug made it." That sort of recognition is manna from heaven for a politician. It tasted even better than the potluck food. After I enjoyed my dinner, and Tony pushed a few items around his plate for a while, I gave my pitch to the group, answered a few questions, and we were on the road home.

I enjoyed campaigning in greater Minnesota, and looked forward to these trips, for several reasons. The people were much like the people of Sioux Falls, South Dakota, and the surrounding farming area where I grew up. I understood them, and they understood me. They were glad to see any candidate who made the effort to come to them and they showed it. They resonated to my message. The local media were eager to air my views. I liked being on the road, and I liked seeing towns, such as International Falls and Thief River Falls, that had previously seemed only slightly more real than the fabled Brigadoon. I liked small town cafes. Looking back, I realize now too that the trips were part of a campaign that at the time was rolling in high gear. The end of these trips always left a feeling of accomplishment from making so many stops in so few days.

The physical and mental effort was grueling, to be sure. At least I was able to recharge in the car between stops. The rhythm of the car moving along the open road, the physical and mental energy expenditures, the feeling of well-being from friendly receptions and a job well done—all these combined to make nodding off in the car at any time of the day easy. People wonder what goes on in the car between stops on a campaign trip. That's easy. The campaign aide drives. The candidate sleeps.

★　★　★　★　★

The time had come, decided manager Gail Sutton, for me to meet the state capitol press. She arranged for former state party chair Bob Weinholzer to introduce me to them. Bob and I joined up in the basement of the state capitol. As we walked slowly along the hallway toward the press room, Bob gave me fast-paced advice about who would likely be in the room and their individual interests and quirks. When we reached the door, Bob had not completed his briefing, so we continued walking. While Bob kept talking, I stopped listening. What seized my attention was the ceiling. Like many older buildings, the state capitol basement had a low ceiling. As we walked into a little-used area, I had to lean sideways more and more as the ceiling became lower and lower. How would I impress the reporters as I listed sideways? The situation reminded me of another cartoon I had taped onto a bookshelf in my office. The cartoon showed a tall man and a short man talking. The tall man was scrunched over sideways, knees bent, so he was facing the short man at about the same level. The caption was "A tall man showing proper respect in a conversation." Eventually, Bob and I turned back to the door of the press room and entered. I was relieved to see the ceiling was much higher than the ceiling in the hallway.

The press room was a long straight hallway lined with filing cabinets and stacks of old newspapers. On both sides of the hallway, between the cabinets and piles of papers, doors opened to individual offices on both sides.

Through the first door on the right, Eric Eskola, the political reporter for WCCO radio, was at his desk. The desk was piled high with sound equipment, stacks of papers, and used coffee cups. Surrounding him were more filing cabinets, more newspaper stacks, lamps, and political memorabilia. The lamps gave a warm glow to the room. Eskola appeared hardly to have enough room to get back and forth to his desk. I had the impression of an animal cozy in its den. He jumped to his feet when he saw us, and after a little small talk, said "We'd better get something on tape." He dodged his way back to his desk, retrieved his tape recorder, and recorded my answers to his questions about the campaign.

A few steps farther along the hallway, on the other side, was the door to the *StarTribune* office. It had three desks—a lot roomier, but still a little cluttered. Dane Smith and another political reporter were there. They glanced at my press release about the summer trips and took notes as they asked several questions. Who was my primary Republican competition? How were the travels going? What have you heard about the Democrats? Have you been in touch with Dave Durenberger?

Bob and I stopped by the other offices in the press room, but no one was home at Associated Press, Minnesota News Network, and Minnesota Public Radio. We turned two corners and walked into the large office of the St. Paul *Pioneer Press*. It had the feel of recent occupancy, so the two of us waited a few minutes to see if a reporter would return from a bathroom break or short errand. When no one did, we put our press release on a desk and left.

While Bob and I were waiting in the *Pioneer Press* office, we looked around at the photos on the walls. The one that caught our attention was a photo of Dave Durenberger dressed for a night on the town in Washington. He was wearing an expensive overcoat draped loosely around his shoulders and tight-fitting calfskin gloves. The photo must have spoken to the reporter who had tacked it to the wall. It also spoke to me. Durenberger wouldn't be able to run again because he had "gone Washington."

★ ★ ★ ★ ★

Our family vacation for the year was a week we squeezed out of the campaign in early August at a small family resort in western Wisconsin called Hunky Dory. It was a little tame for our four children, but Mary and I liked the week away from the stress of campaigning just fine.

With only a week remaining in the summer before I would be tied down by the start of fall classes at Hamline, we had an opening for one more multi-day trip. Gail decided to send Tony Sutton and me north and west again. This trip started at six a.m. Monday morning and ended at 10:30 Wednesday evening–only 65 hours and 750 miles on the road this time.

The first day started with breakfast in Cloquet, the scene of my ice water soaking following the first BPOU convention nearly six months earlier. We then drove to nearby Duluth. A television station recorded an interview for the evening news; we also stopped for interviews at four radio stations. The media stops surrounded another successful lunch in Duluth, hosted by loyal supporters Jack and Therese Vaughn, with twelve around the table.

A big group at a table requires a careful decision about where to sit. A seat at the head of the table asserts strength and control. A seat at the middle of one of the long sides of the table conveys openness and closeness, and it also shows confidence of not needing to seize the head of the table. When I worked for Chief Justice Warren E. Burger at the Supreme Court in Washington for two years a decade earlier, the Chief always took a middle seat. Everyone in the room loved being close to him. I always tried the same strategy at political meals.

Tony and I drove 90 minutes northwest to Grand Rapids for a dinner with activists. The start time came and went. No one showed. We thought we were skunked. Finally, two activists arrived. Both committed. At least once we got the people in the door, I sold the product.

We started the second day with another 90-mnute drive to Bemidji for breakfast. Alice Fuglestad, the Beltrami County chairwoman and an energetic supporter, turned out seven additional activists. The managing editor of the Bemidji *Pioneer*, Brad Swenson, also attended. Apparently, my gaffe about Dave Durenberger going off the reservation had not done serious damage—or he hoped to get another hot quote. After breakfast, Swenson walked downtown with Tony and me. He said he was glad to see me back so soon. He mentioned former governor, Democrat Rudy Perpich, in contrast to the current governor, Republican Arne Carlson. "I can't remember the last time Carlson was here," Swenson said. "Perpich was here so many times we felt as if we had to beat him off with a stick."

After yet another 90-minute drive west to Detroit Lakes for lunch with two activists and three more media stops, we arrived in Wadena for dinner with activists. County chairman Andy Kessler, a member of my kitchen cabinet, and his wife were there. A year later, after the campaign ended, he called and asked if he and his wife could stop by my home on a Saturday morning to talk. He was coy on the subject. Of course, I would be glad to meet with two loyal supporters. When he got around to business, he told me that with all the contacts I had made in the campaign, I would be perfect to join them as an AMWAY distributor.

Our third day on the road included breakfast in St. Cloud (Sue Turch, Noel Collis, and Shirley Borgerding were back with us), lunch in Little Falls (county chairman Nick Fillah committed on the spot), and dinner in Willmar, with several media stops interspersed. Our last media stop of the day was at the newspaper in Paynesville, a town of some 2300.

I had already realized the existence of an unwritten rule for small town

*media. A visit from a statewide political candidate was an honor to the town.
Reporters invariably wrote soft articles on my visit and mentioned some of
my political views; sometimes they threw in a barb or two, but always in the
middle of a substantial, friendly article. Even the papers on the Democrat-
stronghold Iron Range printed positive, generous stories about my visits to
town.*

*The idea fascinated me. Why should anyone care what I thought more
than a random person off the street? Could any bozo declare himself a
candidate for a statewide office, blow into town, and receive a nice story, with
photo, in the local newspaper? Could any ordinary person, who decided to run
for office, have local television and radio broadcast his or her views on issues
of the day? My views apparently were more valuable and newsworthy than
those of any citizen pulled in at random because I had taken the initiative
to run and had gathered a reasonable amount of support to be considered a
serious candidate.*

The editor of the Paynesville *Press* didn't follow this rule. Tony and
I sat quietly in the main room of the newspaper before we were shown
into editor Linda Stelling's office. She didn't seem impressed to see us.
She announced "My standard policy is I'll give a visiting politician one
free-ride interview. You come to town, and I'll write a story on you once.
After that, you can't just come to town and get a story. You have to make
news to get into our paper."

"OK. Fair enough," I responded.

"If you're going to be back here closer to the election, you might want
to wait until you come back for your one free story."

The decision was easy. I had no plans to be back in Paynesville
anytime soon. "Fine," I said. "Let's go ahead."

A week later, the only mention of my visit to town was an item in
Stelling's "Viewpoints" column. It said I hadn't made a good impression
as I had ignored the people in the front room of the newspaper while
waiting to speak with her. She commented that people other than editors
vote. It advised that politicians "should want to talk with as many people
as possible" and they should "spend more time walking up and down the
streets instead of sitting in offices talking with one person."

Stelling apparently believed a political candidate who pays attention only to people who can help him is an elitist who probably swears at waitresses and badmouths store clerks. A man of the people visiting a newspaper office, eating in a restaurant, shopping in a store, or walking down the street, will shake every hand. She had a point, but only a small one.

The problem is another point of view was drilled into me early in life by my dad, who sold men's suits for a living. In other words, he was a retail store clerk. More than once he came home from work in Sioux Falls and mentioned one politician or another had come into the store. "George McGovern came into the store to see Frank [the owner] today," he said.

"Oh," I contributed.

"Yeah, the slippery SOB went around the store shaking hands with everyone in the place. I had to shake hands with him. Those guys are always running for office. They always have their hands out. They won't leave you alone anywhere."

Think you are showing respect for people in their workplace by not bothering them and some think you are an elitist ignoring them. Think you are demonstrating the common touch by shaking hands and greeting all the people in a workplace and some think you are a grandstanding empty shirt. You can't win for losing, as my dad also used to say.

★ ★ ★ ★ ★

The next morning was an Elephant Club breakfast at the Minneapolis Hilton in honor of Senator Dave Durenberger. Since Mary and I had followed National Committeewoman Evie Axdahl's advice to contribute enough to join the Elephant Club, we were on the guest list. Steve Clark received Mary's ticket as a partial reward for all his work.

The guest speaker was Senator Alan Simpson from Wyoming. I was eager to hear Simpson speak for several reasons. He was assistant minority leader in the Senate and a national Republican spokesman. He had a rapid-fire, barbed wit and was willing to use it freely, so he was hugely entertaining. He was a plain-spoken western individualist, a man from a state bordering South Dakota, so I felt a kinship to him. In short, I was a fan.

At the end of the program, as usual, several audience members clustered around the speaker, Simpson. One by one they wandered away, their inquiries answered. I was undecided whether to eavesdrop politely to learn from his handling of the questioners, or to tell him I was running for Senate. Finally, the last of the questioners drifted away and the two of us were alone. "Hello, Senator," I said as I stuck out my hand. "I really enjoyed listening to you and just wanted to introduce myself. I'm Doug McFarland and on the assumption that Dave will not be running for reelection, I've been running for the Senate."

Simpson was a tall man himself, perhaps 6' 5", with much the same body type as mine. We looked at each other with that bond of unspoken affinity that especially tall people have for each other. The Senator eyed me carefully up and down. I waited for his reaction. Finally, he spoke: "Is that suit off the rack?"

"Yes, it is." I held out an arm and he rubbed the fabric. I added "It's a Hart, Schaffner & Marx. I'm lucky that I'm almost a perfect 46 extra long."

"Looks like it fits you well. I have to order all mine custom."

Now this was a subject I could converse on with some confidence. A bit of my dad's experience in selling men's suits had transferred to me. Simpson seemed interested too. He probably was tired of talking politics.

"You know, Senator, I can buy a suit almost any place in town. It's shirts that I have a terrible time finding."

"Yeah? What size do you wear?"

"Seventeen-and-a-half, thirty-eight."

"Well, I'm just thirty-five, but I still have to order custom."

"We have a store here in town you would love," I told him. "It has tall men's stuff, and unlike most tall men's stores, it's all high quality. You can find shirts or anything there. It's like a kid going into a candy store because you know everything fits. The name is the Foursome. If you ever have any time here in town, you should try it."

While I was giving Simpson this little unsolicited commercial, I noticed a Durenberger aide in the back of the room spot the two of us deep in conversation. From the way he jumped when he saw us, I could tell he thought I was horning in on the speaker there to honor Durenberger and trying to co-opt Simpson for my own campaign. He almost ran across the room to us and immediately said "We need to keep you on schedule, Senator. You have to leave now."

"OK. Thanks," Simpson said. He wished me "Good luck." I watched the two of them as they strode out of the room. The Durenberger aide was whispering animatedly into Simpson's ear. Later, I enjoyed speculating about the report the aide must have given Durenberger himself. "We get Simpson into town and that bastard McFarland tries to undercut you at your own event. I hope Simpson turned him down cold." I wonder whether Simpson ever told him we had discussed the politically charged topic of clothing sizes for tall men.

★ ★ ★ ★ ★

At the end of August, I took a weekend off from the campaign as Mary and I drove our oldest daughter Amy to Valparaiso University in Indiana for her freshman year. Parents of college-age children know what a surprisingly painful event that was.

We arrived back home for fall semester classes at Hamline. My negotiated teaching schedule favorable to campaigning was classes at ten a.m. and three p.m. on Mondays, Tuesdays, and Thursdays. Gail could schedule campaign events at any of the three mealtimes; four days were entirely open. Even so, multi-day trips during the workweek were now out. One-day travel schedules became the norm.

The first Wednesday, Gail Sutton, Steve Clark, his wife Leslie (who was eager to see the campaign trail), and I made a southern circuit of Red Wing, Northfield, Faribault, and Chaska. The reporter for the Northfield *News*, Brett Rabe, came to the activists' luncheon. The mixture started badly; Rabe didn't feel right attending a private, partisan luncheon. I agreed to conduct the interview first so he could get his story and leave. I also expected the activists at the table might find listening to a newspaper interview interesting.

After a few questions and answers, Rabe asked "I've heard you think you've been getting lousy coverage from the media. Is that right?"

"No," I answered, genuinely surprised, "I don't know where you heard that. I've been quite pleased with the media coverage, at least in greater

Minnesota. I have to say I'm unhappy with my treatment in the Twin Cities, especially by one unnamed paper, but the newspapers and other media outside the Twin Cities have been treating me great."

The transformation was immediate. From a hostile, hard-bitten inquisitor, Rabe became a friendly, sympathetic questioner. He asked several more questions and took a few photos. The next day the newspaper ran a warm article, with large photo, under the headline "Just call him 'Senator' McFarland." The photo caption even listed the Clarks among the local activists who had come out to see me, making the group appear larger.

The following Saturday morning we hosted an open house next to I-694 in the northwest corner of the Twin Cities. We had a hotel ballroom. We had bagels, sweet rolls, coffee, and tea. We had my family and many of our well-known party supporters there, including Bob Weinholzer, Tony Sutton, and Ron Carey. We had a good turnout. In contrast with the greater Minnesota events that started at a set time, this was a three-hour open house, with activists arriving and leaving through the morning. Finally, I thought, instead of miles of travel and meals with handfuls of activists, we were cracking the vote-rich metro. My heart may have been in greater Minnesota, but the votes were in the Twin Cities.

★ ★ ★ ★ ★

The end of August was the annual Minnesota state fair. I had always pictured the state fair as a politician's cornucopia: thousands of voters coming to the candidate daily instead of the candidate chasing after two or three voters at a time. I expected to spend twelve hours a day for all twelve days of the fair pressing as much flesh as possible. Again, expectation did not meet reality.

People attend fairs for the animals, the midway, grandstand shows, and food. Fairgoers are not there to talk politics or see politicians. When a candidate tries plan A to greet people as they pass the party booth at the fair, the voters either scurry by or even cross to the other side of the street. Those that do stop to talk are almost all either committed supporters or committed opposition troublemakers. The politician can move on to plan B. If the voters won't come to the candidate, the candidate must go to the voters. The candidate, trailed by a scrum of volunteers, abandons the party booth and strides the fairgrounds with hand outstretched. The average fairgoer, concentrating on eating cheese curds, a corn dog, a pork chop on a stick, ice cream, or mini donuts, is accosted by some annoying person wanting to shake hands. Hey, I'm trying to eat here. Plan B is like telemarketing without the telephone.

The situation is worse for an aspiring candidate. Officeholders can rent booths and candidates with party endorsement can use plan A to work at the party booth. All others must fend for themselves. The only option is plan B: gather a half-dozen supporters, arm them with signs on sticks to wave, and walk around the fairgrounds shaking hands and distributing literature. The only positive aspect of the plan was that we could easily find our way home at the end of the day. All we had to do was retrace our route by following the trail of all the discarded pieces of our campaign literature. After a couple of days of this wasted effort, we decided the state fair would not be the "great Minnesota get-together" for us.

CHAPTER ELEVEN

The High-Water Mark

With the turning of the calendar from summer to fall, political activity began anew. The first major event was the state party convention on September 18 in St. Cloud, 50 miles northwest of the Twin Cities. Even though this off-year convention was more than a year before the general election, the state party executive committee voted to conduct an official straw ballot. We were excited. Day after day, week after week, month after month, a candidate wonders "Am I running helter-skelter about the countryside with knowledgeable political people laughing up their sleeves at me, or am I riding the crest of a true grassroots political surge sweeping towards office?" The straw ballot at the state convention would be the first reliable answer.

As both Gail and Tony Sutton kept reminding me, "politics is perception," so we wanted the convention delegates to perceive we had the most active campaign in the state. That meant I had to continue to trudge down to the basement most evenings, pick up the telephone, and call around the state. We mailed a pre-convention letter to all the delegates and alternates. I continued to appear at various party meetings around the state. We were trying to get the buzz going that "McFarland is everywhere."

By now, I had answered nearly every question scores of times and could rattle off campaign themes and supporting evidence without even thinking. The most-asked question was a snap. No matter who I called or where I went, the first question almost invariably was "How's the campaign going?" Let's see, how to answer that toughie? How about "Great!"

Our volunteer team was large and growing. Late one Sunday afternoon, Gail asked me to come over to Ron Carey's house, but she wouldn't tell my why. I arrived to find a team painting all kinds of signs and posters for the upcoming state convention. Stacks of completed signs—some for taping to the walls and some attached to wooden sticks for waving by delegates—leaned against the basement walls. People were busily painting still more signs. Ron showed me the biggest surprise of all: a stack of 18 Styrofoam panels, each four feet by eight feet. When arrayed, the 18 panels spelled out in huge red letters "McFarland," with smaller, black letters below that said "Our Next Senator."

"We're going to string these high above the convention floor," Ron said. "Nobody's going to miss them."

"No, I guess not," was all I could say.

The candidate is supposed to fire up the volunteers, but with this show of dedicated work and support, the volunteers fired up the candidate. I went home ready to work both day and night, and to go anywhere and do anything.

★ ★ ★ ★ ★

My primary pre-convention task was to write and practice my speech. The writing came easily. Each candidate was allowed only ten minutes, and the speech had to leave room for applause breaks. Not a problem. Our campaign themes were well-established, so I hit each one with sure-fire applause lines; by now, I knew exactly what lines would bring cheers and applause.

Next came the practicing. Just as she had done months earlier for my congressional district convention speech, Gail assembled a handful of our loyal supporters to conduct a critique. My first effort showed that I had improved from months of speaking experience, yet all was not well. The critics were consistent. "Be more animated in your delivery." "Be more enthusiastic." "Make the listeners believe you truly believe what you're saying." "Show more passion." "Fire up."

I delivered the speech a second time with more passion. Better, they said, but still needs more fire. After watching the video of the speech, I tried again. Still more passion, they said. We tried again and again.

Their concern was they wanted me to wave my arms and emote to show the depth of my convictions. My concern was the line between passion and parody is thin. My natural speaking style was conversational, and when I tried to ratchet it up, I moved more toward bombast and herky-jerky than enthusiasm. My mind told me I would be delivering a statement of political principles, not charging up the audience at a rock concert. Still, I respected the opinions of these friends. I promised them I would practice plenty in the three days remaining before the eighteenth—and try for more fire.

★ ★ ★ ★ ★

The big weekend finally arrived. While the convention was officially scheduled to begin Saturday morning, unofficially it began Friday evening with candidate hospitality suites at the Holiday Inn in St. Cloud. Our campaign team arrived Friday afternoon to find rumors and questions already flying hot and heavy on both governor and senator.

Did you hear Governor Arne Carlson is coming to the convention instead of giving the delegates the cold shoulder? Does his challenger Al Quist have a chance? What do you think of this other conservative candidate for governor Dick Kimbler? My response to all of these was easy: I'm staying out of that race.

How about the Senate? Will Dave Durenberger try to hang on? He knows the convention will conduct a straw ballot; can he risk an embarrassing loss? If Durenberger gets out, will anyone else jump into the race? How about an 800-pound gorilla such as former Senator Rudy Boschwitz or former Congressman Vin Weber or even current Congressman Jim Ramstad? No, I answered, they've said time and again they're not running. How about Rod Grams, the only other Republican Congressman in the state? No, I responded, Rod was first elected less than a year ago and the party needs to hold that seat; Grams jumping to a run for the Senate would be a dumb thing to do. How about a woman; the Democrats are bound and determined to run a woman; do we have one? Well, I said, we have state senator Joanne Benson, but she isn't widely known. No one else is out there.

I repeated time and time again I expected Durenberger to get out eventually. That's why I was running. As for other candidates, both Bert McKasy and I are running strong, and we can carry the Republican message. What I didn't tell the questioners was that this matchup was just fine with me. I can beat Bert.

I would have been delighted to arrive in town for the beginning of the convention Saturday morning. Instead, I first had to go through the ordeal of the hospitality suite Friday evening: three solid, high pressure hours of standing in one place answering questions, with back muscles growing tighter and tighter and voice getting raspier and raspier. That's no way to spend the evening prior to delivering the biggest speech of your life. Yet we had no choice. Politics is perception. Failure to host a hospitality suite would lead the delegates to think my campaign was falling apart. That wasn't an option. By the time we closed the hospitality suite around ten p.m., and Mary and I plodded off to go to our room at another motel, my voice was a steady rasp and my back felt as if it would never loosen again. I probably looked like Frankenstein's monster lumbering across the parking lot to our car.

The convention started Saturday morning at nine o'clock. Our family—Mary and I, and the three of our children in town—arrived at the St. Cloud civic center early and entered our campaign war room, a meeting room near the great hall. We had it easy. My schedule included only two tasks: a private meeting with Vin Weber in the morning, and a ten-minute speech to the convention in the afternoon. The rest of the family was there to appear on stage during the speech.

Manager Gail Sutton had taken care of everything else. Our team had fully slimed the convention hall with posters and signs. A wide variety of home-made signs, fresh from Ron Carey's basement, were ready on the convention floor. A sharp literature piece, touting my summer travels, prominent party supporters, and conservative positions, was placed on every chair. Volunteers stood at the hall entrances to push a lapel sticker onto every person who would take one. A team of more than 100 floor workers, with the dual tasks of reporting convention floor trends to Gail in the war room and lobbying their delegations for votes, was assembled in a nearby room, waiting for last-minute instructions.

Gail said "Doug, our floor team is already pumped up, but I want you to give them a final pep talk before we send them out to the floor."

The floor workers broke into a round of applause when we entered. All of them, including many party leaders from across the state, were decked out in McFarland for Senate red and white tee-shirts. Their faces were flushed. Many were almost giddy with excitement. They were ready to storm the convention floor to have some fun and get some payback for all their hours of dedicated party work. Seeing them, I was giddy, too.

Before I could open my mouth, Gail announced "Doug, Joanne Muller from Hibbing has one question she wants to ask you."

Even though taken aback, I responded "Sure."

"Doug," asked Muller, "would you vote for a constitutional amendment outlawing abortion?"

I managed to stammer out "Well, uh, yes." Muller must have demanded of Gail that the question be a surprise as one last test on her key issue. Looking back over the years, I realize now that Gail, a strong social conservative, may also have wanted to be sure herself of my steadfastness on the issue. My answer might have sounded tentative, but it was the right answer and it didn't waffle or squish. I had an immediate vision of the wrong answer causing this red-clad mini-army of volunteers to place their literature and signs down on the floor right then and there and spurt out of the room onto the convention floor, symbolizing the bleeding out of my campaign.

"OK, then," Gail said, "we're ready to go." She barked out final instructions and cast the workers into the swirl of the convention.

A few minutes later, Mary and I followed the workers through the side door onto the convention floor. We stayed in the shadows amongst concrete columns at the side of the hall. A jolt went through us. The job Gail and our volunteer crew had done was beyond belief. Our red and white posters were in all the choice locations. Delegates with red shirts peppered the floor. Strung high above was a rope holding the huge Styrofoam letters spelling out "McFarland Our Next Senator." Wow! Since politics is perception, the delegates would perceive we were crushing the opposition.

The St. Cloud convention

★ ★ ★ ★ ★

I was also thrilled because Vin Weber had finally agreed to meet with me. We would get together behind the stage after he addressed the convention at ten a.m. Gail and I waited in the dark area at the side of the convention floor to listen to Weber's speech. I didn't want him to ask me what I thought of the speech and have to say I didn't listen to it. As soon as he was finished, Gail and I hustled along the darkened path outside the concrete columns to the front of the convention hall and stepped around the side of the huge, blue curtain that hid the unused area of the arena floor from the delegates.

Weber was sitting on a folding chair, already holding court for a favor-seeker. Another two were lined up waiting to see him. Jack Meeks motioned for Gail and me to take our place in line. After several minutes, our turn arrived. I took the folding chair facing Weber and leaned close to him.

I complimented his speech. We talked a few issues. I told Weber how much I wanted his support. Weber was noncommittal. He suggested in a subtle way that he did not appreciate seeing in the newspaper the quotation from Gail linking him to the failed Jon Grunseth for governor campaign.

Probably the best thing for me to do at that point would have been to apologize profusely. "I didn't say it, Vin, and I'm sorry anyway. Gail said it; she was just trying to be funny, and she's also deeply sorry. I never believed it. Vin, you're my man." Instead, I found myself patting his thigh as I blurted out "Oh, Vin, you know how competitive Gail is. It didn't mean anything."

Even this weak apology seemed to mollify him. I told him how much I needed his help, especially with fundraising. "Vin, I know what kind of sources you have, and what you can do. What I really need is for you to help by raising some money for me." Weber said he wasn't backing anyone in the Senate race yet. He declined to make any calls himself, but he did rattle off eight names of Minnesota large contributors. He said "These are some conservative people who have been good to me in the past and probably would be willing to help you." A good start.

"You can tell them you got their names from me." Even better.

"Tell them I said you were a good conservative." Best!

I walked away with a list of Vin Weber-certified conservative fat cats and his seal of fundraising approval. I felt as if I'd won the bronze medal of the political Olympics. Plus, I could now see a distinct possibility existed that Vin Weber might eventually sign onto our team. Now that would be the gold medal.

★ ★ ★ ★ ★

Only one item of morning business of the convention interested us. Gail had thought we were finally ready for a straw ballot, so our people on the state executive committee had voted to place an official straw ballot for senator and governor on the convention agenda. Gail anticipated a motion to cancel it. Delegates supporting the re-election of Governor Arne Carlson didn't want a straw ballot. Delegates still supporting Senator David Durenberger didn't want a straw ballot. We didn't know whether Bert McKasy wanted a straw ballot.

When a delegate did move to cancel the straw ballot, our people carried the debate on the convention floor. Gail was ecstatic. "Not only is the straw ballot going to stay," she crowed, "but also the delegates are going to see that we are the ones pushing it. That will show them our muscle." The motion to cancel the straw ballot failed badly.

Soon after the motion failed, word filtered into our war room that Dave Durenberger had asked to address the convention. The option of staying on the sidelines was now gone; he was on the straw ballot. Durenberger spoke to the convention. He would not be a candidate for re-election! Another major roadblock vaporized!

I was also happy because a major reason I decided to run was that I didn't want a person with ethical problems representing our party on the ballot. Durenberger was out, and I had played a large part in forcing him out. Win or lose in the end, I felt satisfaction that my campaign had already been a success.

That doesn't mean I disliked the man or disrespected his work. He had been a good Senator for many years, at least until he had "gone Washington." Shortly after his speech, I chanced on Durenberger outside the hall. I was surprised to find my eyes misting over as I laid a hand on his back and said "Dave, I know this was hard for you, but you did the best thing for the party."

He responded softly "I think I did the best thing for myself."

★ ★ ★ ★ ★

The convention broke for lunch. Since the candidates' speeches and the straw ballot were the primary afternoon business, we couldn't relax. One of our workers made a run to a fast food restaurant with a bulk order while the rest of us continued to push. Gail and others worked delegates.

Mary, Stuart, Katie, Wesley, and I looked for a small, private room so I could practice the speech yet again. Gail's admonition "This one needs to be a barnburner" echoed in my mind.

We walked up the stairs to the second level of the civic center, but the conference rooms were locked. The best we could find was a cluster of chairs at the far end of the hallway, mostly isolated from the hubbub of the first floor. Mary sent Stuart back to the war room to tell Gail where we were.

During my doctoral studies, I learned that classical Roman rhetoricians believed memory was as important as content or delivery of a speech. With that in mind, I memorized all my speeches, including this one. Delegates always seemed impressed that I spoke without notes or a text. Of course, delivery of the same speech many times imprinted on the memory. This speech was one-time-only. One of my worst fears was to look out over the assembled delegates and have my mind go blank, so I had one printed copy of the speech in the left inside breast pocket of my suitcoat, and a backup emergency copy in the right inside breast pocket.

The five of us sat alone isolated on the second floor. I read through the speech again carefully, checking emphases. I stood and delivered it quietly to the family. We all rested a while. A worker dropped off our fast food lunch. I read through the speech again and again and delivered it again and again. Mary said it sounded fine. I sat back in a chair and closed my eyes, trying to keep my breathing slow and my mind clear. Every so often a delegate, likely seeking a rest room, appeared at the head of the stairs, saw our small group sitting in silence, and retreated down the stairs. Time dragged on: we waited through afternoon convention business and speeches by the three candidates for governor—Arne Carlson, Allen Quist, and Dick Kimbler.

Finally, Gail appeared at the top of the stairs. Time for the senate candidate speeches. The culmination of a year of work. Time to get it done or time to be done. We all walked through the side door into the convention hall and stood in the semi-darkness amongst the concrete columns. We listened to Bert McKasy's speech to be sure he wouldn't pull any surprises.

John Palmer, the convention chair, announced me as the next speaker, and our family bounded up onto the stage to the loud approval of the delegates. We all waved, and I stepped to the microphone. In truth, the speech was more style than substance. I mentioned the federal budget, health care, agriculture, education, and term limits. I hammered my campaign themes of honesty, common sense, straight talk, trust, and hard work. I thanked recent Republican Presidents Ronald Reagan and George Bush to cheers and applause. I took shots at recent Democratic politicians to hoots and laughter. I promised to protect the rights of the unborn, and the delegates roared their approval. I reminded the delegates of my humble roots, and quoted another tall Republican, Abraham Lincoln, at both beginning and end—no need to be subtle.

In what seemed like ten seconds, the ten minutes was spent. To the cheers and applause of the delegates, Mary, our three kids, and I waved broadly from the stage. I bounced down the steps into the center aisle. Delegates on both sides shouted approval and stuck out their hands. I grasped as many hands as possible, yet I tried to keep moving to reach the last row of delegates before the applause came to its end. Gail was waiting. I anxiously asked what she thought. She said it was a home run. Of course, my manager would say that.

We all retreated to the war room. By the time word came that the straw ballot results were ready, afternoon had shaded into evening. We all stood again amongst the concrete columns at the side of the floor, waiting to hear the results. Convention chair John Palmer announced the Senate vote as McKasy 351, McFarland 487 . . . I couldn't hear any more as Gail was shrieking into my ear. I wanted to shriek too. Less than a year earlier, I was a political nobody. Today, I had helped to shoulder aside a sitting Senator and won my party's straw ballot.

I stood there basking in the results and the broad smiles from nearby seated delegates when Gail pushed me forward. "Look," she pointed to the press section at the front of the hall and rasped, "there's Leon up front with the press trying to spin the results for Bert. He's probably telling them the vote didn't mean much. Get up there!"

When I reached the front of the convention floor where Bert McKasy's manager Leon Oistad was holding forth for reporters, the reaction reminded me of a comedy scene from a movie. The crowd of reporters buzzing around Leon melted away from him and congealed around me within seconds. Leon was left standing with his mouth open, having lost his listeners in midsentence. He was a good enough sport to smile.

The reporters peppered me with questions. "What does this win mean?" "You beat McKasy 40 percent to 29 percent. Was that what you expected?" "To what do you attribute your win?" "What's next for your campaign?" "What do you think of the results for governor?" I answered every question. Like an athlete after winning the big game, I didn't want to leave the locker room and go home.

Finally, the reporters were done. Mary and I wandered toward the back of the hall, which by now was nearly empty. A lingering delegate here and there shouted congratulations. We passed governor candidate Al Quist, who was giving a radio interview. He had lost to Arne Carlson, 40 percent to 37 percent. Even so, he had a serene smile. Referring to the state endorsing convention the following year, he said "Next June, we will win." We passed Bob and Georgiann Stenerson; Bob looked at me with newfound respect, but Georgiann remained cool. Well, I guess you can't win them all.

Our family loaded into the minivan for the drive home. Gail and other volunteers, who would stay to take down the signs and decorations, stood on the sidewalk and waved as we drove slowly away. Other delegates, in their cars and on foot, waved and shouted.

Ecstasy. The highest of the high moments of the campaign. As I told reporters, this vote put us on the map. It would help with fundraising a great deal. We were on the way now. Our tide was rising. What I didn't know was that we had reached the high-water mark of the campaign.

CHAPTER TWELVE

Where's The Payoff?

One would expect a raucous drive home from St. Cloud, but it was silent. With the end of the adrenaline rush of the convention, Mary, our three children, and I were spent. Stuart, Katie, and Wesley slept, and I used my remaining energy to stay awake at the wheel.

After arriving home too late for the six o'clock news, we ordered a Chinese takeout dinner and waited eagerly for the ten o'clock news to see how the television stations would play our big win. We flipped channels to try to catch every report. The coverage was good: Republican convention, Senate straw ballot win, delegates cheering. One of the stations even showed a wide angle shot of the convention floor with the huge McFarland Styrofoam letters clearly visible high above.

Television was a good start. Next morning's newspapers were the real payoff. Audiences for late Saturday evening television news might be slim, but hundreds of thousands of Minnesotans would read the Sunday morning statewide editions of the *Pioneer Press* and the *StarTribune*.

The previous Saturday, the Democratic party state central committee meeting had included a straw ballot for Senate. Ann Wynia had won that straw ballot with fewer than 100 votes. The *StarTribune* ran a banner headline and photo on the front page of the Metro/State section proclaiming Wynia's victory. I anticipated more. With a real straw ballot at a full state convention, I hoped for a headline on page one.

Never before or since have I been more eager to read the morning newspapers. Like a kid waiting for Christmas morning, I had trouble sleeping. I was lying in bed awake when I heard a car engine pass the front of our house, signaling the delivery of the paper. I rolled out of bed and padded out to the street to retrieve the newspaper.

The convention took a banner headline on page one of the *StarTribune* all right. It proclaimed "Carlson narrowly wins straw poll." The story was incumbent, popular Governor Arne Carlson had almost been beaten by right-wing, fire-breather Allen Quist. The story quoted various party leaders about the race. The page featured photos of both Carlson and Quist in action at the convention.

Buried in the middle of the story continuation on page 14A was a mention that a straw ballot for senate had also been conducted with McFarland beating McKasy, the "only two official candidates in a field that will undoubtedly get more crowded." A single photo highlighted the page: McKasy shaking hands with a delegate. For 100 votes, Ann Wynia earned a banner headline and a large photo. For 500 votes, I earned a deprecating comment on an interior page with a photo of the man I had crushed.

The *Pioneer Press* was only a little better. Again, the big news was the straw ballot for governor, but at least the front-page story carried the sub-headline "McFarland gains most votes for Durenberger Senate seat" and the jump page contained face shots of all four candidates.

The greatest triumph of the campaign transformed before my eyes into a scene from a horror movie. I wanted to scream as the flesh of the smiling, friendly face on the screen melted away to reveal a leering skull underneath.

Many times during the campaign I had been the calm eye of the storm while my manager Gail Sutton swirled and thundered around me.

This time the roles were reversed. I called her and demanded to know whether she had seen the morning newspapers. "Can you believe what the *StarTribune* did to us again?" I asked.

"Yes, I can," she replied. "Did you really expect better for a conservative?"

"Well, they've gone over the top this time," I raged. "Last week Wynia gets a headline for a hundred votes and this week I get nothing."

"Yeah, I guess it is bad even by their standards."

"It wouldn't look good for me to call Dane Smith, but I want you to call him first thing tomorrow. He didn't write the article, but he controls their political coverage. We have to call him on this. Point out to him the headline last week with the treatment this week. I suppose I can understand that Quist and Carlson were the bigger story, but the photo of Bert is too much. They run one photo, and it's of the guy who lost."

"Damn right I'll call him," Gail said as she warmed to the task. "You're right. We shouldn't let them get away with this sort of thing."

Gail did call Dane Smith the next morning. She reported back that he hadn't realized the unequal treatment or the problem with the photo of Bert. Now he understood. Great. Now I had another concrete example when people asked "What media bias?" With that, Smith's new understanding, and a dollar, I could buy a cup of coffee.

★ ★ ★ ★ ★

By this time, I hardly had a dollar, and in any event wouldn't have wasted it on coffee. We had given priority to raising political support over raising money. Surely, we had attempted to raise money, but as a variant of the old joke goes, we wanted to raise money badly and that's just what we did.

Bert McKasy seemed to have the opposite strategy. He was concentrating on raising money. Occasionally, a supporter passed on to me a flyer for one of McKasy's fundraising events. He had hosted several, and I had hosted none. We didn't know how much money he had raised, but it certainly was far more than I had. Plus, Bert had more personal wealth to throw into the campaign. In sum, Bert had the money, and I had the delegates. The result was I beat him badly in the straw ballot. This seemed to me at the time like a fair trade.

Now the time had come for us to shift gears and collect the financial payoff of our efforts to amass political support. Our theory all along had been that with political support would come political muscle. We had just flexed that muscle to body slam the opposition at the state convention. With political muscle would come financial support. Now the purse strings were bound to loosen. We turned our primary effort from gathering political support to gathering dollars.

Our first postconvention event was a luncheon with several young attorneys at a major Minneapolis law firm. Erik Kaardal, a new associate attorney and a strong social conservative, hosted the event. The young attorneys liked what I had to say. I asked them for money. They committed their political support.

Once again, I may have been too understanding. These were attorneys beginning their careers, not grown old and fat in their wallets over the years. Even so, I could have said "Look, I know you're just starting out, but I also know each of you can contribute at least $100. I want to see at least ten checks for $100 each on that table in front of me by the end of lunch." I'd heard stories of well-known politicians who didn't hesitate to make that sort of appeal. It might have worked, but it would have shown a lack of class. I left that luncheon with my class intact and pocket empty.

Another problem dogged our fundraising. Many people thought the Senate field was not yet complete. Rumors continued to rise that with Durenberger out, a real candidate would come forward. One afternoon I tuned in to a radio talk show. The guest was former Senator Rudy Boschwitz. The host said "What about you getting into the race, Rudy? I know you'd like to get back to the Senate."

"No, I'm not running. I may run again in the future, but not this year."

"You'd like another shot at Paul Wellstone, Rudy, is that it?"

"We'll see when the time comes."

"Well, then, Rudy, how do you assess the current field of Republican candidates?"

What would he answer? I had known Rudy for many years as a mutual political supporter and as a friend. Boschwitz said "I have to give credit to the two candidates we have out there running for us now. They're working hard, but I think the field is not complete."

"What do you have for us, Rudy? Who else do you expect to get in?"

"I don't have any names. I just think we haven't seen all the candidates, and the eventual nominee for our party isn't in the race yet."

"Who?"

"I don't know. Just someone not in the field yet."

"When do you think this person will jump in?"

"I don't know. Sometime soon, I would think, or it will be too late."

Wonderful! That'll help my fundraising a lot. Now potential contributors will wait for the anointed one to emerge from the mists of nowhere to accept the acclaim and the nomination of the party at some unknown point in the future. I was disappointed, annoyed, and curious. I called Boschwitz at his office and asked, "Rudy, I heard you on the radio this afternoon, and you said you thought someone else would enter the Senate race soon. Do you know anything I don't know?"

Rudy was flustered. It's happened to me, too. Who knows how far a comment will travel or who might be listening? "No, no, I don't know anything about another candidate," Rudy said. "I was just making a general comment."

I wasn't quite ready to let him off the hook. "You sounded pretty definite. Are you sure you don't know of someone thinking of running?"

"No, I was only saying it's relatively early yet. Others might get in."

"Well, Rudy, you said you thought the eventual nominee isn't even in the race yet. Do you have any inside information?"

"No, no, just that a lot of names are floating around. I don't know anything definite."

Rudy had merely been speculating while facing an anonymous radio microphone. The wiser course for me from the beginning would have been to swallow my irritation and not call. Rudy was a friend. More importantly, he retained a huge amount of goodwill among state party people, and he had been chairman of the national Republican Senatorial Campaign Committee. I wanted and needed his help.

"OK, well, thanks then, Rudy. I just thought that, well, you know, you said you knew of someone, and you know how important that would be to me. I wanted to be sure you didn't know of anyone in particular. I was concerned." After a little small talk, we both rang off, Rudy to return to his role as elder statesman of the party and me to return to my role of scrabbling for contributions.

★ ★ ★ ★ ★

Manager Gail Sutton picked Wednesday, September 29, as the day to announce my candidacy for the Senate. Since the formal announcement is the one time a candidate is assured substantial, favorable coverage by the major media, Gail had been saving this event. The previous spring was too early. Summer was too empty. That left fall or winter. Her initial plan was to announce shortly after Labor Day so I could ride the publicity boost into the state convention. When she concluded that we would do well at the convention without the boost, Gail decided to bet on a win in the straw ballot. Announcement shortly after the convention would make the biggest splash.

The next question was where to announce. One logical location was a Hamline University classroom to remind everyone of my background. We kicked around more exotic locales. A few years earlier, former governor Rudy Perpich had announced his campaign for re-election at the headwaters of the Mississippi River in Itasca some three-and-one-half hours north of the Twin Cities. Gail nixed any exotic locale. "Reporters hate to travel" she said. "They hated to have to go to Itasca for Perpich's announcement. We don't want them mad at us." She decided on a plain vanilla location: a room in the state office building across the street from the state capitol. "The media will love it," she said. "They can walk to it from their offices. They may give us some more play this way."

The last question was what time of day to announce. Gail decided a mid-morning press conference gave the media plenty of time to prepare stories for the evening television news and the next morning newspapers. It also gave us time the same day to drive to other towns and announce again for the benefit of their local media.

On announcement day I would emerge into the awareness of the general public as a serious, substantial candidate for the U. S.

Senate—unless I put my foot into my mouth at the press conference. To prevent any foot-in-mouth situation, the day before I practiced answering questions from "reporters" Gail Sutton, Bob Weinholzer, Ron Carey, Steve Clark, Chris Bakeman, Rich Villella, and Orlando Ochowada. We all kept at it until they ran out of things to ask.

By 9:30 a.m. on the big day, reporters and supporters packed state office building room 5, the size of a grade school classroom. Red and white McFarland campaign signs covered the walls. A media informational packet graced every chair. Many state political reporters were present, including Eric Eskola of WCCO radio, Jack Coffman and Bill Salisbury of the *Pioneer Press*, Pat Kessler of WCCO television, Gene LaHammer of the Associated Press, and Dane Smith of the *StarTribune*. Several television cameras pointed at the rostrum. The enthusiastic crowd of my supporters jammed into the small area behind the rostrum to provide both vocal support and a background for photos and television. Gail had done another magnificent job.

The buzz of the crowd broke into a cheer when our family walked into the room. I took my place behind a rostrum adorned with a dozen microphones. The warmth and excitement of the supporters floated me through the formal announcement. The themes were family, long-shot campaign, hard work, major issues, honesty, common sense, and key supporters. Our supporters cheered lustily and often.

Steve Clark was assigned to call for questions from the reporters. After about 15 minutes of questions, Clark tried to call the press conference to an end. Unfortunately, his timing was a little off. He stepped in right after I mentioned the National Endowment for the Arts as an example of a federal program I would eliminate. Eric Eskola rose from his chair, thinking my handlers were trying to protect me from an embarrassing answer. I held up a hand to Clark and told Eskola that I wanted to eliminate the NEA because the federal budget was in crisis, we had to take tough looks at every program, and art ought to be funded privately. I did not say it should be eliminated because it funded blasphemy such as a crucifix in a jar of urine masquerading as art. Eskola calmed down. False alarm. No real news there.

Some candidates make a two or even three-day media swing out of the formal announcement, flying around the state to repeat the announcement live in Rochester, Mankato, Duluth, Moorhead, and additional towns. We drove to Rochester and back home. I had to teach two classes the next day.

That evening and the next morning proved Gail right. We did get uniformly good stories from the media. Maybe the reporters were glad they didn't have to drive up to Itasca.

CHAPTER THIRTEEN

Dress For Success

The first Saturday of October was another kitchen cabinet meeting at our house. We invited the kitchen cabinet plus our core team of campaign workers to join us for lunch followed by a game of touch football in the back yard. The older folks in the kitchen cabinet were not touch football players, but the younger workers, who had been carrying the physical tasks of the campaign, loved it. Both groups raved about Mary's lunch, and we all had a great time. The Kennedys had nothing on us.

About this time, word on the street began spreading that Republican Congressman Rod Grams was eyeing the Senate seat. Only the previous election, he had left his job as a television news anchorman with the intent of running for the state senate in a southern Twin Cities district. Party professionals Leon Oistad and Dave Hoium talked him into moving to a northern suburb to run for the sixth district seat in Congress instead. When the Democratic incumbent became part of a national scandal involving overdrafts at the House of Representatives bank, Grams became a hero to Minnesota Republicans for winning a Congressional seat that had been firmly in Democratic hands.

For everyone who asked, I easily ticked off the reasons why I didn't expect Grams to shuck the House seat to run for the Senate. The move would be high risk for him. Instead of a relatively safe re-election, Grams would have to face two solid, active campaigners for the Republican nomination, and then beat the Democratic candidate in a state that trended Democratic. Further, running for the Senate after less than one year in the House would appear to be naked, blind opportunism, which doesn't go over well with voters. Many party activists had told me they were irritated by the prospect because they had worked hard to help Grams win the House seat, and he would likely be handing it back to the Democrats.

Gail relayed reports that Grams was gathering support for a Senate run by meeting over coffee with activists in his own sixth district. We also heard Grams had commissioned a statewide poll that found he had 70 percent statewide name recognition (to 39 percent for me and 19 percent for Bert McKasy). Even when these reports arrived, I still didn't believe Grams would run. It just plain wasn't a smart, canny political decision.

What I didn't realize was that Rod Grams wasn't politically smart and canny. Worse, he was listening to bad advice. He had fired both Leon Oistad and Dave Hoium, the two political pros who won him the House seat, six months into his term when they crossed a young, good-looking, ruthless, politically inexperienced female staffer who had grabbed onto and held tightly to his imagination. He was taking his political advice from her.

★ ★ ★ ★ ★

At the state convention, Vin Weber had given me the names of eight potential large contributors. Three couldn't fit me into their schedules. Four more parroted the same old refrain with a new addition: I like what you have to say, Doug, but it's too early to get behind a candidate. By the way, what do you hear about Rod Grams possibly running?

The single exception was Bill Cooper, the chief executive officer of TCF Bank. Gail and I arrived at the TCF executive offices in downtown

Minneapolis for our 11:15 meeting. I had never met the man, and didn't know what to expect, other than that he had once been a cop in Detroit before he moved to Minnesota to make his fortune in the financial world, and that he had been a generous contributor to several Minnesota Republican candidates.

Cooper looked like a tough cop. About six-two with a ruddy face and lean body, he appeared to be able to don a uniform right then and there and report for duty. The man had a businesslike, almost brusque manner about him. Our initial conversation revealed he was not one for making small talk. Almost right away, Cooper asked me "What do you think is the number one issue facing our nation today?"

I had called on scores of potential contributors, and none had asked this question in this blunt fashion. I didn't know whether to trot out the safe response of balancing the federal budget or to take a chance. I decided to take a chance.

The Center of the American Experiment, the Minnesota conservative think tank founded by Mitch Pearlstein, had recently sponsored programs on the topic of the American family. I had also attended monthly meetings of a discussion group known as the Hamline Dialogues. Even the liberal members of the Hamline Dialogues resonated to statistics that showed the explosive growth of illegitimate births at all levels of our society, and especially in minority communities. Studies clearly showed that children growing up without a father were disadvantaged. That was a large part of what "family values" was all about.

I swallowed hard and answered "I think the number one problem facing us today is the rising illegitimacy rate and the breakdown of the American family."

Cooper's face lit up. His whole manner changed from hard-bitten former cop to the concerned parent that he also was. He agreed this was the most important issue in the country today. Cooper practically had his checkbook out then and there.

Before contributing to my campaign, Cooper wanted to know what I thought about the possibility of Rod Grams getting into the race. He said "I contributed to Rod when he ran for Congress last year, and served on his finance committee, so I feel a certain loyalty to him."

I answered honestly with my standard response. For various reasons, my best guess was Rod would not run.

Cooper pulled open the drawer to his desk, opened his checkbook, and wrote a check for $1000, the maximum single election individual contribution to a candidate for federal office. Gail and I could hardly contain ourselves. I hadn't even asked for money, and the man was handing us a maximum check. Even more exciting, Cooper said his wife would almost certainly also want to make a $1000 contribution. He ended the meeting by saying "I might well be willing to serve on your finance committee."

Gail and I floated out of the office. This was the big break we had been desperately pursuing for months: a major business leader willing to put his name and reputation on the line for my campaign. Other business leaders would soon follow. The money would begin to flow. The payoff from the straw ballot win was about to begin.

On our way out, Gail asked Cooper's secretary if we could use the telephone; she wanted to share this wonderful news with Tony Sutton back at our campaign office.

Tony had news for us too. Watching Gail's face as she talked on the telephone, I thought someone had died. "What?" I demanded. "What is it?"

"Grams announced he's going to run."

"Damn."

Five days earlier, I had announced my candidacy as the party frontrunner. Now, in one second, I had slipped back into the pack baying at the tail of the leader. Now, all the potential major contributors who wanted to see what Rod Grams would do had received their answer. The fundraising window that had been open for only two weeks following the state convention had slammed shut. Both Gail and I believed in our hearts we could beat Grams politically, but we both knew in our minds we didn't stand a chance against an incumbent member of Congress financially.

We looked at each other. "What do we do now?" I asked.

"The first thing we do is cash this check before Cooper gets the news" she said.

"Yes," I agreed, "but I don't think we'd better hold our breath waiting for that second $1000 from his wife."

★ ★ ★ ★ ★

The next evening our calendar called us back to the political side of the campaign. The Stevens County party leadership was holding its monthly meeting in Morris. [Reminder: a Minnesota map showing congressional districts and some cities is in the Appendix.] Gail had promised Laura Carrington, the county chairwoman, a high school teacher, and one of my most committed and important supporters, that I would attend one of their earlier meetings, but a conflict intervened. Now we had to keep the promise.

Three of us—Gail and I and our chaperone—drove 160 miles due west to Morris for the 7:30 meeting, schmoozed everyone there for a half-hour, and then drove 160 miles back home. That's 320 miles of driving to meet with a dozen people for a half-hour. Of that dozen, perhaps three would eventually be elected delegates to the next state convention. Of those three, I already had commitments from two. The math worked out to a seven-hour trip for one potential delegate. Looking back, I see that wasn't too smart. At the time, I was willing to go anywhere and do anything to get one vote. Politics by retail.

After the appearance, county chairwoman Laura Carrington followed us to the car. She thanked us for coming, and then surprised me by saying "Doug, when you come here, you always wear a coat and tie."

"Yes, of course." I didn't quite see where she was heading.

"Well, I want you to know we all appreciate it," she said. "Bert McKasy was here last month, and he had on some sort of plaid flannel shirt. He must think we're a bunch of hicks out here in outstate, and he can dress down that way and impress us. You can bet he doesn't dress that way when he makes an appearance in the Twin Cities."

"No, I don't think he does," I went along. "Well, Laura, I certainly don't dress differently when I visit greater Minnesota."

"I know that, Doug, and that's one of the things I like about you. We're as sophisticated here as the people in the Twin Cities, and you respect us."

"Of course."

As we drove off into the night, I felt like cackling. Bert had tried to dress down to connect with the people in Morris, and his tactic had backfired. He had been too obvious. What I didn't tell Carrington, or anyone else outside of our inner circle, was that my graduate study in speech-communication was paying another dividend: knowledge of nonverbal communication (by the way, anyone who calls it body language is most likely a quack) helped me to craft carefully my own appearance for every campaign event.

After traveling to the destination in casual comfort, I stepped into a gas station or convenience store men's room (or ladies' room when the other key was missing). The first thing was to take off my thick glasses and pop in contact lenses. Instead of looking distant and bookish, I became a welcoming person with an open face and a twinkling eye. Next I changed out of my golf shirt and wash pants into a suit or sport coat with slacks, dress shirt, and tie. The result was a high-octane politician ready to meet the people. I spent a lot of time in men's rooms across the state.

For years, I had worn a bow tie. It had become something of a trademark. A few people at my early campaign appearances, especially in greater Minnesota, had said "I'm not sure about that bow tie." Why take a chance? From then on, I wore a standard long tie to every political event. Mary bought me some for my birthday. A friend of mine at Hamline soon began to claim he could tell whether I had a political appearance that day by whether I showed up on campus wearing a bow tie or a long tie. Actually, I had worn a bow tie to teach classes earlier that day but switched to a long tie for the event in Morris. The long ties all were predominantly red, a strong, trustworthy color. That's why nearly every male politician at every level from city council to President usually wears a red tie.

Other clothing items were also calculated. I had one pair of "political shoes," black leather lace ups with a square toe and some stitching. I always wore a long-sleeved white dress shirt with a standard collar. Someone might think short sleeves were too casual. *Today, male politicians on the stump seem to wear any kind of shirt and often display an open collar with no tie. I still think that's the same mistake of too obviously dressing down in the attempt to connect with voters.* My closet contained several older white dress shirts that were reserved for political events; political appearances often produced flop sweat, and I didn't want to sweat out a new dress shirt. I wore only a wedding ring on the left hand and a ring given to me by my parents upon law school graduation on the right.

Since a delegate might think a candidate in a fine suit is getting big for his britches, I never wore an expensive suit to a political event, even the state convention. Maybe the exception was I did wear a good suit to the Elephant Club luncheon where I encountered Senator Alan Simpson. The occasion called for something to try to impress people I hoped would be large donors.

My political hero, Bill Frenzel, served ten terms in Congress from the third district in suburban Hennepin County. I don't remember ever seeing him dressed in anything other than a navy blue blazer and heather gray slacks. I wore my blue blazer and gray slacks political uniform often, too. Other times, I wore navy blue or charcoal suits. Sometimes I felt safe dipping down to the bottom of my closet. I liked to wear a comfortable, shiny, royal blue, summer-weight suit that I had found on crazy days clearance at the Foursome for $99. That's what I had on in Morris.

My loyal supporter Linda Carrington thought that Bert McKasy tried to dress down outside the Twin Cities, but that I wore the same type of dressy clothing for appearances across the state. I was not about to tell her that Bert's flannel shirt likely cost more than my suit.

★ ★ ★ ★ ★

The next day I had lunch at a suburban motel with a volunteer who had asked to see me; Gail agreed based on a vague hint he might make a contribution. He didn't make a financial contribution, and he had no professional political experience, but he had plenty of free advice on how to run the campaign.

That's the great thing about politics. Everyone has a different opinion about how to run a campaign, and every one of those opinions is right. Outside of election day months into the future, or constant polling, the candidate has no way of separating the advice gold from the advice iron pyrite.

★ ★ ★ ★ ★

In contrast to various volunteer advisors, I sought out advice from people who had been through the political wars as candidates themselves. Running as a candidate gives perspectives that even professional campaign managers do not have.

Al Quie, a Member of Congress for several terms, a Minnesota governor for a term, and a grand old man of the state Republican Party, agreed to meet me for lunch. A big man who looked like the Norwegian farmer he had been before entering politics, Quie's face, manner, and life were as open as one of his farm fields. He was a man of strong convictions and strong Christian faith. At the time of the Watergate scandal, Quie, a Member of Congress, offered to serve the jail term for presidential advisor Chuck Colson, who was a fellow member of a prayer group.

Quie had a tremendous natural advantage in politics. People instinctively liked him. Bill Frenzel had this advantage also. I think of movie actors whose next film I can't wait to be released. People just plain like being around them and listening to them talk. Maybe the right word is charisma. A lucky few people have it. I should be so lucky.

I had first met Al Quie when he was leaving Congress to run for Minnesota governor. His competition for the Republican nomination was David Durenberger, whose only political background at the time was as chief of staff for a former governor. Quie smashed Durenberger in the early delegate count, so Durenberger dropped out of the gubernatorial race and accepted the consolation prize of the party nomination for a partial term in the U.S. Senate. Both won in a big Republican election year sweep. Durenberger went on to two re-elections. Quie was not so fortunate. He decided not to run for a second term when his popularity declined along with state revenues in a recession. He had reached a deal with the Democrats controlling the state legislature to balance the budget, but many Republicans thought he had been suckered into raising taxes as part of that deal.

The wheel had come around. Durenberger was now on his way out, and I was sitting down with Al Quie over lunch to seek his advice and— if all went well—his support. Quie remained a revered figure to state Republicans and almost a mythic figure to state conservative Christians. His endorsement would be a big boost with a huge number of delegates.

Out of politics, Quie was wearing a western-style shirt and cowboy boots. We each slid into our own side of a booth at a pancake house. Quie casually stretched out sideways with his back against the wall and his legs resting on the seat. The conversation eventually turned to the topic of the day when I asked for his advice on how to run a statewide campaign.

"Before we talk about that," he said, "I want to ask you to answer a hypothetical for me."

Uh, oh. *Politicians hate to answer hypotheticals since they almost always involve either hot button issues or strange, bizarre facts, and often both. Often, the question is designed to entrap.* I was taken a little aback that a friendly fellow politician would ask me a hypothetical, but I had no choice. I said "OK."

"Let's assume you're elected to the Senate. You know the deficit situation of the federal budget is bad."

"Of course."

"Say it gets worse," Quie continued. "A group comes up with a plan to balance the budget. It involves plenty of spending cuts, and it also includes a tax increase. Could you vote for it?"

Terrific, I thought, he's asking me to make the same mistake he did. I said "I want to balance the budget with spending cuts alone. I will not vote to raise taxes."

"Yes, I know that's your position, but what if cuts alone won't do it? Could you vote for a tax increase?"

This conversation wasn't going the way I had hoped, but he still wasn't trapping me. "I just don't think that situation is likely. Cutting spending is the way to balance the budget."

"OK, but here's the situation," Quie persisted. "You just plain can't cut any more. The only thing left is a tax increase. The numbers are that it will balance the budget. Could you vote for it?"

I hesitated. My campaign as a fiscal conservative was based on spending cuts alone. Tax increases were anathema to conservatives. I was certain in my mind that the federal budget was so bloated with spending just crying out to be cut that more taxes would not be needed. Yet Quie had crafted a hypothetical that seemed to have only one reasonable answer. Finally, I said "Yes. On the assumption that we have cut all spending possible, the tax increase is as small as possible, I am convinced it is absolutely necessary as a one-time deal, and I'm sure the Democrats aren't trying to snooker me, I could vote for a tax increase."

Quie shifted around in his seat and faced me. He apparently was now ready to give advice on politics and governing to a reasonable person instead of a rigid, stick-to-the-script ideologue.

We had an enjoyable and beneficial lunchtime conversation Eventually, I asked him for his support. As expected, he declined, saying the time was too early. He was right. A commitment from a party activist a year before an election was one thing; the commitment of a former governor, perhaps the most respected man in the state party, that early was another.

One last thing showed me Al Quie did understand the plight of a politician on the make. Instead of letting me pick up the lunch tab, he insisted on paying his half.

★ ★ ★ ★ ★

As October wore on into November, a year before the election, we racked our brains for potential money sources. We pushed personal connections. Ron and Sheila Johnson hosted a neighborhood party three blocks from my house. Ron and Diane Low, my next-door neighbors, hosted a party, and nearly everyone on our street came and contributed. Steve Michel hosted a reception for friends at Calvary Lutheran Church of Golden Valley, where Mary and I had been active members for many years a decade earlier. Jim Krause hosted a reception for people we both knew through connections to Bill Frenzel. Len Pratt and other fellow coaches from the board of directors of the Little Lakes Little League met with me over breakfast and made contributions. The help and trust and smiles of these friends and neighbors gave me a tremendous boost, and the memory remains one of the warmest of the entire campaign.

The drawback was that few friends and neighbors were political fat cats. The contributions came in amounts of $25, $50, and $100, which was generous for nonpolitical people. The problem was the people we needed to reach were the political types who could comfortably pull $250, $500, or $1000 from their pockets.

Gail Sutton and Steve Clark continued to work the telephones to line up meetings. They reported that nearly everyone sang the same song: Doug seems to be OK, and I like what he has to say, but, you know, I gave a big chunk of money to Rod Grams just last year, and, uh, feel I should maybe stay with him this one more time.

★   ★   ★   ★   ★

Autumn of a non-election year is not an active time in politics, yet regular party meetings and special events continue. We were out of and back to the Twin Cities in October and early November like a jack-in-the-box: 360 miles roundtrip to Morris, 360 miles roundtrip to Fergus Falls, 180 miles roundtrip to Mankato, 150 miles roundtrip to St. Cloud, 170 miles roundtrip to St. Peter, 200 miles roundtrip to Olivia, 180 miles roundtrip to Mantorville, and another 360 miles roundtrip to Fergus Falls for a seventh congressional district rally and fundraiser.

The return trip to Fergus Falls produced two highly encouraging developments. First, the Fergus Falls *Daily Journal* reported on the rally under the banner headline "[Republican] rally brings out candidates." The story lead, with photo, reported that Doug McFarland had attended the rally and added a couple of my quotes. I had become a newsworthy commodity! Competitors were mentioned briefly later. Bert McKasy had two quotes. State senator Gen Olson, who was thinking about joining the race, was identified as a "farm woman" who "plans to explore candidacy." Rod Grams, who didn't attend, didn't merit a mention.

Second, I no longer needed to work a room. The room worked me. Instead of moving around from group to group to stick out my hand, I stood in one place as the activists flocked around me with their hands outstretched. I've seen this before. People seeking a touch and a personal word gravitate around a well-known politician. I've certainly been one of those gravitating toward the political force. Now I was the force. Both these developments seemed to be tangible measures of success in a business with few tangible measures.

Back in the Twin Cities, I taught classes, spent a full day at an agriculture forum, spent another full day at a conservative summit, and attended numerous evening party meetings. Every "free" night went to more calls on the telephone in my basement.

★ ★ ★ ★ ★

Concentration on politics became easier. A giant distraction seemed to have gone away. The female student at Hamline law school had gone ahead and filed a complaint of "harassment" against me months earlier. Waiting for the story to hit the news, or for a resolution, had been torture. Every time the complaint came to mind over the summer and fall, my stomach churned. In the past, I had read and heard stories about charges made against public people, and each time wondered with a smirk how much was true. The best an innocent person can hope for is to be only the butt of cruel jokes and gossip. The worst is instant transition from public person to private person.

Now eight months had passed since the complaint was filed, and we were more than two months into the next academic year. The story had not appeared in public. I had heard no more about it, and I wasn't about to ask. This thing just might go away after all. In the end, it did go away. The powers that be at Hamline did not even ask me for a response. I never—to this day—have heard another word about it.

CHAPTER FOURTEEN

You Wanted To See A Sign From God?

Nearly every candidate for federal office hires a political consulting firm in Washington. These firms had been writing and calling for months; the calls increased following the straw ballot win at the state convention in September. I referred all the letters and calls to Gail Sutton. She kept saying the time was too early to hire a firm. Finally, she said the time was right.

Gail decided to hire a brand-new, two-member firm in Washington. They and we were both new kids on the block. They couldn't yet attract established candidates, and we couldn't afford a large, well-established consulting firm. We signed a contract with Norm Cummings and Ed Brookover. They seemed competent. That was important. They were willing to work cheap. That was vital.

The candidate also makes a pilgrimage to Washington to consult with the chosen firm and to see and be seen by the national political operatives and money sources. Gail scheduled our pilgrimage for Tuesday, November ninth, exactly fifty-two weeks prior to election day. The Republican Senatorial Committee was conducting an all-day National Issues Conference for Senate candidates on Thursday the eleventh. We also intended to do our own political spadework before and after the conference. The centerpiece of our visit was a reception, arranged by Cummings and Brookover for late Friday afternoon, for me to meet several Senators and many potential major donors.

As campaign manager, Gail would make the rounds with me. We required a chaperone. Gail's husband Tony decided to go. Tony had never visited Washington. No one was a bigger political junkie than Tony Sutton, and for a political junkie never to have seen Washington was a remarkable omission. Tony was beside himself with anticipation. I enjoyed watching his face light up whenever he thought about the coming trip.

The three of us arrived Tuesday morning. Gail and Tony went off to do the tourist thing for the day. I took the metro from the airport directly to the Supreme Court. A decade earlier, when I worked two years for Chief Justice Warren E. Burger, I had discovered the exquisite experience of a haircut by Johnnie Shaw, the Court's barber. This time again, Shaw seemed to linger over snipping every single hair as he filled me in on the latest news from other friends at the Court. A session in his barber chair was almost worth the trip alone.

Early that afternoon I arrived at the northwest Washington home of Paul Arneson, a Washington political consultant who Hamline law faculty colleague Larry Bakken said was willing to offer some free advice. The two of us chatted for an hour as he probed my plans. He seemed interested in joining our team. I told him about the Friday reception and invited him to come. Arneson smiled wryly and said "That's the sort of thing I do, too, and I don't think Ed Brookover would appreciate seeing me there."

I took the metro back to Capitol Hill to make the rounds of the Minnesota Republican Congressional delegation. The previous election had not been good to the party: Republicans held only one of two Senate seats and two of eight House of Representatives seats. Since the staff in the offices of Senator Dave Durenberger or Congressman Rod Grams would not likely be pleased to see me, the only call to be made was the office of Congressman Jim Ramstad.

Specifically, I had an appointment to see Ramstad's administrative assistant Maybeth Christiansen, who had made the transition from Bill Frenzel's staff when Ramstad succeeded Frenzel as third district Congressman. While I wasn't close to Ramstad, I had known Frenzel and Christiansen for two decades. *Bill was the man who taught me that the most important thing for a politician to know upon arriving at any campaign event is the location of the rest room.* He was one of those lucky few who could slide wry phrases into a political talk with the polished ease of a magician pulling rabbits out of a hat.

Maybeth and I sat in her office and reminisced. I mentioned that years earlier, Bill had taken Mary and me on a Capitol tour that included the Senate floor. His reverence for that place had been almost palpable. I said to Maybeth "We both know Bill wanted to run for the Senate. He could have had the nomination for the asking the year Durenberger and Boschwitz both got into the Senate, and he would have won. Why didn't he take the chance?"

She gazed into the distance, thought a moment, and said "I guess he just thought of the Senate as too big."

Great. The Senate was too big for our political giant. What was Maybeth thinking about this political midget sitting in front of her trying to pull himself from the mire of obscurity by starting at the top and running for the Senate? I didn't ask, and she didn't say.

"How will you run?" Maybeth asked. "Aren't you worried about painting yourself too far to the right to win the election?"

I knew exactly where she was coming from. Bill Frenzel was well-known for his moderate views, which his former staff reflected. As one of Frenzel's boys, I could have been expected to share them. I repeated the age-old Republican bromide, "Run to the right to get the nomination; run to the center to win the general election. I think Bill used to do that some, too."

"But, Doug," she continued, "you're running a pretty conservative campaign. Aren't you worried you'll run so far to the right you can't get back?"

"That is a concern. You're right. But I think I'm OK so far. I've been looking for an issue or two where I can take a more moderate position without offending my conservative base." I was speaking too freely, but I trusted Maybeth. Too soon, the time to leave arrived.

★ ★ ★ ★ ★

Gail and Tony Sutton, our two consultants, and I met for dinner. The five of us went over the plan for the next three days. While Ed Brookover placed the final touches on the Friday afternoon reception for Senators and donors, Norm Cummings would show Gail and me around town.

Wednesday went by quickly. Cummings ushered us in to an hour at the American Medical Association, two hours at the National Republican Senatorial Committee, and an hour at the U. S. Chamber of Commerce.

That afternoon I made a private side trip to the Heritage Foundation for an appointment with Edwin Meese III. I had met Ed Meese when I arrived in town to work at the Supreme Court nine years earlier. Mary and I found a furnished townhouse to rent in suburban Vienna, Virginia, and a nearby Lutheran church to attend. The first Sunday morning I looked around the pews and saw a fellow who looked a lot like Ed Meese. Couldn't be. Meese was the right-hand man to President Ronald Reagan. What would he be doing here? Of course, people living in Washington had to be somewhere. Ed Meese and his wife Ursula were in church. After the service, I introduced myself to him as a fellow law professor. I expected him to smile and say "That's nice. Keep in touch." Instead, he talked my arm off. Over the next two years, I came to know Ed as an open, friendly, warm human being. I remember him standing shyly a year later to receive the applause of the other congregants on the Sunday morning after he was confirmed as Attorney General of the U.S. Harry Truman famously said "If you want a friend in Washington, get a dog." He never met Ed Meese. Ed remains in my memory as the most genuine person I ever met in Washington.

Ed Meese and friend

When I parted from Norm Cummings and Gail Sutton on the sidewalk to enter the Heritage Foundation building, Cummings seemed to be in a state of disbelief that a national Republican icon like Ed Meese would take the time to meet with me. He was even more amazed when I reemerged with Ed's promise to come to Minnesota to raise money for my campaign. I wasn't surprised. I knew the man.

★　★　★　★　★

The Republican issues conference began at 8:30 a.m. Thursday morning at the Omni Shoreham hotel in northwest Washington. A score of other Republican senatorial hopefuls and I flipped through our huge loose-leaf briefing books and settled in for a day of lectures. The speakers, backed by the materials in the briefing books, talked about taxes and spending, foreign policy, defense, the environment, education, health care, and social issues.

The issue that stuck with me was Social Security. The speaker's main point was that Democrats run with the issue against any Republican foolish enough not to stand foursquare in favor of Social Security. He showed us a television attack ad used in the previous election against a Republican candidate who, in a general discussion of closing the federal budget deficit, had made the bland statement that everything was on the table. The attack ad shouted that the Republican was out to renege on our nation's promise of Social Security to seniors.

The ad was designed to scare seniors. It scared me. I remembered back a few months to my appearance on the Paul Stacke radio program in St. Cloud. A caller had ripped me for daring to suggest that I might be willing to hold Social Security cost-of-living benefit increases to less than inflation. Had I already handed an opponent the ammunition to shoot me?

As the speakers began to drone on, I surveyed the room. Separating the candidates and the staff aides was easy. The candidates were sitting, looking relaxed. The staff aides were hustling about, whispering furtively into the candidates' ears from behind, or running off on errands.

More difficult and more intriguing was separating the sheep from the goats amongst the candidates. The issues conference was open to all potential party candidates. Some of those attending were serious sheep on the fast track to the party nomination. They were polished and articulate. Others were clearly goats, wasting their time and money at the conference, deluding themselves into thinking they had any chance at the party nomination. They were amateurish and even tongue-tied. The same separation became even clearer at the closing reception. The candidates were on display as they worked the room: they worked each other, the speakers, others' personal aides. Some were slick. Some weren't.

I did my best at putting on sheep's wool, which required a strong dose of will power. After a long day of briefings, I wanted only to retreat to the side of the room to gather my thoughts and observe. That was out of the question. The last thing I needed was for others to see me standing off by myself, looking aloof, and have the word circulate that tall guy from Minnesota can't work a crowd. I threw myself into the melee.

Working a reception really wasn't that hard. Advice from my U. of Minnesota persuasion professor Bill Howell always carried the day. He said

"Wait until the person you are talking to says something, then say 'That's interesting. Tell me more.'"

★ ★ ★ ★ ★

The schedule for Friday started strong and continued to build through the day toward the evening reception. Norm Cummings, Gail and Tony Sutton, and I began at the Washington office of the *StarTribune*, where we talked with bureau chief Tom Hamburger. He asked several tough questions and I answered them directly. As the questions continued, Cummings became increasingly uncomfortable. He clearly was accustomed to political answers that circled round and round the question until finding a safe, bland spot to land. My campaign themes were honesty, common sense, and straight talk, so the answers were unexpectedly direct. In the corner of my eye, I saw Cummings move to the edge of his seat, eyes bulging, seemingly ready to leap forward at any moment to grab my ankle to keep me from placing my foot firmly into my mouth. In the end, he didn't have to make the leap. After all, I had been answering questions for more than a year and was by then pretty well able to find solid ground for placing my foot down.

We next took a taxi up to Capitol Hill to meet with reporters for the national political newsletters *Roll Call* and *Cook's Political Report*. These publications meant nothing to delegates in Minnesota but everything to politicos in Washington. To be considered a serious national candidate, I needed to impress these reporters favorably.

We were excited that Charlie Cook himself interviewed me. I told him and another reporter about my background, key issues, the campaign, and the big win in the convention straw ballot. He probed some issues. Since the horserace aspect of a political campaign is always the most interesting read, Cook soon turned to a discussion of the competition. Cook asked "Rod Grams just announced he's in the race. What effect do you think that will have?"

"I'm going to beat Rod," I predicted boldly. "He's getting in too late. You have to remember Minnesota is a caucus state. I've been working for over a year now, and I have hundreds of delegates already committed to me." Well, that might have been a slight exaggeration, but Cook wouldn't know. "Rod, Bert McKasy, and I will be competing for the remaining delegates, and there just aren't enough left out there to go around. Rod's not going to catch up."

"How about McKasy?" Cook asked. "He was chief of staff to Durenberger and he seems to know what he's doing. He's been out there a long time, too."

"Yes, I heard Bert made his trip through here a couple of weeks ago." I decided to push the matter a little and asked "Did you talk to him?"

"Yes. He was here and we interviewed him, just as we are interviewing you."

"Well, I'm going to beat Bert. He isn't going to go over with the delegates."

"How do you know that?" said Cook.

"He's dull."

Cook's roar of laughter showed his assessment matched my own. Bert had many positive qualities, but charisma was not one of them. Had Cook followed up, I could have said anyone who looked at the two of us would have picked Bert as the professor, not me. Small, wiry, large glasses, thinning hair, bright, and serious, Bert had a professorial air. Also, he was more of a policy wonk than a politician.

What I would not have added is Bert would be a great Senator—likely a better Senator than I—if he could be appointed to the office. The trouble is a Senator is elected, and to be elected a candidate needs to get people excited.

A candidate who could get people excited was Rod Grams. A former television anchorman, Rod could deliver lines to stir a crowd. Rod looked the part of a Senator, and he had a big physical advantage over both Bert and me: he stood about six-two, nearly six inches taller than Bert and six inches shorter than my height. That's tall enough to impress people, but not so tall as to intimidate half the voters. Rod Grams was a great candidate. Unfortunately, after election a candidate must serve in office, and Rod wasn't made of Senatorial timber.

My assessment was this. Rod was the best candidate. Bert would be the best Senator. I hoped to be the best combination.

★ ★ ★ ★ ★

Norm Cummings and Ed Brookover, Tony and Gail Sutton, and I met for a late lunch at the J. W. Marriott hotel; from our table looking out onto Pennsylvania Avenue, we watched the early afternoon parade of pedestrians pass by. We assessed the day so far as a success. Cummings did mention my direct answers made him cringe a little, and he suggested that we might want to work on softening them. Even so, when a candidate made a jaded Washington reporter like Charlie Cook laugh out loud, that had to be good.

As we ate lunch, rain began to dampen the sidewalk. Someone mentioned the forecast for later in the day was freezing rain. We hoped that with luck the freezing rain would hold off until evening when our day was complete.

After lunch, Gail and I hopped into a cab for the ride to Capitol Hill. Cummings had scored for us a three o'clock meeting with Senator Phil Gramm, the chairman of the Republican Senatorial Finance Committee. Gramm was the man with the money. The cab pulled up to the Richard Russell Senate Office Building, the oldest and grandest of the three Senate office buildings, and Gail and I dashed into the building through what had become a steady rain. The temperature seemed to be dropping by the minute.

The door opened into Gramm's impossibly large private office. Gramm sat at his desk at what appeared to be 40 feet away. The ornate ceiling was at least two stories above our heads. Gail and I strode quickly across the expanse of plush carpet to meet the Senator as he rose from his chair and came around the desk to greet us. The three of us arranged ourselves in overstuffed chairs around a coffee table already stocked with coffee, hot water, and cookies.

We made the usual small talk. I didn't bother trying to work in the usual explanation of how a professor, an inhabitant of the ivory tower, could be taken seriously as a political candidate because Gramm had been a professor of economics. He already understood that a professor might get the notion into his head to enter politics. One thing I did make sure to work in was that Minnesota was a caucus state. Consequently, we had been focusing on political support of the delegates—with great success— and were only now turning our attention to fundraising. I mentioned we were eagerly looking forward to a major reception later in the day to introduce me to Washington money sources. Gramm said he knew about it and would try to stop by.

After a few minutes, Gramm began to probe my reasonableness and political savvy. Al Quie had probed these things a few weeks earlier in the guise of questions about support for a tax increase. Now Phil Gramm probed them in the guise of questions about the Minnesota political climate. It was political deja vu.

"OK, Doug," Gramm began, "what makes you think you can win in Minnesota?"

"I've got a great campaign manager here in Gail Sutton, and already have the commitments of hundreds of people who will likely be delegates to the party convention next June. There are only two other candidates—"

"Yes, but I'm not talking about the party nomination. I'm talking about the general election."

"Well, Senator, you already know that this is shaping up to be an excellent Republican year. This is the midterm election for a Democratic President, and the President's party historically loses seats in the Senate and House. With Dave Durenberger dropping out, I'm going for an open seat."

"Yes," Gramm said, "but isn't Minnesota a tough state for any Republican to win?"

Now I saw where he was going. "You're right, Senator," I said. "Minnesota has been a pretty Democratic state, but it's not as bad as the popular image. True, in presidential elections, Minnesota has gone Democrat even in Republican landslide years. But you have to remember that in nearly every one of those elections, we had a favorite son on the national ticket—Hubert Humphrey in two elections, and Walter Mondale in three. And, of course, both of them won a lot of Senate elections in the state, too. They're out of the picture now. I don't think Minnesota is as Democratic as you might think. The playing field is a lot more level."

"All right," Gramm said slowly as he pursed his lips. He seemed to be a little exasperated that he couldn't pin me down. Maybe that was because as another professor I was also familiar with the classroom dynamic. Anyway, I wasn't evading him, just standing up for Minnesota

Republicans. He tried again. "Let's take personalities out of it. Say you have candidate X, a Democrat, running for Senate in Minnesota against candidate Y, a Republican. Who wins?"

"OK, with that hypothetical, a generic Democrat running against a generic Republican, with no other factors such as personalities or issues, I'd have to say X the Democrat would win."

"All right then," Gramm said. He didn't turn to face me as Al Quie had done in the pancake house booth, but just as clearly, he was now ready to get down to business.

After discussing issues and strategy for a while, Gramm, in his soft Texas drawl, told a story about his view of elections. "Imagine yourself in a great hall full of people there for a feast. The people are there to eat and drink. At one end of the hall, you have your buffet and your head table set up; you're trying to speak to the crowd. At the other end of the hall someone else has a buffet and head table set up and is trying to make speeches. You want the people in the hall to eat from your buffet, not the other one. You're competing for the attention of the people in the hall. The people don't much care which food they have or who's speaking. They just want to eat. So, you try different things to catch their attention. Fancy foods. Nice presentation. So does the other side. Finally, the spotlights flick on and all attention for a moment is focused on the head tables. That's election day. Then the lights go out and the people go back to eating and drinking and ignoring the politicians again. One day comes and the people in the hall have to choose one buffet or the other. Are you with me?"

"Yes."

"OK, then, how do you make sure they come to your buffet and not the other one?"

"How?" I asked.

Gramm smiled. "By raising enough money and spending it to catch their attention. You need to have the better buffet."

I was thinking through this analogy when Gramm asked the one question I feared. "How much money have you raised so far for your campaign?"

Since politics is perception, perceptions will differ on a candidate's whole package: appearance, political savvy, speech delivery, press dealings, one-on-one ability, answering questions, charisma, guts, stamina, electability. One thing that is not perception is the ability of a candidate to raise money. It is an objectively measurable benchmark of a candidate's political skill and the viability of a campaign. A candidate who can't raise money is not a viable candidate.

Out of a campaign built on straight, honest answers, I didn't want to give a straight, honest answer to this question. A truthful answer would have made the chair of the Republican Senatorial Finance Committee think he was wasting his time looking at nothing more than a nice head of hair. I tried not to gulp as I said "You mean total?"

"Yes, since the beginning."

How high could my answer go before it left the area of fudging and wandered into outright deception? "A little short of $100,000." I exaggerated the figure a little, and of course didn't mention that nearly half of the money had been raised by the simple and successful fundraising technique of reaching into my own pocket.

Gramm's face took on a look of consternation. A hundred thousand in campaign money was chump change to a man used to Senate campaigns costing millions of dollars.

Before all the air escaped from my campaign balloon right then and there, I quickly added "I know that doesn't sound like much, but you need to remember two things. First, Minnesota is a caucus state, not a primary state. The nomination will be decided by the delegates at the party convention, not a money-driven primary. I won the state party straw ballot just two months ago, and I won it big. The delegates are behind me, and their endorsement will follow. Whoever wins the endorsement at the party convention next June will win the primary in September. That's going to be me."

Before Gramm could argue, I raced on. "Second, you and I both know that the money will be there. Whoever is our party's candidate won't have any trouble raising plenty of money to finance the race. The money always comes in during the election year. This is an open seat and a real chance for a Republican to win. The money will be there."

My answer may not have been the whole truth and nothing but the truth, but it had a lot of truth in it. Gramm didn't seem totally convinced, but he appeared to be satisfied for the time being. When the meeting wore down after nearly an hour, Gramm repeated his intention to stop by our reception later.

★ ★ ★ ★ ★

Friday afternoon at five was the ideal time for a reception. Ed Brookover had invited all sitting Republican Senators, and several had responded they were coming. He had also invited representatives of many interest groups that traditionally support Republican candidates, and he was ecstatic that more than 30 were coming. Of course, the real mutual attraction was between the sitting Senators and the lobbyists. I would be the third-party beneficiary. While the Senators and lobbyists were busy working each other, they would also size up whether I was worthy of their political and financial support in the near future—no endorsements or checks expected today, thanks anyway.

To say this reception would make or break my campaign was an overstatement, but it was crucially important. The rest of our trip to Washington could not have gone better. Now the time had come for the climax.

Gail and I left Senator Gramm's office around four and walked down a flight of stairs to the ground floor of the Russell building. We looked out the glass doors to First Avenue and stared disaster in the face. While we were meeting with Gramm, the temperature outside had continued to drop. The steady rain had become freezing rain. We looked at a winter wonderland of ice.

Having worked in Washington for two years, I knew immediately what this meant. Rush hour traffic in Washington was a hassle on an ordinary clear, dry day. As soon as the lightest snow, or even a heavy rain, began falling, everyone from Cabinet secretaries to janitors thought only of one thing: leaving early to beat the rush. Friday added to the early exodus, and ice multiplied the panic effect. By five p.m., Capitol Hill would be a ghost town. Our reception, the keystone event of the trip, my best and brightest chance to meet Republican Senators and serious donors, was going to be a total bust. We would be lucky if one person showed.

I thought of Cary Humphries. A year earlier, he had a mild heart episode that he took as a sign from God not to run for the Senate. If that internal murmur constituted a sign from above, then this massive ice storm certainly did. I stood on Capitol Hill, looking out from the grandest Senate office building there, and saw the sign. God was telling me quite clearly that I would not be a United States Senator.

Of course, I didn't throw up my hands and howl "It was fun while it lasted." I didn't even tell Gail what I was thinking. The two of us merely exchanged a favorite expletive or two as we emerged onto the sidewalk and began slip-sliding our way the few blocks north toward the site for the reception in a Republican Senate campaign building.

Inside, Ed Brookover had everything ready to go. The room was a perfect size to hold 50 people. The hors d' oeuvres and the hard and soft drinks were set out. All was warmth and welcome.

Outside, all was ice and early winter evening gloom. One of us walked to the front door of the building every so often and returned to report no change. The freezing rain continued.

Five o'clock came and went. Not a single person arrived. Several had called to withdraw their acceptances. I didn't expect them to bother. Everyone in town knew what this weather meant.

Finally, around 5:30, the Senator from Montana walked into the room. He set the pattern for himself and two other Republican Senators who also appeared over the next half-hour. He strode in through the door, looked with raised eyebrows around the empty room, decided he couldn't reverse course as he'd already been seen, shook hands with me, sampled a bite or two, engaged in a minimum of polite conversation, made his excuses, and left as soon as possible. Why should a sitting Senator hang around with four people who aren't constituents?

Most of the time, Ed Brookover, Tony and Gail Sutton, and I stood around and divided our time between small talk and trips to the front door to survey the scene outside. Brookover was beside himself. His carefully planned and prepared event, expected to be a booming success, was an utter disaster. Brookover apologized again and again, but I knew exactly where the fault lay. Ice.

After six, about the time we were all thinking of giving up and leaving, Senator Strom Thurmond of South Carolina, followed by his chief aide, tottered through the door. His arrival brightened the room; the President pro tem of the Senate had taken the trouble to come. I had met Thurmond a decade earlier when I worked at the Supreme Court. At that time, I heard him speak several times at events involving the courts, and he always had a prepared text. That was a lesson in hard work. Now, the grand old man was near the age of 90, yet he still had the fortitude to come out in an ice storm. I was grateful.

Thurmond helped himself to a plate of chicken wings. We talked a little about the Court. He didn't seem inclined to talk policy or politics, and I wasn't either. The two of us carried on an extended conversation about the merits of various kinds of barbecue sauce for wings. For the first time, I heard him speak without a text.

So ended the reception on Capitol Hill. Poet Robert Frost wrote "Some say the world will end in fire, Some say in ice." My political world ended in ice. Even so, the dream had not yet ended in my head. We would push forward.

★ ★ ★ ★ ★

Back home, we heard that another competitor was emerging. Gen Olson, a state senator from Minnetrista, a town half suburb and half farmland west of Minneapolis, was making the rounds of the district meetings to tell activists she was thinking of running. That meant she was running.

Olson had been in the state senate for many years and was well-known and respected in the party. She was astute, pleasant, and well-liked. She was conservative. She was a woman, a strong positive since the Democrats were likely to nominate a woman. On the other hand, Olson had ordinary features and was a little plump. She was no more than an adequate speaker. Her message was the same as the three of us already running. The question was why she thought she could make a dent in the race.

What I didn't realize at the time was that Olson had a ready-made base constituency in the Christian, social conservatives in the party. She had been a champion of social conservative causes in the state senate for many years. *Bert McKasy, Rod Grams, and I were conservatives, all right, but the problem was that over the years many candidates had talked the talk to gain social conservatives' votes and then betrayed their trust after election to office. Social conservatives had been burned time and again, and they were wary. Many told me they were waiting to see whether any of us would walk the walk as well as talk the talk. Gen Olson had already walked the walk. That made her a serious contender.*

★ ★ ★ ★ ★

Near the end of November, the *StarTribune* conducted a poll that asked voters around the state to respond to the names of nine potential candidates for the Senate. All nine candidates had similar "favorable" and "unfavorable" numbers. The key column was "don't know name." The higher the number in that column, the less statewide name recognition. That meant the score was akin to a golf score: lower was better.

The four Democrats in the poll were Tom Berg (a St. Paul lawyer), Linda Berglin (a state senator), Collin Peterson (the seventh district Congressman), and Ann Wynia (a former state senator). The five Republicans were Rod Grams, Bert McKasy, Pat McGowan (a state senator), Gen Olson, and me. The numbers were as follows:

Rod Grams	41%
Collin Peterson	61%
Doug McFarland	69%
Tom Berg	71%
Linda Berglin	72%
Pat McGowan	73%
Gen Olson	78%
Bert McKasy	81%
Ann Wynia	84%.

Wonderful news. Thirty-one per cent of voters statewide recognized my name, the best number of all the candidates in both parties behind the two sitting Members of Congress. Our campaign was succeeding. At the other end, Ann Wynia, who had won the party straw ballot and was the insiders' favorite to be the Democratic candidate, was dead last in statewide name recognition.

What's in a politician's name? Shakespeare's Juliet may have thought "That which we call a rose by any other name would smell as sweet," but I believe a candidate's name can help or hurt a campaign. Take a name like Grams or Peterson or even McFarland. Easy to recognize. Easy to pronounce. Easy to remember. Then take a name like McKasy or Wynia. Looking at McKasy in print, a voter thinks Mick-Casey is running. The same voter listens to the news and hears a story about Mack-a-see. Who's that guy? The name recognition is diluted between the candidate and the phantom. The same can be said for Wynia. Is it Winn-e-ah, or Wine-e-ay, or Wine-yah?

The first name also matters. Of the nine candidates, only two first names—Collin and Linda—could not easily be shortened. The other seven of us used one-syllable first names, and six had to shorten their two-syllable first names to do so: Rod instead of Rodney, Gen instead of Genevieve, Doug instead of Douglas, Pat instead of Patrick, Tom instead of Thomas, Bert instead of Albert, and Ann. A one-syllable first name has a solid sound. A voter can get his or her mouth around it. It's a name of the people.

Our society has become more informal in manners, dress, and all aspects of living. So too in politics. The town hall debate passed through the one-minute commercial into the sound bite. The shorter, the better. One syllable is the norm. Even Hubert Humphrey's son abandoned instant name recognition to run for governor in Minnesota as Skip, not Hubert III. A good name means a lot in politics, in more ways than one.

I'm a junior. When I was growing up, my dad was Doug and I was Douglas. Today, for my legal writing, the name is Douglas. That doesn't suit a political campaign. Doug it is.

CHAPTER FIFTEEN

Take This Hospitality Suite And Shove It

On the first three days of the month of Christmas, my campaign scheduler brought to me: hundreds of political Christmas cards to sign, six fundraising appointments, four political appearances, two law school classes, and one session of physical therapy.

The big event of the month arrived on the fourth day, Saturday: the semi-annual state central committee meeting. The most active of the party activists across the entire state gathered in a suburban community center. The last time this bunch had met six months earlier, the members had turned my friend and party chair Bob Weinholzer out of office and voted me third of three in a pseudo straw ballot. Little wonder that I was not looking forward to this go-round.

I was especially not looking forward to the kickoff event of the state central committee meeting, the candidate hospitality suites at a nearby hotel on Friday evening. For many reasons, my feelings toward hosting a hospitality suite had grown with each repetition from interesting new experience to mild distaste to cordial dislike to active loathing.

First, the expenditure of physical energy is enormous. A hospitality suite requires a candidate to stand in place talking with activists for three straight hours. That alone is physically exhausting. The voice starts to go during the last hour. Also, back ailments are aggravated by standing for long periods. Even though people with back problems should stand up straight with a small arch in the back, a hospitality suite requires a tall person like me to lean forward to get closer to the delegates and sometimes literally to hear. Back problems are aggravated by stress. A hospitality suite is three hours of unmitigated stress. I don't think anyone would much like standing for three hours in steadily increasing pain until by the end of the evening the back feels like an iron board and the voice is a sore rasp.

The mental energy expenditure is greater. No one wears a name badge to a hospitality suite. At a party meeting or convention, everyone wears a name badge. A candidate with a little experience can greet Jane Doe like a long-lost friend by surreptitiously eyeing her name badge as she approaches. With her name in mind, I can usually remember her location and key issues, and boom out "Hello, Jane, how are things with the school board in Jackson?" At the hospitality suite, when Jane Doe approaches me, I recognize her face, but have no idea whether she is one of my former students, one of my children's schoolteachers, one of the supportive conservatives from Alexandria, or one of the hostile moderates from Edina. A safe bet is the connection is political, but what? When she says hello, I know enough not to say "Glad to meet you." A few early campaign responses "Oh, we met last month" were enough. So, when she says "Hello, Doug," I answer lamely "Good to see you again." She must realize I can't remember her name. That's not good politics, and it is embarrassing. Sometimes the name eventually comes to me, and sometimes it doesn't. Until the name solidifies, I give half my attention to our conversation and the other half to paging through my mental name book.

Second, and much more importantly, the hospitality suite is a leg-hold trap with no escape. At a reception, a candidate trapped by a persistent questioner can listen politely, respond to a couple of questions, and escape. The cover is easy: "Great to talk with you again. Oh, look. There's Nancy Rademacher from Alexandria. I need to talk to her. Sorry." Walk away. Another option is to make eye contact with a nearby campaign aide who will come to the rescue; Gail was always dependable at this task. At a hospitality suite, the candidate has no option other than to tough it out until the pit bull questioner decides on his or her own to release the bite on your ear. The candidate can't walk away. An aide can't help by moving the candidate because there is nowhere to go.

Who stops by a hospitality suite? Loyal supporters stop by to say hello, but they know the candidate is not there to preach to the choir. The people who stay with questions are either genuine undecideds or another candidate's supporters whose highlight of the evening would be to provoke a damaging answer.

That means the candidate must concentrate on every question and every answer. Some questions are standard fare, such as "Give me some examples of what you want to cut out of the federal budget." Many more questions are obscure, such as "How much are you willing to cut the federal subsidy for sugar beet growers?" I can't tell whether the questioner is a budget slasher or a sugar beet grower. After I stumble my way through an answer to that question—thankfully making a fool of myself to only one delegate and not to a large audience—the questioner asks the next question—often just as narrow and just as tricky. A hospitality suite is a near guarantee of three hours of flop sweat.

The best metaphor for a candidate in a hospitality suite is a coin-operated arcade game I played as a boy. The player uses a toy rifle that shoots a beam of light at a game box some 20 feet distant. Inside the game box is a mechanical bear with three circular light cells, one on each side and one on its belly. The bear slides slowly on all four legs from right to left. When the player hits the cell with a shot of light from the rifle, the bear roars, turns and raises up on two hind legs facing the player, and drops to all fours to begin moving left to right. Another good shot repeats the action in the opposite direction, and the bear once again is moving right to left. A skilled shooter can hit the light cell when the bear exposes its belly in the process of turning. This produces another roar and a turn back to the original direction. Shot. Roar and change direction. Shot. Miss. Shot. Roar and change direction. Shot. Roar and raise up. Belly shot. Roar and return to the original direction. In a hospitality suite, I'm the bear.

Most of all, I didn't like having to pay to be the bear. The hotel room, food, drink, and incidentals cost $500. Our campaign didn't have many $500 bills to spread around, and this didn't buy commercial time, print literature, pay staff salaries, or raise money. I felt that I might as well roll up a few hundred-dollar bills and stuff them into the nearest snowbank.

As campaign manager Gail Sutton was planning for the state central committee meeting, I said to her "Gail, we aren't having a hospitality suite, are we?"

"Of course, we are."

"Let's save the money."

"We can't. We have to have a hospitality suite."

"No, we don't. I'll just stand near the pool and work the crowd there. The delegates wandering around can't miss me. We don't need to spend the $500. We have better uses for it."

"Doug," Gail said, "you know that if we don't have a hospitality suite, everyone there will notice. We'll stick out like a sore thumb."

"They're all conservatives. They'll think we're the only smart ones saving money."

"No, they'll think we're in trouble. And if they think we're in trouble, we will be in trouble. The word will be all around the state within a week. We have to spend the money."

I had to give in. Gail was the campaign manager, and Gail was right. She certainly was not pushing a private agenda, since we could have used the money to help pay her salary for another month. Still, spending $150 an hour to play the bear galled me.

The appearance of the full field of Senate candidates at the Saturday morning state central committee meeting generated a lot of excitement amongst the delegates. Bert McKasy and I had been running all year; both of us had scores of committed supporters. Gen Olson had just jumped into the race; she had instant support from Christian social conservatives. Rod Grams had been campaigning for two months; as a sitting Congressman, his celebrity impressed delegates.

All four of us were running on essentially the same conservative platform. We all favored balancing the federal budget by cutting spending instead of raising taxes. We all were prolife. We all promoted agriculture. We all opposed a national health care plan. Delegates were not going to choose based on issues. Delegates were going to have to choose on other considerations: who could best carry the Republican message, who could raise the most money, who was the most electable, who had the physical stamina, who made the delegate feel warm? This meeting was the first opportunity for these party activists to see all four of us in action, in the same setting, and to begin to make those comparisons.

As for me—carry the message, certainly. Most electable, bring it on. Physical stamina, no problem. Raising money, let's talk later. Make people feel warm and fuzzy inside, not my best talent. Let's hope three of five carries.

In ones, twos, and small clusters, the delegates streamed into the community center. All four of us Senate candidates vigorously worked the delegates as they passed through the hallways. That was the most we could do; since the state central committee meeting was about party machinery, the candidates would not be allowed to address the gathering.

All four Senate campaigns, as well as several other campaigns, had young people stationed at every door to slap their candidate's lapel sticker onto every lapel, shirt, and blouse possible. Some delegates refused all stickers. Some delegates took every sticker and later placed them all in the trash. Some delegates took every sticker and turned their lapels or dress fronts into kaleidoscopes. Some delegates took a lapel sticker only for the favored candidate. These were the delegates we all watched and counted.

The morning started well. My stickers were in the lead. Grams stickers also went well, especially considering he was relatively new in the race.

Prior to the meeting start, as Gail had instructed me to do at every convention or meeting, I worked my way down the line of registration tables, shaking hands and chatting with every volunteer. Mostly, candidates ignored these workers, Gail had told me, and they appreciated the recognition for their work. Even more important, as the registration lines ended and the meeting started, many of them moved into the meeting hall to take their places as delegates.

When the state central committee meeting recessed for lunch, the process reversed. The campaign volunteers returned to the doors of the meeting hall and pushed lapel stickers on delegates as they were leaving. Perhaps a delegate had decided on the Senate race while listening to the morning reports on state party machinery?

Before the meeting convened again after lunch, many of the 300 delegates, plus a score of candidates for various offices, again packed the back hallway. The scene was mindful of a high school dance. The delegates coyly stood around in small groups, chatting with each other, keeping an eye on nearby candidates. Before long, a candidate moved in on the gaggle of delegates, and asked each one for support. When the answer was no, instead of sulking off to the side, the rejected candidate put on an even brighter smile, said "I hope I'll be your second choice," and moved on to the next delegate. When the answer was yes, the couple did not separate and move to the dance floor; instead the candidate asked the trailing aide for a sticker, slapped this public brand onto the conquest, and moved on to another target.

My pitch was quite different depending on the sticker situation of the person I had targeted. "I'm so glad to have your support . . . I see you're supporting Grams, but I hope you'll also . . . I see you haven't made up your mind on the Senate yet, and . . .." Naturally, I was primarily trying to work people with multiple stickers or no stickers.

As I was schmoozing a delegate, I spotted Gail Sutton knifing through the crowd toward me in a panic. She grabbed my elbow. "Doug. Doug." Gail hoarsely whispered "Armin Tesch is wearing a Grams sticker. We've lost him." Tesch, a farmer near Waseca, was the chairman of the first

Congressional district, and his influence extended through the state. I had worked on him over the telephone and in person a dozen times. I thought we understood each other well, but he had evaded commitment. Of course, Tesch never said much. Typical of men of the land, he was a man of few words.

This was bad news, but hardly a cause for panic. By now, I had experienced many ups and downs along the campaign trail. Since the positives never were as good as expected and the negatives were never as bad as portended, I shrugged and asked "Come on, Gail. Are you sure?"

"Yes. Yes. I saw it myself. Dammit, after all that work, we've lost him."

"Well, maybe someone just stuck it on him," I suggested. "Maybe he was just being polite and taking one from a kid."

"No, he's wearing one. We've lost him." Gail's panic grew. Her head jerked back and forth as she scanned the hallway. "Doug, you've got to find Sandy Evenson and get your sticker on her!" While getting my sticker onto the first Congressional district chairwoman would indeed counterbalance the loss of the first district chairman, the idea that after months of sturdy neutrality she would right now take one of my stickers was beyond reality. I said "I don't think Sandy's going to put on anyone's sticker today, and even if she did, I don't think anyone would see that as a balance to Armin. I've worked on her plenty."

"Go try again!" Gail pointed. "There she is. She's over there."

"No, I'm not going to run over there and look like I'm panicking."

Gail calmed down a little, but she wasn't ready to let go. "At least go talk to Armin" she said. "See if you can sound him out."

"All right. I'll go talk to Armin."

I talked with a delegate or two as I worked my way over to Tesch. The two of us started with the usual political chit-chat. Soon enough, I got to the point. "Armin, I'm a little disappointed to see that Grams sticker on you."

"Yes, well, I decided to go that way" Tesch answered.

"Armin, I don't think Rod can offer anything that I can't offer. Why would you want to jump on board with him now?"

"Doug, you remember that GOP agricultural task force we were both on last summer?"

"Yeah."

"Well, you didn't seem to know much about agriculture."

Talk about the best laid plans of mice and men! I said "Armin, the reason I asked Bob Weinholzer to appoint me to that task force was because I realized I didn't know much about agriculture. I wanted to learn from the experience and the knowledge of the other members—like you." I didn't add that Bob had told me he was also appointing Tesch to the task force, which would be another opportunity for me to try to get close to him.

"Well, all right, then" Tesch said.

So now we understood each other, but he was still wearing a Grams sticker.

A few months later, the St. Paul *Pioneer Press* ran a column making fun of politicians from both parties who were "scraping their experience barrels for anything that might appeal to rural voters—whether or not they know which end of a cow gives milk." For my turn, the column noted "Doug McFarland, a Hamline Law School professor and former aide to Chief Justice Warren Burger and with a law degree from New York University, claims an A+ grade on his position on agriculture. His promo material says he will 'fight for farmers, small town businesses, and the way of life they represent.'" The column made me laugh. It probably didn't make Armin Tesch laugh.

★ ★ ★ ★ ★

Ken Starr—former federal judge, former Solicitor General of the United States, and future special prosecutor in the Bill Clinton Whitewater case—came to town in December to raise money for my campaign. I knew Ken as a friend and as a truly good guy from my days at the Supreme Court ten years earlier, a time when Ken was always mentioned on the short list for appointment to the Court himself. Had President George H. W. Bush followed through and nominated Ken Starr to the Supreme Court instead of David Souter, an unknown state court judge who was reputedly chosen in large part with the expectation of easy Senate confirmation, the history of our nation would be far different.

Gail Sutton asked our Washington consultants Norm Cummings and Ed Brookover for advice on how best to use Ken Starr. They advised to schedule three events: a big-money reception, a small-money activists' event, and an event for local lawyers, since Ken's fame was in the law. We also had to schedule around an appearance he was making on behalf of a local corporation. That was just fine, since the corporation was paying him a large honorarium and covering all his expenses for the trip.

Ken Starr and his wife Alice arrived early Monday morning on the corporation's private jet, and I caught up with them on their arrival at a downtown Minneapolis hotel. Alice was a Republican political operative herself, having worked in fundraising in Virginia. Ken shared with me that he had seriously considered running for the Senate from Virginia in the coming election, and he had not yet totally abandoned the idea. In other words, both were politically astute.

They weren't quite so astute about Minnesota weather. Ken announced that "his tootsies" were freezing from the street slush that had seeped in through a hole in the sole of one of his shoes. His first order of business in town was to purchase a new pair of shoes.

The schedule for the evening began with the what was supposed to be the big money reception at the downtown Minneapolis Athletic Club. About 20 of us sat around a large conference table as Ken answered questions. After subtracting Mary and me, and Ken and Alice, the total at the table was about 15 contributors. Of the 15, several had already given me money and were in for free. In other words, the big money reception was a fiasco.

The reception for lawyers was much better. A roomful of people stood around to listen to Starr speak and answer questions. The money came in, but following the familiar pattern, the amounts were not large. At least the large, enthusiastic group gave us all a boost. Mary told me later that she had found herself at the side of the room visiting with the bartender. He noted all the "Lawyers for McFarland" signs on the walls, and asked "Who's this McFarland that he needs so many lawyers to help him?"

Ken Starr with Doug and Mary McFarland

The next day's activists event made the big money reception look like a smashing success. The response rate was poor. Ken Starr was a big name to lawyers, but not yet to the public. Gail moved the event from a hotel to my home so it would be more personal and intimate. It was personal and intimate all right. Maybe 20 activists sat on folding chairs in a large circle in my family room batting the breeze with Ken about law and politics. Ken gamely answered their questions and put on a bright face. The few who came told me they thought the event was absolutely great. The hundreds who didn't come didn't think so.

Ken and Alice Starr must not have thought so either. Word filtered back to me that Alice, as a fundraising professional, thought we should have cancelled the big money roundtable when the RSVP rate was low. Instead we had desperately forged ahead into two embarrassing scenes. I didn't ask either one of them for an assessment of the campaign based on what they had seen. I did send to their home in Virginia two mail-order live lobsters as a token of thanks.

★ ★ ★ ★ ★

Two days later, I attended a luncheon of the Corner Club, a group of people in business who met every month at the downtown Minneapolis Club to hear a guest speaker and discuss issues of the day. Orem Robbins, the CEO of an insurance agency and a member of the club, had invited me to speak. Once again, this success was produced by a personal contact: Robbins was a member of the Hamline University board of trustees. He told me the group had several members who might contribute to my campaign.

Twelve Twin Cities business leaders and I sat around the table. I gave them a short version of my stump speech and answered their questions. Even though I pushed hard for contributions at the end, none were forthcoming. Maybe I was overly optimistic. This group heard a guest speaker every month. I thought I was there to squeeze money out of them; they probably thought I was there to have a speech squeezed out of me.

I was also disappointed when Harold Stassen, a member of the Club, didn't show as expected. Stassen was a great man. After being the boy wonder governor of Minnesota in his 30s, he had gone on to many more successes, including signing the original United Nations charter and serving as president of the University of Pennsylvania. When Stassen returned to Minnesota from service following World War II, everyone had expected him to breeze to election to the U.S. Senate. Instead, he reached too far too soon when instead he ran for President and lost the 1948 Republican nomination to Thomas Dewey. After that, Stassen ran for President again and again, becoming a national joke. In recent years, he had taken to wearing a toupee that sat on top of his head like a flattened version of the state mascot gopher. What people missed in the laughter was the incredible record of achievement of the man.

When Stassen didn't show at the luncheon, Robbins told me to call Stassen's law office so I could meet with him personally. I called that afternoon. Even though I thought of Harold Stassen as a great man, the feeling apparently was not mutual. He never called back.

Perhaps he didn't want to be dunned for a contribution. The more likely explanation was he was disgusted with what he thought were my politics. Stassen was a Republican moderate who had been run out of party leadership because of his prochoice position on abortion. I remember attending a party convention at which the former governor and presidential candidate had asked to be elected a second alternate to the national convention. John Nance Garner once said the vice presidency wasn't worth a pitcher of warm spit. Well, a second alternate slot wasn't worth a pitcher of cold spit. Even so, the delegates denied this small honor to the man who had carried so much water for the elephant. Harold Stassen likely assumed I helped the door hit him in the rear on his way out. I never had the opportunity to tell him I voted for him.

★ ★ ★ ★ ★

The end of the year brought forth some political speculations by columnists in the Twin Cities' newspapers. One I liked was a column in the *StarTribune* by Nick Coleman in which he predicted political events for the coming election year. For October, Coleman wrote "First-term Congressman Rod Grams, the ex-TV anchor, abruptly withdraws from his campaign for the U.S. Senate. 'After careful reflection,' Grams says, 'I realize I am unqualified for the Senate and, further, that I have not the faintest clue as to what I am doing in Congress.' Grams then quits Congress and studies to become a hair stylist." One I didn't like as well was a column in the *Pioneer Press* by Bill Salisbury: "In the Senate race, my early pick is U.S. Rep. Rod Grams, the first-term Republican from Ramsey. Why? He's the most telegenic candidate in the field. I'm not just being cynical. Grams simply has more crowd appeal. He was kind of a klutz when he first entered politics two years ago, but he has quickly developed into one of the slickest public performers in the state."

The Senate race even made the sports pages. A column by acerbic Patrick Reusse in the *StarTribune* headlined "The trouble all started when Bud Grant left." Reusse wrote "Let's face it, folks: Do you think a dim bulb such as Rod Grams would have had the audacity to announce he was running for the U.S. Senate if Bud still coached the Vikings?"

The closest I came to a mention in any of these columns was in a piece by Steven Dornfeld of the *Pioneer Press*. In analogy to the fairy tale Snow White and the Seven Dwarfs, he wrote "The Republicans do not have seven dwarfs running for the U.S. Senate, only three or four. Compared to candidates like freshman Rep. Rod Grams, the former TV anchorman, even the tarnished Dave Durenberger still looks pretty good." Later in the column, he referred approvingly to the "intellectual firepower" of Democratic Senate candidates Ann Wynia and Tom Berg.

The next day I mailed Dornfeld a personal, handwritten note:

> Let me make two comments on your editorial yesterday. We haven't met yet, so you appear to be mistaking me for other candidates.
>
> 1. On the intellectual firepower in the race, you have confused the Democratic candidates with me. Please see enclosure [my resume].
>
> 2. On the three or four dwarfs, you have confused me with the other Republican candidates. I'm 6'8".

Dornfeld apparently did not share my sense of humor. At a reception a month later, Evie Axdahl, our national committeewoman, excitedly called me over so she could introduce me to the influential newspaperman. He must have remembered my note. As he reluctantly extended his hand to grasp mine, Dornfeld's face showed all the enthusiasm of putting his hand into a pile of fresh, steaming Minnesota manure.

CHAPTER SIXTEEN

The Winter Of Discontent

As the election year began, I redoubled my efforts to try to broaden my base of support. Since we were still working on obtaining the party endorsement, that meant reaching out to Republican moderates. The problem was they weren't reaching back. Primarily, they weren't buying my prolife position.

This was difficult for me to understand. First, all four Senate candidates were prolife; the moderates weren't going to get a viable prochoice Republican candidate. Second, I was as reasonable on the issue as they could hope for, and I had often spoken of my dream of being the person to bring the two factions of the party together on the abortion issue. In retrospect, that was a pipe dream, but it was my dream. Third, I actually was the most moderate of the four Senate candidates. Early in the campaign, I had made a lot of mileage with activists by making fun of Minnesota's other Senator, Paul Wellstone, because he consistently showed up in rankings of most conservative to most liberal Senators as number 100 out of 100. Occasionally, an activist asked me the follow-up question "Where would you like your name to appear, Doug? Somewhere in the top five? Number one?" I always surprised the questioner with the answer "Right around 25 to 35. Certainly conservative, but not too far either way." Early on, I even told people I was a "moderate conservative."

I hadn't uttered that phrase recently. Now the answer to my politics was just plain "conservative." The campaign was relentlessly driving me right. Countless party activists were saying things to me such as "I'm supporting you, Doug, as you're a true conservative," or "I'm going to vote for the Republican Senate candidate I think is the most conservative," or "You can't be too conservative." At the same time, the party moderates were offering no political support and no money; many wouldn't even deign to meet with me. Which way is a candidate going to move? The answer is simple physics.

When we found ourselves alone, sometimes I said to Gail Sutton that I should take at least one liberal position on one issue to show people that I was not a rigid, doctrinaire conservative. Minnesota voters had demonstrated in the past that they liked politicians who—like Dave Durenberger, as I said in Bemidji—went off the reservation once in a while. I usually introduced the subject by saying "Gail, we have to think about the general election as well as the party endorsement."

Gail always answered "Yeah" as she went right on planning the next trip or doing whatever else she was doing.

"I mean it. We need to show voters I'm not at the far-right end. I need to come out with at least one non-conservative position."

"OK," Gail answered. "What do you suggest?"

That, of course, was the question. I couldn't and wouldn't come out in favor of higher taxes or increased federal government spending. The major social issues were out of the question. The range of acceptable issues on which I—a new kid on the political block—could break ranks with the party faithful was narrow indeed.

"How about free speech?" I suggested. "I'm a strong First Amendment man. I could take the position that I'm rock solid in favor of free speech, which includes all forms of expression."

"Doug, do you really want to come out in favor of pornography?" Gail asked as she continued to work without bothering to look up.

"Well, uh, no, no, of course not. That's not what I said. I said I'm in favor of free speech."

"All I heard was you're in favor of pornography. That's what conservatives will hear."

"Well, OK, then, what issue do you suggest?"

"I don't know," Gail answered. "I don't think we can take a chance on any issue that I can think of."

"I've got it," I announced. "I'll take a moderate position on gun control."

"No! Absolutely not!" Gail finally looked up.

"Yes, that will work," I said. "I can come out in favor of controlling handguns in cities. You and I both know that the real rub with gun control is people want their hunting rifles. I won't touch rifles. I'll just talk about handguns in large cities. Our people won't be thrilled, but they won't be too worked up either."

Gail said "No! That's just handing a wedge issue to Bert or Rod. They'll take gun control and run with it. That's all you'll hear the rest of the campaign. And the rest of the campaign won't be far off."

"You think so?"

"I know so."

"Oh, all right, not gun control. What issue, then?"

"I don't know right now," Gail said. "I'll think about it."

In the end, I never thought of an issue that Gail agreed would pass muster on the conservative don't-care-that-much scale, and she never suggested one. What I realized only in retrospect was that Gail was advising me as a committed social conservative. No wonder I couldn't come up with an acceptable mildly moderate/liberal issue.

All along, I knew my best hope to appeal to party moderates was endorsement by Bill Frenzel—my mentor in politics, former third district Congressman, former ranking Republican on the House Ways and Means Committee, a consultant at the Brookings Institution in Washington, and the most-respected Republican moderate in Minnesota. I knew the chances that Frenzel would endorse me were between slim and none, especially so early, but I hoped he would remember I had done a lot of volunteer work on his early campaigns. At that time, his prochoice position had not made me flinch; maybe my prolife position now would not make him flinch. Frenzel knew I admired him; I hoped he knew I was a reasonable person. A telephone call was worth a shot. The first Tuesday morning of the election year I dialed his direct telephone number at Brookings.

"Frenzel," the deep, familiar voice rumbled over the receiver. I smiled to hear it again. We exchanged some small talk about the campaign. He got down to business first when he asked a hard-edged question with a smile in his voice: "Doug, how did you get to be so conservative?"

"Bill, I've always been conservative, but I'm a party man first. That's why I never had any problem working for you." I'm not sure he bought entirely all that answer, but it was almost entirely true.

I told him that I had been looking for an issue or two on which I could take a more moderate stance, and then I asked for his advice on how to appeal to party moderates. We batted a few ideas around. Eventually, I got to the point. "Bill, I just can't seem to make any headway at all with the delegates in the third district—your old district. They seem to think I'm too conservative. Do you have any ideas for me on how to reach them?"

Frenzel certainly knew that the quickest and surest way for me to gain support from moderates in the third was with his stamp of approval. He didn't offer, and I knew enough not to ask. He talked in general about some of the people in the third district.

"Bill, I'm especially interested in district 42, Edina. The delegates there won't give me the time of day. Spud Carpenter is the district chair. I can't get through to him. Do you have any ideas about reaching him?"

The rumbling, slow-paced answer came back: "I've always found that having coffee with someone is a good way to get to know him."

I had to laugh. This wasn't the answer I'd hoped for, but it was a good answer, and it was typical Frenzel. "OK, Bill," I said, "I'll do it."

A week later Spud Carpenter and I met at nine in the morning for coffee at the Perkins pancake restaurant in Edina. Spud was easy to recognize in one of the booths; his combination of bald head with full, gray beard stood out. I'd known him for years, dating back to the Frenzel campaigns. Now

Carpenter was the chair of senate district 42, which was largely co-extensive with the suburban city of Edina in southwestern Hennepin County, the most solidly Republican district in the state. Put the GOP label on the village idiot, and he would carry district 42. At the same time, district 42 was one of the few remaining bastions of moderate Republicanism in the state; social conservatives had not succeeded in rooting out moderates from party positions. Spud Carpenter was proof of that.

The two of us drank coffee and talked politics. Eventually, I asked Carpenter how I could make headway with the people in district 42, and his answer was to declare myself prochoice. This was accurate advice, and it was also worthless advice. On personal principle, I was not going to switch positions on a key issue in a cynical attempt to gather in a few votes. On practical politics, the switch might gain 100 delegate votes in the third district at the expense of losing 2000 delegate votes statewide.

After that, we didn't have much more to talk about. Prochoice people whine that prolife people are one-issue voters. While that complaint has truth in it, they don't say that they are the same. We were at stalemate.

Spud and I enjoyed our coffee and had a nice chat about old times. He didn't offer any help. At that point, I didn't expect any. We both had our constituencies. Nothing personal. I would have to look elsewhere for votes.

After Spud left, Margaret Anderson arrived for coffee at ten. Anderson was the chairwoman of senate district 45 in the western suburb of Minnetonka, the next most moderate Republican district in the state. A decade earlier, our family had lived for eight years in Minnetonka, where I had been a precinct chair and convention delegate. Anderson was also a Hamline law graduate. I thought personal connections and old loyalties might account for something.

Old loyalties don't stand up to new realities. Our meeting quickly became a carbon copy of my meeting with Carpenter. Anderson and I enjoyed our coffee and had a nice chat about old times. She didn't offer any help. I didn't expect any. We both had our constituencies. Nothing personal. I would have to look elsewhere for votes.

★ ★ ★ ★ ★

While I was trying to figure out how to reach party moderates, Rod Grams set off on the opposite strategy. His first major entry into the awareness of the general public as a Senate candidate was to take a hard-right position on abortion. He made a big splash in the news by ripping the Clinton administration for forcing states to pay for abortions of poor women who had become pregnant by rape or incest.

The rest of us on the Republican side of the Senate race thought he'd lost his mind. We were all prolife, but we were not bellowing it to independents and Democrats. No one was painting Grams as a right-wing candidate; he had the brush and bucket of paint and was gleefully doing it himself.

His madness had only one possible method. Grams was trying to get to the right of the rest of us. Leon Oistad, Bert McKasy's campaign manager, said in the *StarTribune* "I hope these campaigns don't get into the position of trying to out-pro-life each other." He added Republicans should bring people together, not drive them apart.

Frankly, what came immediately to my mind was southern politicians in the 1950s and 1960s who tried to outdo each other in opposing civil rights. Many lost elections by being outflanked to the right on intensity of opposition to integration. Grams was raising the same danger to the rest of us on opposition to abortion. Delegates had often told me they would vote for the most conservative candidate, and Grams was flanking to the right.

Grams's gambit did require a decision. Should I also sprint right, or should I risk being outflanked to the right on abortion? The decision was to stay the course. First, I thought, party conservatives already knew I was prolife. Only a week or two later, I would learn that was too optimistic. Second, I thought the flanking effort might even backfire on Grams by making the rest of us look more attractive to party moderates. Third, Leon Oistad was right. I was in politics to bring people together instead of to use wedge issues to drive them apart. I wasn't going to play Grams's game. Finally, at the level of practical politics, winning the party nomination by outflanking everyone on the right would likely be a pyrrhic victory; I wanted to win the general election, not just the party endorsement.

While I tried to reach out to party moderates, incumbent Governor Arne Carlson tried to reach out to party conservatives. He dropped Lieutenant Governor Joanell Dyrstad off his ticket for re-election in favor of state senator Joanne Benson. The only noticeable difference between the two women was that Dyrstad, like Carlson, was prochoice, and Benson was prolife. Whether this appeal by Carlson to social conservative party activists would succeed in deflecting the challenge to his re-nomination spearheaded by Allen Quist would play out over the spring months.

After being pushed off the Carlson ticket, Dyrstad entered the Senate race. She was the prochoice candidate party moderates had been waiting for. That development didn't worry me. Party conservatives would determine the endorsement.

★ ★ ★ ★ ★

Through the winter, we continued to run the campaign on a shoestring. Gail Sutton and Steve Clark continued to operate out of our small one-room campaign office in Roseville. Gail continued to shun telemarketing as a fundraising source. We continued to have isolated successes, almost all from previous personal contacts: Guy Schoenecker, the father of two Hamline law grads, hosted a luncheon for his employees to meet me; Mark Knutson, a friend of mine from church, and his business partners met with me over lunch, and a check for $2000 arrived from Mark's partner and his wife. Law book publisher and friend Dwight Opperman, who I knew from my time at the Supreme Court, and former neighbor and governor candidate David Printy, brought their contributions up to the max. I reached into my own pocket every now and then to throw a little more into the campaign till. We continued to try to break into the money of the Republican business community.

One business leader we pursued was Mike Wright, the CEO of SuperValu, the grocery wholesaler. Wright and I had practiced law together at the Dorsey firm in Minneapolis. A former Gopher football star and a big name in civic affairs, Wright was a major force in the Minnesota business community. He was also a good guy, and he returned my calls. Wright was my best chance for a breakthrough. He agreed to have his political man meet with Gail and me over lunch in the company cafeteria.

Gail and I presented our folder full of literature and position statements. Could Mike make a major contribution? Could Mike join my finance committee? Could Mike make some fundraising calls for the campaign? Could Mike sign a letter to his business colleagues in the Twin Cities asking for money for the campaign?

A day or two later, the political man called with the answer. Wright needed Dave Durenberger's help and vote for food matters pending before the Senate. He didn't want to alienate and offend the sitting Senator by supporting a candidate trying to take his place. Maybe later, as the race developed, he could help me.

I was disappointed but not surprised. I'd heard this answer before. Or maybe, I thought, Mike had made a few calls and heard the word in the business community on McFarland wasn't good. Maybe my disaster at the Edina Rotary months earlier was still haunting me.

Later, another possibility came to mind. The reason for the refusal—that Wright didn't want to offend Durenberger—always struck me as odd. Why didn't he just tell me what everyone else did, the time was too early. Or I needed to demonstrate more widespread support before Mike would get on board. Or Mike wanted to be sure he was betting on the winning horse. Or Mike had a lingering loyalty to Rod Grams. Or even Mike didn't think I had a viable campaign. Why mention lame duck Durenberger? Maybe Mike had called Durenberger's office, and the reply came that he'd better not give any money to that SOB who had come out so early and helped force Durenberger into withdrawing at the state convention in September. Maybe Durenberger's invisible fingerprints were all over the business community's collective refusal to contribute or help me.

Or more likely the campaign was making me paranoid. Members of the business community sized me up on their own and spread the word that I wasn't the candidate to carry the ball for business interests. I prefer the vindictive Durenberger theory to the hapless McFarland theory. Human nature is to look for a hidden, outside source to account for one's personal failings.

★ ★ ★ ★ ★

Mary's dad Daryle Getting drove up from his home in Des Moines, Iowa, the same week to help with the campaign. His father had been an influential Republican state senator in Iowa for many years. Daryle himself was both a life-long Republican interested in politics and a life-long man of the land—farmer, sheep rancher, irrigation systems seller, and commodities broker. He was the stereotypical midwest farmer, with an open, friendly face, and a set of mannerisms that evidenced his life far more than words. A man without guile. A man who interrupted family trips to stop and inspect the condition of the corn crop in far distant counties. A man who knew his agriculture. The obvious place for his help was in my weak area of agriculture. Gail made appointments for the two of us to see the head of the Minnesota Farmers Union and the head of the Minnesota Farm Bureau.

Friday morning, Grandpa Getting and I drove the few miles to suburban New Brighton to meet David Frederickson at the Minnesota Farmers Union. I let the other two men carry the conversation, but I did say that even though I was a city boy, I realized the central place of agriculture in the Minnesota economy and was willing to learn. Frederickson asked why the two of us had come to see him. The question made sense since the Farmers Union always leaned toward Democrats and populists. While I was trying to come up with an answer, Daryle said "We want to see everyone." Hey, good answer. Maybe he should have been the politician.

That afternoon, we drove to Woodbury to see Gerry Hageman at the Minnesota Farm Bureau. This was another get-acquainted meeting, with no support expected or offered. The major difference was that Hageman did not ask why we had come to see him. The Farm Bureau leaned toward Republicans.

I was grateful to Grandpa Getting for shepherding me around to the powers-that-be in state agriculture. A candidate must respond to issues that are vitally important to many and yet beyond the candidate's knowledge, experience, and even personal interests. My knowing the importance of agriculture was one thing; being turned on by it was another.

* * * * *

The following Tuesday morning I was in my office at Hamline preparing for class when the telephone rang. "Doug," Gail shouted, "we've got a problem." The icy fingers squeezed my stomach once again. "Someone sent *Human Events* information that you were prochoice in your campaign for the state legislature in 1976," she continued in rapid fire. "If they print it, you could lose the endorsement."

The icy fingers released. Another issue I had beat down repeatedly. "Oh, hell, that's old news," I said with relief. Every other day one event or another was going to cost me the party endorsement.

Gail didn't slow down a bit. She said "It's not old news to them, and if they print it, it won't be old news to a lot of the delegates."

"We've dealt with this before. We even took a trip up to St. Cloud to meet with Sue Turch, Shirley Borgerding, and Noel Collis, and they were satisfied I'm prolife."

"That may work for St. Cloud, but that leaves 1500 delegates across the state who haven't heard it. They read it in *Human Events,* and you're cooked. We'll never be able to convince them otherwise."

"Slow down, Gail. What makes you think they're going to see it? How many of them do you think subscribe?"

By now, she was frustrated. "Look, Doug, *Human Events* is practically a Bible to social conservatives. It can't elect you, but it can damn sure beat you. And it doesn't make any difference how many subscribe. One of our opponents will helpfully reproduce anything they print and mail it to every delegate and alternate in the state."

Gail was right about that. The other Senate campaigns would certainly see that delegates learned of any problems another candidate had.

She was also right that we needed to respond immediately. Rod Grams was trying to flank all of us to the right on abortion. If a magazine or newspaper printed a small blurb that even suggested I was not 100% prolife, at the next party meeting an activist would approach me, photocopy of blurb in hand, to ask whether I was prolife. No matter the same activist had heard me declare my position a half-dozen times already. A beaten-down "revelation" never stayed beaten down. We needed to respond immediately and powerfully to every attack on any major issue, and especially on the issue.

I said "OK, Gail, what do you want to do?" Today the answer would be email or even a face-to-face chat on a cell phone. Back then, such options were not available.

"I have the fax number for Peter Coffman at *Human Events*. Ron Carey has told him you're reliably prolife, but Coffman needs some backup information. I'll get together some information and get it to you this afternoon. You can fax it to him yourself with a cover note."

"Fax it? Can't we just mail it? Doesn't faxing it look like we're worried? You're sure all of this is necessary?"

"Yes, damn sure. Doug, we need to do this today."

I faxed a cover note, some sample pieces of my literature, and the names of some of my prolife supporters to Coffman. He did not print an article, a note, or even a blurb questioning my prolife position. Another crisis averted.

★ ★ ★ ★ ★

Near the end of January, the St. Paul *Pioneer Press* published a poll surveying statewide name recognition for the major candidates for governor and senator. The higher the number, the better for the candidate. The paper reported nine individual scores on the Senate. The Democrats were Tom Foley 67 percent, Collin Peterson 43 percent, Tom Berg 33 percent, Linda Berglin 33 percent, and Ann Wynia 14 percent. The Republicans were Rod Grams 66 percent, Doug MacFarland 35 percent, Gen Olson 16 percent, and Bert McKasy 7 percent.

Good news: another strong showing. Two of the highest three finishers were male Democrats; they wouldn't be around in November, as the Democrats appeared determined to nominate a woman. The only contender ahead of me was Rod Grams, and high name recognition could be expected for a sitting Congressman. I scored fourth overall in spite of the misspelled name. The most exciting of all the numbers of the poll were the abysmal scores for Ann Wynia, who was the odds-on favorite to win Democratic party endorsement, and Bert McKasy, whose 7 percent statewide name recognition was even lower than the 9 percent racked up by respondents who "recognized none" of the names. As I said before, a good name matters in politics in more ways than one.

★ ★ ★ ★ ★

We were now into the election year, only five months prior to the state convention and nine months prior to the election. Despite many successes, including activist commitments, a straw poll win, and positive polling numbers, the campaign was still in the same small, one-room office with no money in the bank and no particular prospects of raising much soon.

Maybe I should have pulled the plug on the campaign. That's a mighty hard thing to do for a candidate after the investment of a full year of his life. Gail Sutton and Steve Clark had also given a year of their lives. Hundreds more Republicans had become my friends and committed supporters and workers. Many Democratic friends had given me money and encouragement. I was being propelled forward by the collective hopes, goodwill, and trust of thousands of people. The campaign now belonged to all of them.

Also, as Gail and I looked ahead, we could still see a possible win. We could limp through both BPOU and congressional district convention seasons on a tight budget, I could continue to accumulate delegates at retail, and we could enter the party state convention in June with a chance to win in a five-way race. My campaign had not caught fire, yet neither had the others. Even if another candidate took the lead, I could be the second choice. Enough delegates might not be for me, but no one was against me. Party endorsement required 60 percent of the delegate votes. The convention could deadlock and turn to a compromise candidate. Money would flow to the endorsed candidate. Nothing was wrong with my campaign that some serious money would not cure overnight. You can't win if you're not running.

CHAPTER SEVENTEEN

Just Can't Wait To Get On The Road Again

February in Minnesota is for the strong of heart. Snow covers the ground. White steam escapes the nose and mouth with every breath. People of sane mind stay indoors. Like a hibernating animal, the political season awaits the spring. Established politicians and officeholders can respect the rhythm of the season and stay home. Aspiring politicians can't afford to wait for spring. No matter what season or what weather, we will be on the road to your town and at your door. We're more reliable than the post office.

For February, Gail scheduled three major road trips, all chock full of meet-and-greet meals with party activists interspersed with media stops at local newspapers, television stations, and radio stations. The plan called for three days west and southwest, three days north and northwest, and two days south and southeast to every nook and cranny of the state.

Normally, whatever Gail told me to do, I did. She was the manager; I was the merchandise. No so for this month of road trips. When Gail told me the plan, I balked. I had by now been on enough road trips to know what a draining experience they were.

Road trips are compressed, intensified microcosms of the campaign. Giddy euphoria alternates with panic and dread. High! Low. High! Low. High! Low. The pattern of the road trip is the pattern of the campaign. The candidate attends a new play each and every hour without knowing whether it will be a comedy or a tragedy. Slogging forward through successes and failures in a campaign over days and months is tough. Dealing with alternating periods of ecstasy and agony several times in a single day is tougher.

The daily highs—

I loved being on the road. Outside the Twin Cities in small town America, I felt at home. I often found myself humming the Willie Nelson tune "On the Road Again." Rushing from place to place, usually running just a little behind schedule so I could shake one more hand or answer one more question, I had a warm glow of working hard and accomplishing much. Every day on the road felt like Friday.

Conversations with party activists usually went well. I already knew many of the activists who showed up at our meal events. We were old friends beyond the awkward get-acquainted stage of conversation. Many of these friends had already given me their trust through their commitments, and these trips produced new friends. More often than not, I came away from a meet-and-greet with more committed supporters.

The media stops—crammed up to nine in a single day—were even better. We arrived at the newspaper office or radio station to be greeted by the reporter as manna from heaven. News was walking in the door to fill blank pages or empty airtime. Arriving a little late was not a problem; these folks were accustomed to the vagaries of the schedules of itinerant politicians. After an easy interview, we were on the road again.

The daily lows—

Breakfast, lunch, and dinner—and sometimes afternoon coffee. Actually, the low was not the meet-and-greet meal itself. Once the event was finally underway, the conversation around the table usually was friendly and supportive. The low was the anticipation.

Let's take lunch. Our office sent postcard invitations to more than 100 party activists in the counties surrounding the luncheon location, but we had no idea how many would take time out of their day to show up for lunch—Dutch treat, of course. For a noon lunch, I began stewing over an internal monologue at least a half hour earlier. Who will bother to come out for lunch? Anyone? We were here for breakfast only a few months ago. Why would anyone bother to come out again? Maybe when they saw me before, they left laughing up their sleeves. Will Delores be there or is she going to Bert McKasy? Will I remember the names of people who came out before? Will anyone ask a trick question? Will someone expose my weakness on agriculture? Will a hidden Rod Grams supporter try to embarrass me?

We arrived at the local café perhaps ten minutes before noon. That's when the stewing intensified. For crying out loud, no one's here. Are they all drifting to Grams? Olson? Maybe it's a late arriving crowd. Will anyone show up? Maybe not. Maybe that would be the best. Zero is far better than the dreaded one. Then the dreaded one and I will have to work like dogs to carry on a conversation for an hour or so, and as soon as the one gets home, he or she will start spreading the word all around town that McFarland can't draw flies. The minutes pass like hours. Nearly noon. Still no one. Of course, political events never start on time. Past noon. Is my campaign dead in the water? Now I hope no one shows. Let's get out of here before that dreaded one appears.

Oh, wait, here come two. Great, it's not one. Hello! Should we order now, or should I suggest we wait for some more? That will look foolish if no one else comes. Should I start my pitch and have to repeat it for anyone else who does show up, or should we make small talk for a while? The waitress must be seeing her vision of a big group with big tips vanish. So embarrassing. A turnout of only two in a big county like this. I might as well pack it in now. People are voting with their feet and all of them seem to be kicking me in the butt.

No, I have to persevere. The game is won by those who show up. Where's our county leader? Isn't she at least going to show? Oh, what a relief. Here she comes. And here are another two. We might as well order.

From that moment on, the lunch morphed into a high. The problem was the anticipation. Maybe it was simple stage fright. Maybe it was lack of perspective; Gail kept saying we shouldn't expect much of a turnout in the middle of winter. Maybe it was fear of rejection. Maybe it was plain old introversion. What I do know is that sitting in the dentist's chair looking at the long needle dripping Novocaine is about the same as sitting in a small-town café wondering who will show up. And this was three or four visits to the dentist every day.

By this time, I had a full-blown love-hate relationship with these road trips.

When Gail told me the plan for February, I said "OK, Gail, but can't we at least change the scheduling? Let's keep the media stops and eliminate the meal events."

"Why would you want to dump the meals? You're out there to see the delegates."

"No, I'm out there for the media stops."

"No, you're out there to meet the delegates. This is the best way to meet them."

"Gail, you know how gut-wrenching these meet-and-greets are. I'll probably see only a couple of delegates for breakfast, but a stop by the local paper and the whole town will know I was there. That's the real value of these trips."

"Yes, Doug, but you can't ignore the delegates. They want to know you're courting them. We can't have them read in the paper you were in town and ignored them."

"Well, OK," I conceded, "but let's at least stop scheduling meals. Let's schedule a few coffees instead. You know, mid-morning or mid-afternoon. No wonder people don't come when they have to pay for an expensive meal. If we schedule coffees, it'll be cheaper for them and more informal. They're more likely to come out."

"No, this is the way it's done."

"If we have only coffee, there'll be less expectation if we get a crappy turnout."

"No."

"Gail, I have a definite feeling of been-there, done-that about these trips. Imagine the party activists. Why should they come out in the dead of winter and buy themselves an expensive meal to see me again so soon?"

"Doug, we need to do this."

"But, Gail, we're getting lousy turnouts. We aren't doing much good."

She pursed her lips and explained to me as if to a child "This is the standard way to court delegates. They all want to be courted. All the other Senate candidates are traveling around the state doing the same thing. If we're not getting good numbers, then they aren't either. This is the way it has to be done."

And so, it was. Gail was the campaign manager. I was only the candidate, who just needed to suck it up and get back on the road.

★ ★ ★ ★ ★

Shortly before our first trip, I took a call from Dennis McGrath, a reporter for the *StarTribune*. He said "I hear you're planning to travel around the state in February."

"Yes, that's right."

"Well, I'm thinking of doing an article on politicians who campaign in February. It reminds me of Paul Wellstone. I think one reason he won was that he slogged around the state in the dead of winter making himself known and getting delegates early on to support him. That's one hidden secret of his win."

"OK" I ventured.

"And I think that Linda Berglin on the Democratic side and you on the Republican side seem to be following his formula, running a grassroots campaign by getting out and seeing the delegates. I'm thinking of riding along with either Berglin or you on a leg or two of one of these trips in February. I haven't decided which one yet, and it depends on if we can fit our schedules together. Would you be interested?"

Is this a trick question? Let's see. Do I want free media in the *StarTribune*, the largest circulation newspaper in the state, that will probably liken my campaign to that of Paul Wellstone, who won an upset victory in the last Senate election? Let me think about this one. Yes, the answer is yes! Ride with us anytime.

We compared schedules. One big problem was that I was staying on the road overnight instead of returning to the Twin Cities at the end of each day. McGrath said he would see what developed.

★ ★ ★ ★ ★

Chris Bakeman, one of Gail's crew of young guns on the political make, and I left on the first of the three trips before dawn in subzero cold early Wednesday, February 2. We started our day with breakfast in St. Cloud. Zero party activists came out to greet us. That got my mental demons off and running. Nothing like starting a three-day campaign swing with a zero. At least Dennis McGrath wasn't along to report on it. Of course, had McGrath been traveling with us, Gail would have made sure the place was packed.

After the ritual gut-twisting of breakfast anticipation and an empty table, we stopped by the St. Cloud *Times* and two radio stations. Lunch at noon in Alexandria was more pleasant. Chris and I found five county activists already waiting for us at the Traveler's Inn on Main Street. The food was good too, especially the pie. Gail always asked the locals which café to use. Early afternoon coffee produced ten activists in Morris. Fantastic. After another radio station, late afternoon coffee in Benson turned out three. Good for a small town.

We arrived in Montevideo an hour ahead of our scheduled dinner at six, so the two of us stopped at the Hardee's for yet another cup of coffee. Even though the plastic seats were hard and uncomfortable, it was a good place to unwind and relax a little. Some relaxing. I worked harder for that hour trying to keep a rising sense of panic out of my mind than I worked for an hour talking to activists. I had a bad feeling. We were returning to the scene of a highly successful dinner only a few months earlier; and we might be going to the well again too soon. Even Scott Van Binsburgen, the energetic young activist who had been our guide around town on the previous trip, had told Gail he had other plans for the evening.

Bakeman and I arrived at the hotel private dining room a minute or two before six to find a large rectangular table set for a party of 14. I said "Dammit, Chris, I told Gail to be sure to have the hotel set a small table. We can always expand, but this way we'll look bad if only three or four show up." I needn't have worried. We were the only two people in the room. Six o'clock came and went. The gut tightened. Six-ten. Tighter. Six-twenty. Tighter still. Six-thirty.

Finally, I couldn't take waiting any longer, and went exploring through the hotel lobby into the restaurant. Immediately, I recognized six people in a booth. Scott Van Binsburgen, his parents, and a local activist were meeting with Republican state House leader Steve Sviggum and his aide. The last thing I wanted was for them to see me alone. I considered for an instant spinning on my heel and hustling back out, but with my size couldn't expect that none of them had seen me. I had to approach.

They said Van Binsburgen was thinking of running for the state House. Sviggum was there to encourage the effort. We had a nice chat about our parallel evening events. Of course, the party leader of the state House and his chief aide had to realize why I was talking to them instead of hosting my own event. That was far worse than the zero turnout.

The first day of our swing west and southwest ended 15 hours and 240 miles after it began, with successes at six media stops, lunch, and two afternoon coffees bookended by disasters at breakfast and dinner. I knew we should have scheduled coffees.

The second day started with breakfast in Willmar. Gary Swenson, our key man in the area, stopped by early to say hello. At least he didn't stay long enough to see another zero turnout. Afterward, we did some good in town at two radio stations and the West Central *Tribune*.

On to Marshall. Chris and I were enthused about an appointment to meet with Marv Schwan, the president of Schwan's food, the largest business in town, and a generous Republican donor. Chris called in to check with Gail, and she said Schwan had cancelled. I was more than disappointed; I was mad as hell. We had made the appointment weeks earlier, and Gail had scheduled it as a highlight of the day. Now he cancelled the day of the appointment. That set off my paranoid fantasies again. Had Durenberger got to him? Had Grams got to him? Had the business network told him not to bother? The two of us stopped by the reception desk of his business anyway and asked the receptionist to tell him we were there. It was pointless, except I was irritated enough to want to embarrass him a mite. Of course, he didn't see us, so we left the fundraising packet we had been carrying for him with the receptionist.

A campaign dishes out countless large and little, unexpected nicks and downers such as the Schwan appointment. Of course, a campaign also dishes out countless large and little, unexpected boons and uppers. We were amazed that eleven activists showed for lunch in Marshall. Half were students from Southwest State University and most of the other half were farmers, including Rick Bot, who chuckled about my stumbling attempt to answer his question on agriculture at this same café a few months earlier. The interests of the two groups didn't match well, but we all had a great conversation. After lunch, Chris and I hit a radio station and the Marshall *Independent*.

By late afternoon, we arrived in Sioux Falls, South Dakota, a few miles from the western Minnesota border. We were there because Sioux Falls television stations covered the entire southwest part of Minnesota. The reporters at all three television stations gave me wonderful coverage. Of course, I had a natural hook with them, having grown up and graduated from high school in Sioux Falls. I was home.

The thought crossed my mind, not for the first time, that I should just chuck Minnesota and run for the Senate from South Dakota. A lot less competition. A Republican state. The entire state is like small town and rural greater Minnesota, which is my type of place, and none is like suburban Minneapolis, where I couldn't get any traction at all. Well, too late for that.

We drove 30 miles east back into Minnesota for dinner in Luverne. Turnout of two. When is a turnout of two only a little better than the dreaded one? When the two are a married couple. That counts as one.

After dinner, Chris and I drove another 30 miles east to stay overnight in Worthington. This leg of the trip fully matched Dennis McGrath's expectations about candidates slogging through the dark and cold: the temperature was ten below zero, and the wind chill was unmentionable. We stayed in the same room in a motel that had seen better days. The arrangement was uncomfortable, but conservatively frugal. The room did have two beds. I'm not that cheap.

Breakfast in Worthington with six activists at the Gobbler Café was a great start to the third day on the road. Media stops across the southwestern counties filled the morning and afternoon on both sides of lunch (with the dreaded one) in Fairmont. Finally, we turned north to Hutchinson, where a table of four activists, including party fundraiser extraordinaire Wilma Grams, awaited us for dinner. Eager to see her political friends in Hutch, to welcome her warriors back from battle, and also to pad the dinner count, Gail drove the 60 miles west from St. Paul to Hutchinson to join us for dinner.

The southwest swing was a triumph of media coverage: seven newspapers, 13 radio stations, and three television stations in three days. All of it free media. Progress with party activists was decidedly mixed. We had huge turnouts and shutouts. Overall, 45 people came out for 11 meals or coffees. An average of four per event, in miserably cold weather, wasn't bad. The problem was that the images that stuck in my mind were not the large groups but instead the zeroes.

Chris Bakeman and I arrived back at my house around ten-thirty Friday night. First thing Saturday morning, Gail, Mary, and I drove 100 miles back to Willmar. When Gary Swenson stopped by our breakfast there only two days earlier, he had urged strongly that I should attend their town event on Saturday. I was so blitzed from the three-day campaign swing that I have absolutely no memory of the Saturday trip to Willmar or the event. But I was there. My calendar says so. Go anywhere and do anything for a vote. Politics by retail.

★　★　★　★　★

After a little rest on Sunday, and teaching classes for my day job at Hamline on Monday and Tuesday, I was ready Wednesday morning for another February three-day campaign swing. This time both Gail Sutton and Steve Clark went along. Gail needed to get out of the office. Steve was along as the chaperone and as a reward for all his—mostly volunteer—hard work.

This trip was north and northwest. What made the prospect of driving north on icy roads in frigid, dark February even more daunting was the plan to turn northwest into the vast emptiness of the seventh congressional district.

Day one began in 5:30 a.m. darkness for the two-hour drive to Duluth. We got off to a good start with a lovely group of ten for breakfast; Therese Vaughn, the chairwoman of the eighth congressional district, and her husband Jack always turned out a lot of folks. Our success in town continued with a meeting with University of Minnesota-Duluth College Republicans, which was covered by the press.

We next ventured north by northwest into the Iron Range, the treasure house of Democratic votes in Minnesota. Even though a Republican stood as much chance of being elected on the Iron Range as did a foreign terrorist, the Mesabi *Daily News* and the Hibbing *Tribune* again welcomed us. Lunch in Hibbing with three. Mid-afternoon coffee in Grand Rapids with one. Maybe coffees weren't such a good idea after all.

On highway 2 from Grand Rapids to Bemidji, we stopped in Deer River to call on the Rajala family at their lumber business. We weren't stopping to inspect the timber. The Rajalas were a rare breed: major Republican donors in the northern part of the state. Naturally their big issue was federal policy toward cutting of forests. I allowed as how trees were a renewable natural resource, so as long as a lumber company had a renewable forest program in which it planted more trees than it cut, no problem. Right answer. Like what you have to say, Doug. Too early for a contribution. Keep in touch.

Our last event of the day was dinner in Bemidji, and as usual we were behind schedule. Darkness came early in February. Solid walls of fir trees lined both sides of the road. We sped along highway 2 in isolated blackness. I was driving, but all of us kept an eye out for a deer to bound from the woods in front of our car at any instant. At least for the hour I wasn't frenzied with anticipation about the Bemidji dinner. All I could think about was watching for deer and willing the car not to have a breakdown on this frigid, desolate stretch of road.

We broke free of the trees about ten miles outside Bemidji, and I pushed the gas pedal harder. Almost there, and only a half-hour late. Just as we were entering town, the answer came to the question of what else can go wrong. Red lights began flashing behind us. The state trooper walked up to the driver's window of our minivan. He could see the three of us plus piles of campaign materials through the large side windows. I tried to put on my best politician's smile. "Hello, officer." "Well, we're out campaigning. I'm running for the Senate." "Yes, we have a dinner just into town here in Bemidji. Several of my supporters are waiting for us. That's where we're going." "Oh, a warning?" "Yes, I will be careful." "That's great. Thank you."

We hustled into the hotel dining room in Bemidji 45 minutes late, and our mouths fell open. Sixteen people leaped from their seats to greet us. They were fired up and ready to talk politics. Alice Fugelstad, our organizer in Beltrami County, had put together the most successful meet-and-greet meal of the entire campaign.

The previous thought that we might cut the dinner event short to get a good start on the two-hour drive yet to come that evening vanished as soon as we entered the room. We would stay with these folks as long as they wanted. We talked. We ate. I gave a little speech. Activists asked about their important issues. Gail gave a little speech. Steve Clark gave a little speech. All of us talked some more. Two hours flew by. No one left early. The room took on a warm glow. We had all the time in the world. We didn't want this warm feeling of success to end.

Finally, the time came for us to take a reluctant leave. Well after nine p.m., we started northeast on highway 71 for the 122-mile drive to International Falls, located hard by the Canadian border. Our next event was breakfast in the Falls, so we had two rooms reserved at the Super 8 motel there.

The line in one of my favorite Christmas carols, "Good King Wenceslas," is "Sire, the night grows colder now, and the wind blows stronger." The temperature was nearing the predicted low of 25 below zero, and the wind was waxing mighty strong. We were on the way to "the Icebox of the Nation" in the middle of a February night. The two-lane highway rolled through frozen forests and marshes. Everything in all directions was a dull, frozen white. This drive made the earlier hour from Grand Rapids to Bemidji look jolly in comparison.

The only positive was that trees did not line both sides of the highway so we could see into the distance. We met one car during the two hours. We saw the headlights and tried to guess how far away it was. By the time we finally met, we had logged ten miles; that means we probably saw the headlights 20 miles away.

I've been on many lonely drives in my life, but this one takes first place. Pitch black, no moon, no stars. Twenty-five degrees below zero. Howling wind. Middle of a bleak February night. Seemingly no towns. No other cars on the road in either direction. The springs on our minivan creaking and cracking in the cold. On and on in the frozen emptiness, mile after same mile. On and on, listening for the slightest strange sound in the engine, hoping against hope that the car wouldn't break down. Finally, we pulled into International Falls shortly before midnight and claimed our rooms at the Super 8. Our day ended after 18 hours of campaigning covering 440 miles.

Yet it hadn't quite ended. The next day, breakfast was at 7:30. That left over seven hours for the minivan to set outside overnight in the bitter cold. I set the alarm clock for three-thirty a.m. When it sounded, I threw on some clothes, went outside and started the car, ran the engine for about five minutes, and returned to bed. The car started right up in the morning. That's the glamour of campaigning in Minnesota in February.

The question might come to mind why I would voluntarily subject myself to such an ordeal. The answer for me personally was easy: the price of admission to public office is high. No one said the campaign would be pleasant and easy.

A question harder to answer is why campaign workers would subject themselves to such suffering? After all, Gail Sutton and Steve Clark were right there in the car with me, mile after desolate mile. For the two of them, the answer was likely much the same. My election would take them to Washington. What about the motivations of more casual campaign workers and volunteers? What do they get out of campaign work that prompts them to invest themselves emotionally and to donate hour after hour? For some, the motivation is similarly personal: become known to the people in the party as a go-getter in order to build a personal political career. Others enjoy socializing with the group, or perhaps hope to meet someone with common interests. Likely the majority of campaign workers believe so strongly in their political philosophies and the direction the government should take that volunteering hours in the cause is worthwhile. Whatever the motivation, campaigns don't turn volunteers away.

★ ★ ★ ★ ★

I woke up Thursday morning raring to go. The schedule for the day featured International Falls, Warroad, and Roseau. These towns near the Canadian border had surfaced every winter in hockey scores and record low temperature reports, and then receded into oblivion with each spring. They could have been as real as Shangri-la, Brigadoon, and Atlantis, and I was eager to see them for the first time.

The day was as good as we could have hoped. Every single activist who came out committed to me. They were excited a candidate would come so far to see them. No one else had made the effort. The problem was the vote total added up slowly. Three commitments at breakfast in International Falls would produce one or two delegates to the state convention; three more commitments at lunch in Roseau would produce one or two delegates. County chairman Marv Kading showed for afternoon coffee in Thief River Falls; we had talked often on the telephone, and this day he committed. One more state convention vote. Two commitments at dinner in Crookston, one of whom would likely be a delegate at the convention, completed the day.

Thursday ended after 13 hours and 235 miles at a motel in Crookston. We broke our usual routine by not driving on after dinner to stay overnight in the town where we would have the next morning's breakfast. Breakfast the next morning was in Moorhead. With my past luck in Moorhead, the motel would probably burn down as we slept.

As Thursday was that good, Friday was that bad. The pattern was set when the dreaded one showed for breakfast in Moorhead. After we labored with the sole activist through the breakfast hour, Gail, Steve, and I stopped by both television stations. Fergus Falls was a carbon copy. Zero for lunch. Stops by two radio stations and the *Daily Journal*. Detroit Lakes for afternoon coffee was a little better. Four prolife activists wanted to know what I could do to promote their issue that the other Republican candidates could not. How to out-prolife the others? You can count on me! I'll do my best. Let's talk taxes.

On the 91-mile drive southeast on highway 10 to Brainerd for dinner, I was in a fragile mood: three activist events for a grand total of five people with zero commitments for the day. The beginnings of a winter storm didn't help at all. It meant our drive home after dinner would be even longer. By the time we reached Brainerd, the air was thick with snow.

Gail, Steve, and I walked out of the blowing snow into the restaurant to find a table set for 16 in a private meeting room. Oh, great. No way we'd get people out in this weather. Six o'clock came and went. Did we want to order? No thanks, not yet. The three of us took turns checking the rapidly accumulating snow outside. No sign of anyone coming to join us for dinner. Six-fifteen, and no change. Did we want to order now? No thanks, not yet. Six-twenty-five, and no change.

At the end of three long days and still facing a two-and-one-half hour drive through a blizzard, I stood up and said "We're getting out of here. Call the waitress." I told her we wouldn't be staying for dinner, apologized for taking her time, and gave her a tip that should have been a lot more. We grabbed our standard on-the-road meal at McDonalds and started south on highway 371 from Brainerd.

Steve Clark took the wheel. I tried to catch a little sleep. No such luck. Steve's cautious nature showed in his driving, and the snowy, windy conditions slowed him even more. He was turning a two-and-one-half hour drive into a four-hour drive. I couldn't relax when all I could think about was stomping on the gas pedal. After 30 miles that seemed to take forever, we reached Little Falls. I told Steve he was tired so I would drive a while.

The rest of the trip was on highway 10, a four-lane divided highway. I pushed the gas pedal hard. We roared southeastward through the blowing snow. A couple of times Steve volunteered that he was rested and would be glad to drive again. Of course, what he really wanted was to wrest the steering wheel out of my reckless hands and end his white-knuckle ride. I didn't intend to scare him, but I did intend to get home fast. No way was I giving the wheel back. We hit a small slippery spot or two, and passed a nasty accident, but we arrived home safely at a decent hour.

For this third day, the totals were 16 hours and 400 miles. That meant the three-day swing totaled 47 working hours and 1075 miles. That's the seventh congressional district, the district where politicians' cars go to die.

* * * * *

A few days later, the three of us were sitting in the campaign office talking. Gail said "Oh, by the way, Doug, Noel Collis stabbed you in the back last night."

"Noel? What did he do?" I asked in surprise. Collis, a physician, had run for seventh district Congress the previous election. Word was that seventh district chairwoman Georgiann Stenerson had pulled some shenanigans to hand the endorsement to another candidate. I had made a special trip to St. Cloud to meet with Collis, Sue Turch, and Shirley Borgerding a few months earlier. I thought he was behind me.

"Well," Gail said, "Noel was at the seventh district committee meeting in Fergus Falls last night and Georgiann Stenerson collapsed. She couldn't breathe."

"Oh."

"And Noel, like an idiot, saved her life. After Georgiann had stuck it to him two years ago. Next time we see him, we'll have to ask what he was thinking."

We all laughed. Gallows humor sounds better in the heat of a campaign. "Having Georgiann out of the way would help us a lot in Moorhead and the seventh district, wouldn't it?" I asked.

"You know it."

The next day, I consulted a physician myself. A neurologist examined numbness in my left leg but found nothing major. The following day, I returned to physical therapy for more work on the muscles knotted in my back. I should also have gone to the dentist to ask about a dull, steady ache on the right side of my mouth. No one could do much about the stomach that was often upset or the occasional case of the jitters. The cost of the campaign.

★　★　★　★　★

While February was dominated by the three campaign swings covering the entire state, the major single event of the month was a Senate candidates' forum, sponsored by the St. Paul Jaycees, at the downtown St. Paul Landmark Center. Since it was to be broadcast statewide on public radio and cable television, all the serious candidates of both major parties showed. For a year I had engaged in family squabbling with other Republicans, splitting hairs about issues on which we were all in basic agreement. I really looked forward to this first opportunity to match wits with some Democrats.

Nine of us sat in alphabetical order, Republicans and Democrats intermixed, at a long table on the stage. For the Republicans, Joanell Dyrstad, Rod Grams, Bert McKasy, Gen Olson, and I took our places. For the Democrats, the candidates were St. Paul lawyer Tom Berg, state senator Linda Berglin, Ramsey County Attorney Tom Foley, and University of Minnesota regent Ann Wynia.

I had seen and heard the other Republicans ad nauseum, but I was eager to see and evaluate the potential Democratic opposition. Berg was the polished downtown lawyer. Foley seemed to be more of a big city pol than a hard-nosed prosecutor. Berglin was the earnest neighbor who became involved in a local issue and ran with it. Wynia was the one I wanted to hear. She was the likely November opposition. I studied her closely as she spoke. Even though she was not impressive physically, Wynia had a strong voice. She gave answers that were thoughtful and well-articulated. She was not a party hack spinning political positions. Wynia would not be a pushover.

My own answers were standard fare. I'd said the same things thousands of times. I could have answered by now on autopilot. My cluster of supporters in the audience cheered my answers; the clusters supporting other candidates groaned. No points scored but no points lost. The debate was fun: spouting ideas in front of a large audience with statewide radio and television coverage was a lot more satisfying than emoting in front of two or three party activists across a luncheon table.

★ ★ ★ ★ ★

The following evening, I appeared in front of the Republican search committee screening Senate candidates. Committee members wanted answers to their standard questions about campaigning, issues, funding, and supporters. They were satisfied with my answers. They should have been satisfied: many of them were already committed to support me.

I have always thought the screening process odd. The committee has no power. Anyone can continue to run even if the committee members decide the candidate is the worst prospect for public office they have ever seen. A candidate travels the state campaigning for a year, and then the committee raises enough questions in a half-hour interview to tell the candidate that he or she is not up to the job? Has any party search committee ever advised a candidate not to run? Well, no problem, the hurdle is low enough to jump.

★ ★ ★ ★ ★

Our third February swing through the state went south and southeast, almost entirely in the more compact first congressional district. We would travel a full day, duck home for the night, be back out for a second day, and be home and done by evening. The good news was no dinner event either day.

The bad news was the first district had been tough for me since day one. Early on, favorite son Gil Gutknecht of Rochester was in the race for Senate. Even after he shifted over to a campaign for the House seat, I had less success in the more moderate first than in the other districts in greater Minnesota.

So many times, I wanted to say to a delegate in the first district, or the third district, "I'm conservative, but I understand the necessity of moving to the middle on some issues. This state wants a person who at least appears to be in the middle. I'm the best chance you have for a moderating influence in this race. You ought to be voting for me."

That statement would have helped me with some delegates in the first and third districts. And it would have killed me in the second, fourth, fifth, sixth, seventh, and eighth districts. People there were advising me to stop being so nice to moderates in the party. Their advice was "Call them what they are: liberals!"

As I mentioned earlier, many times on my trips through greater Minnesota, an activist said to me "Doug, I'm going to vote for the candidate I think is the most conservative." I waited. Often the activist continued "Right now, I think that's you." I smiled and nodded sagely. As the campaign pushed into the late winter and spring of election year, the continuation changed. Instead of saying "Right now, I think that's you," the activist often said "I just can't make up my mind. I really like all four of you. You are all such good conservatives." After hearing this refrain for only the first few of what would become scores of times, I was able to interpret it: "I'm voting for someone else."

Talking moderate to certain activists in the first and third districts would have told them what they wanted to hear, but two little bitty problems prevented that strategy. First, my campaign was based on honesty; I was not going to flap in the wind of the day. Second, a solid conservative was going to win the endorsement. The other three leading Republican candidates were all trying to move the farthest right, so they couldn't be selling well in the first or third either. I would just have to muddle through.

The summary of the two-day swing through the first district was 29 hours of campaigning, 520 miles on the road, four meal meet-and-greets producing a total turnout of five party activists, and 15 media stops. In other words, I talked to three times as many media representatives as party activists. While we were losing momentum with party activists, we were gaining momentum with the media as reporters noted the success we had achieved over the past year.

★ ★ ★ ★ ★

StarTribune reporter Dennis McGrath did publish an article about midwinter campaign road trips. The headline was accurate: "The winter political road is cold, hard and lonely." The article described his ride-along with Linda Berglin, and also quoted me about alternating exhilaration and depression of fluctuating numbers for meal meet-and-greets.

On the Democratic side, Senator Paul Wellstone remembered the winter months as the most trying part of his campaign. "There were nights, he said, when he drove through snowstorms, arriving home at 2 or 3 a.m., wondering whether it was leading anywhere." He got that right! "'It's utterly exhausting,' Wellstone said. 'Now, it's very labor intensive. You don't have a lot of people helping you. You're not getting a lot of media attention. It's a real test to see if people have the fire in the belly, because you have to have the fire to get through this part . . . It's a humbling experience.'" Right again.

For the Republicans, state party chair Chris Georgacas said "It's a good testing process for the large physical and emotional toll the general election process will take on the survivors of this process." That's right, too, although he was a lot more detached than Wellstone, who lived the ordeal of the winter political road.

Ordeal is the right word. Some of the price is physical. Most of the price is emotional. February in Minnesota is for the strong of heart.

CHAPTER EIGHTEEN

The Big Mistake

The election year state convention in June grants party endorsement to candidates for statewide offices. Party endorsement is tantamount to winning the primary election a couple of months later; only rarely will a non-endorsed candidate win the primary. To be a state convention delegate is the goal of every serious party activist. To identify and elect its committed supporters at party caucuses on March 1 to the Basic Political Organizational Unit (local district) conventions in March and April, and from those conventions to the state convention, is the goal of every statewide political campaign.

Ideally, we would have spent two months leading to caucus night burning up the telephone lines to identify my supporters, create slates of McFarland delegates, and get those delegates to the BPOU conventions. Of course, an ideal campaign requires money, which we didn't have. What we could afford was mailing small caucus packages to the precincts around the state. Each package contained a letter from me to be read at the caucus plus some campaign literature. We had to take potluck for delegates elected to the BPOU conventions.

So would the other Senate candidates. As far as we could tell, of the five candidates for Senate—Joanell Dyrstad, Rod Grams, Bert McKasy, Gen Olson, and me—and the three candidates for governor—Arne Carlson, Dick Kimbler, and Allen Quist—only one campaign engaged in a major effort to get its people out to the caucuses. That was the Quist campaign.

We all kept our ears to the ground for rumblings from the other campaigns. No one was better at this than Gail Sutton. She was always on the telephone collecting political intelligence from around the state. She talked to Evie Axdahl in St. Paul, Gayle Belkengren in Minneapolis, Therese Vaughn in Duluth, Alice Fugelstad in Bemidji, Laura Carrington in Morris, Bob Crane in International Falls, Linda Pettman in Mankato, George Cable in Chisago, Mary Kiffmeyer in St. Cloud, Sue Jirele in Waseca, Tim Wilkin of the Young Republicans, and a host of others.

The story leading into caucuses was that of Allen Quist, a largely unknown farmer from St. Peter, taking on incumbent governor Arne Carlson. From the information Gail gathered, Quist was building support with party activists like a juggernaut. He was rallying so many seasoned party activists to his campaign that we were left scrambling for our own volunteers. Even as a neutral observer, I had to be impressed with Quist's successes. We could all see the Quist campaign starting to roll. Carlson was running scared; the proof of that was his dumping of Joanell Dyrstad in favor of Joanne Benson as his running mate.

The fuel firing the Quist campaign was committed social conservatism. Long-time Republican activists were ready to go to cultural war with him. The direct loser would be Carlson, but all of us running for the Senate wondered whether we would be indirect losers. How would the Quist phenomenon affect the Senate race? If Quist succeeded in electing his people at the caucuses and local BPOU conventions, where would these delegates come down on the Senate candidates?

At times, I was jealous of the passion Quist was generating among the party faithful. I was scrapping for a vote here and a vote there, and Quist seemed to be collecting commitments by the bushel basket. I could have tried to try to tap into the same passion. I didn't because my assessment was that Quist was drifting too far to the right to have much chance in the general election. I wanted to win both the party endorsement and the election. The analogy in my mind was that Al Quist was the baseball manager who burned up his best pitchers to get to the title game and then had nothing left in the bullpen to win it all. I was trying to struggle through the preliminary games without burning out my best pitching so I could compete in the title game. I would keep the same pitching rotation and play on.

Caucus night came and went quietly. We had considered whether I should blitz around the Twin Cities, speaking at as many caucuses as possible, and decided the results wouldn't be worth the effort. The time frame was too short for many stops, and the key party people already knew me. I attended my own precinct caucus at the nearby middle school, and later by arrangement called in to comment on caucus night on WCCO radio with Eric Eskola and Dark Star. My fate was being decided in thousands of small rooms across the state, and I couldn't do a thing about it.

★ ★ ★ ★ ★

By early spring of the election year, interest groups were beginning to take notice of the election. I filled out questionnaires from many groups. Some, like the conservative Eagle Forum, were easy. Others, like the generally liberal AFL-CIO, were tough. What did I think of right to work laws? Under what circumstances should an employer be permitted to hire replacement workers? Would I support repeal of the Taft-Hartley Act? Hell, I needed a labor lawyer to explain the questions to me, let alone figure out how to answer them.

Even though I knew my chances of gaining labor support were next to nil, I wanted to try. As Grandpa Getting had said to the liberal Minnesota Farmers Union, we wanted to talk to everybody. Also, I had sympathy for labor. My dad had sold suits for a living. I had worked highway construction one summer and driven a city bus another summer. I wanted to tap into labor support. There was no reason labor should always support Democrats. The problem was that I didn't even know what answers they wanted to hear, let alone whether I could give them without alienating Republican business owners. I called former state party chair Bob Weinholzer, who had some background in labor, for advice and filled in the answers to the questionnaire as best I could.

A few days later, I took my turn before the AFL-CIO vetting committee at a downtown hotel. Here's my history. I have empathy for working people. I will work with you. I want your support. Nice, but what about specifics? Would I support an increase in the minimum wage? I knew the "right" answer to that one but knew I couldn't say yes without alienating business support. Hah, with the zero support I'd been getting from business leaders, I should have said yes. How long a cooling-down period would I support in a major strike? I had no idea what the "right" answer was and stumbled through a response. Would I support the right of public workers to strike? I knew my answer was "wrong" as I told them a public worker takes on a public trust and should not be allowed to strike. One of the committee members rose from her seat and announced "I'm a teacher, and the union has done so much for us. It certainly has made my life much better."

How to respond to that? I said "I don't want to give you the impression I'm anti-labor because I'm not. I want to work with you, and I will always be available to meet with you and listen. I'm from a family of working people myself." Of course, that exhortation didn't cut much ice. While they didn't laugh me out of the room, they didn't give me their support either.

★ ★ ★ ★ ★

During these days leading up to the election year BPOU conventions, I was always after Gail Sutton to raise more money. In one sense that was unfair: she was a political manager, and other campaigns had both a political manager and a professional fundraiser. In another sense, it was fair: a year earlier Bob Weinholzer convinced me to hire Gail because she could raise money in addition to managing the campaign.

Certainly, Gail had done everything possible with the larger potential contributors. We had been through the Republican fat cats list time and time again. We had met with as many as would meet with us; we had met several more than once. We had added new names to the list. We had convinced several to host events for their friends or employees to meet and support me. We had called back asking for more from those who had already contributed.

We also had squeezed as much as possible out of the primary funding source for my campaign, which was personal friends, relatives, neighbors, and contacts. Our squeezing had by now exceeded the level of putting the touch on a buddy to the level of acute embarrassment. The time had come to try other potential funding sources.

We tried a mailing to Hamline law school alumni asking them to support their old prof. It raised little more than howls of protest from a few of them that I had been allowed to use a school mailing list for political purposes.

Two of my friends and fellow graduates from Macalester College, Democrat Q. T. Johnson and Republican Dan Peterson, signed a letter to everyone else in our college graduating class. I knew that wouldn't produce much, as most Mac grads were liberal Democrats, but it was worth a shot.

We sent a letter to other Supreme Court Fellows alumni, even though most of them were professors and not flush with cash. It did return a little money.

The Root-Tilden Scholarship at New York University School of Law was given to 20 people each year who were committed to public service. Gail decided to mail a fundraising letter asking for $250 to my graduating class plus the two classes before and the two after. She gave me the list to make follow-up calls. I knew fewer than half of the names in the other classes, but I called every one of them. A bit embarrassing, but we raised some good money.

The worst was when Gail handed me a list of the managing partners— the administrators—of the 100 largest law firms in Minnesota and told me to call them. She seemed to think the managing partners controlled the firm's money. I knew this was a loser. First, each partner at a law firm made his or her own political contributions; we could just as well call any lawyer at each firm at random. Second, chances were only 50-50 the managing partner was even a Republican. Third, busy lawyers would not react well to cold calls from some bozo candidate they didn't even know. Still, I didn't want to dampen any of Gail's fundraising ideas, and I needed to be working as hard as she was. Gail told me to make the calls, so I did.

This string of calls was agony, the most embarrassing thing I did the whole campaign. Of course, the calls raised next to nothing. The only thing the calls accomplished was to give the impression to legal opinion leaders around the state that I was a candidate desperate enough to make a cold call to them. Almost all of the partners took my call, which was positive in itself, but they politely declined to accept my kind offer to participate in the campaign. For example, George Mikan, the famous basketball player, was on the list. I called and asked to speak with him. He came on the phone. I told him what I wanted. He said he wasn't really into politics and was apologetic that he couldn't help. I thanked him and hung up. What else was there to say?

The fundraising stone we still had left unturned was telemarketing. I kept telling Gail that other candidates had major telemarketing operations calling every night. Bert McKasy had been at it for a year. Rod Grams had jumped into the race in December with both feet and a telephone. Al Quist's gubernatorial campaign was humming along nicely on telemarketing dollars. We knew these other candidates were active because we kept receiving reports from our people that they had been called. The others must have been making money. Why weren't we?

A year earlier, both Gail and her husband Tony Sutton had explained that telemarketing was risky. The marketer charged a flat fee for each call made, plus a percentage of money raised. I wasn't well enough known to make telemarketing profitable. Now, I said to Gail, I've been on the campaign trail for a year, and have 35 to 40 percent statewide name recognition. We have to take the chance. At the least, we get a political contact from the call. Gail checked with some telemarketers again, and again said it was too risky.

I tried another tack. If we can't hire a professional telemarketer, why can't we just talk a supporter into letting us use the telephones in his or her office for a few evenings and have some of our volunteers make fundraising calls? Finally, Gail told me she had found a small law firm that would turn over its telephones to us every evening for a week. Telemarketing with no downside risk! We would raise money—and make political contacts. Things were looking up.

After the first three nights, I eagerly asked Gail "How much money have we raised?"

"Not much."

Huh? "I don't understand. Why not?"

Gail seemed reluctant to answer. Eventually, she said "We've been polling potential convention delegates on their choices for Senate and governor. We haven't been asking for money."

My mouth actually dropped open. I knew Gail was a political operator, not a fundraiser, but this was a shock. "Gail, I thought we were using the telephone bank to raise money, not to do polling!"

"Well, I thought we really needed some polling numbers."

"Crissakes, we need money more. We have two nights left. Let's use them to make some fundraising calls."

"OK, if you say so" Gail responded. For all I know, she probably continued polling the next two nights. I didn't ask again. She was the manager.

As an aside, today we would exploit the internet for both campaigning and fundraising. Candidates set up a campaign website and collect a boatload of small contributions. We had a lot of supporters without large incomes whose small contributions would have helped a lot. We did not do that because the internet was largely an unknown. I remember being asked by a friendly questioner at a candidate forum what I would do about regulation of the internet; I hardly knew what he was even talking about and my answer must have shown it. At least he took me aside after the event and helpfully suggested I should bone up on this coming subject. That may make the campaign seem to have been back in the dark ages, but the exploding growth of the internet only makes it seem so.

★ ★ ★ ★ ★

The primary political task for me was to write my speech to give at as many Basic Political Organizational Unit conventions as I could reach in

March and April. It emphasized election year opportunity, quoted Abraham Lincoln, mentioned conservative stances, and included two sure-fire shout-out-and-applaud lines. One was "I know *Roe v. Wade* is wrong, and when the American Bar Association endorsed *Roe*, I quit! You can count on my prolife vote and advocacy." Rod Grams was not going to out-prolife me in this round of conventions. The other hot response line involved President Bill Clinton: "Character counts. The last election we tried to tell the American people to look at character. They didn't, and now we have a President who cares less about foreign affairs than his own personal affairs." That line went over like gangbusters everywhere except in my old suburban home district 45 in Minnetonka, where a woman from the audience commented loudly "Oh, that's mean." I retorted "Well, he deserves it."

Since the winner of the Republican Senate endorsement at the state convention would be one of four peas-in-a-pod conservatives, I struggled to give the delegates a reason to choose me over the others. The best I could do was "It's not just voting right on the issues; it's also who can lead in the Senate. Here's another reason. I have never been and never will be a career politician. In fact, I'm the only candidate in this race who is not a professional politician, trying for yet another rung on the career ladder. You know, it makes sense that politician begins with 'p' because they are interested in pay, perks, pensions, and padding staffs. I'm not. I want to go to Washington to serve you, not myself." That bit of fluff wasn't much to distinguish me from the others, but the local district convention speech was not the time or place to go negative. Even that mildest of nods toward negativity earned me a few unappreciative comments from supporters of other candidates who cornered me after the speech at the conventions.

Convention season began in earnest on Saturday, March 9. I know several things with certainty about this day. The first thing is Mary, Gail, and I spent the entire day from dawn until well into the night hitting every possible local BPOU convention we could cram into the hours available. The second thing is we started northwest in the vast seventh district and worked our way southwest into the friendly second district. The third thing is we appeared at eight or nine conventions and drove over 500 miles. The fourth thing is I have absolutely no memory of the day; despite racking my brain, I am unable to remember a single event or convention from the entire day. Now that seems passing strange. Two possible explanations come to mind.

One, Mary tells me she believes we started the day with the Clay County convention in Moorhead. With my previous disastrous experiences in Moorhead, I wouldn't be surprised to have blocked the entire day from my conscious mind.

Two, over the past year, I had swept comprehensively around the state four times, and had also made hundreds of separate trips to meetings and events in all corners of the state. The routine was getting a little old. I had a feeling of deja vu all over again and again and again. The fifth appearance in a town did not sear itself into memory.

During the weekdays following the first convention Saturday, Gail relayed reports about the results of the delegate elections to the upcoming state convention. In this first round of BPOU conventions, challenger Allen Quist was mopping the floor with incumbent governor Arne Carlson. She also heard from key people in local districts with conventions yet to come that the same result was expected across the state. All indications were Quist was easily going to win party endorsement, which required 60 percent of the votes, on the first ballot at the state convention in June.

Good for Quist. More power to him. I would have said good for Carlson too, had he been winning. The outcome of the gubernatorial race didn't matter to me. I could live with either one. A majority of my people were also Quist people, but I had many Carlson people behind me too. I had told everyone I was staying out of that race and I meant it.

Local BPOU conventions would begin anew Friday evening in Minneapolis, starting off what would be another full Saturday. In the meantime, on Friday morning I was in my office preparing for class when the telephone rang. That sound set into motion the big mistake.

"Doug, Doug" Gail said breathlessly.

Oh, no, what now? What new disaster?

"Doug, I heard that Bert's going to endorse Quist!"

"Bert McKasy's going to endorse Quist?" I laughed out loud. "That can't be right. Why would he do that?"

Gail's words spilled out even faster. "Yes, Bert's going to endorse Quist! He's going to endorse Quist and scoop up all the Quist delegates!"

"No, Gail, that doesn't make sense. He'll just alienate all the Carlson delegates."

"Doug, there aren't going to be any Carlson delegates. Quist is going to win big. When Bert endorses him, all the Quist delegates will go to Bert too. They'll give him the Senate endorsement!"

"Gail, it can't be that bad."

"It is that bad. This is really, really bad news. This will cost you the endorsement."

I wasn't ready to buy into her thinking. A lot of events in past months had been going to cost me the endorsement. Still, I asked "Well, what can we do about it?"

"We can beat Bert to the punch and endorse Quist first!"

Wow! My eyes popped wide open. I hadn't expected that. I shook my head side to side. "Oooh, I don't think so" I said. "I've told everyone I'm staying out of the governor's race." Telling everyone I didn't have a candidate in the gubernatorial race was the smart political position, plus it had the added advantage of being true.

"Doug, I think we have to do it, and we have to do it soon before Bert. You can't just say 'Me too.' The first candidate to endorse Quist will get all his delegates."

"Oh, no, I don't think this is a good idea, Gail. What makes you think this isn't just another wild political rumor?"

"It's not" Gail said. "It's reliable."

"Ahh, crap. I can't think about this now. I have to go teach class."

"Well, call me back as soon as class is over. We have to act fast. Bert might even endorse Quist today."

"Gail, I don't like this. Have you talked with anyone about it?"

She answered "We have to keep it close. If Bert finds out, he'll beat us to the punch."

"We'll have to take that chance. Call some of our closest people—the ones who can keep their mouths shut—and sound them out about this. Report back to me."

I went off to teach class. After it was over, I called Mary with the news. Her initial reaction was the same as mine: bad idea.

Gail called back early in the afternoon. She said "I've talked to some people, and I don't think Bert is going to do it today, so we have a little time. We can talk about it on the way to conventions tomorrow."

I said "OK, but what about the idea itself? Do our people think it will fly?"

"Yes," she responded, "they do. And I do. I think you should schedule a press conference and endorse Quist. If you did it today, we could take advantage of it at the BPOU conventions tomorrow."

"I sure as hell am not going to do it today" I said. "I'll think about it overnight and we'll talk about it tomorrow."

Here I made a small mistake that helped create the big mistake. I should have made some calls myself and sounded out people whose political instincts I trusted. I didn't, partly because we didn't want any leaks, and partly because Gail told me she was collecting advice. I admit too that I didn't like to make telephone calls; I was glad to leave the calls to Gail. I trusted her political instincts and even more her political network.

I thought about the idea for the rest of the day. We didn't want to act precipitously, but we couldn't let Bert strike while I dithered. I'd always prided myself on being able to make decisions quickly. This one I couldn't get my mind around. My instincts shouted no, but my advisers said yes.

Decision-making in a campaign is chaotic. Over earlier years, I had always pictured political campaigns as unfolding according to some master plan. Events always seemed to fit into the plan as if foreordained. Now a candidate, I was in the middle of a maelstrom, making daily decisions based on rumor, fragmentary information, guesswork, or even ignorance. Instead of following a master plan, Gail and I were in a chaotic, no-holds-barred struggle to react to daily crises. Acting on this type of information and with this type of time pressure, we were bound to make mistakes—a lot of mistakes. Fortunately, most of them didn't cost much. Whether to endorse Quist or to remain neutral seemed to be only another in the long string of tactical decisions we made under time pressure, on inadequate information, over many months. In fact, this was the big mistake of the entire campaign.

★ ★ ★ ★ ★

Saturday morning Gail arrived at our house well before seven a.m. The first thing she wanted to know was whether I had decided to endorse Quist. I told her I hadn't decided.

"Well, let's talk about it today," she said. "Bert will be on the road all day today too, so he won't be endorsing Quist today, but we may need to act tomorrow to schedule a press conference for Monday."

The three of us—Gail, Mary, and I—hit the road for our second full Saturday of BPOU conventions. Gail had arrival and departure times scheduled for eight conventions beginning in the city of Rochester (Olmstead County) and ending in the small town of Rushford. Because Olmsted County was the big Republican prize of the day, every statewide and local candidate was there. We had to sit through speeches by almost every one of them. That made us run late all day. Even so, we hit conventions in Dodge Center, Owatonna, Mankato, Albert Lea, Brownsdale, and Rushford. Our only miss was Faribault in the middle of the afternoon; we pulled into town to find the delegates emerging from the elementary school.

I don't remember much about this day of conventions either, except for small snippets about one or two of the halls. I know this was our day because I still have the schedule on a yellow pad sheet with the conventions checked off.

If the conventions have blurred together in my memory, I have to wonder about the memories of the delegates at the conventions. Candidates tear around the state giving speech after speech. Delegates sit through a dozen or more of these speeches., most sounding the same themes. By the end of the day, what does the average convention delegate remember about each candidate? At the time, I believed we were making real progress. We were driving all these miles and being seen and heard by all these delegates. Looking back, I'm not so sure. Was I making a lasting impression on the listeners, or was my appearance merely thrown into the blender of a few hours of convention, so that I became only an ingredient of a candidate puree?

One thing I do remember is that the three of us kicked around the decision about endorsing Quist all day. Gail kept pushing for the endorsement. Quist has slates of delegates at all the conventions, and most of the slates are being elected; he's whopping Carlson at least two-to-one in elected delegates. Quist is going to win the endorsement for governor easily. Yes, the slates are causing some hard feelings and resentment among the Carlson people, especially some who've been active in the party for a long time, but that's politics. We have to jump on the bandwagon and take advantage. We can pick up all the Quist people. Carlson may not even seek endorsement at the convention if Quist has all the delegates locked up. If Bert McKasy endorses Quist before we do, all the delegates will go to Bert.

Against her entreaties, I had no political strategy arguments to make. I had only my own sense that it would be a dumb thing to do. By the time we pulled back into our driveway at ten p.m., fifteen hours and some 570 miles after leaving, I still was not close to a decision.

Sunday evening former state party chair Bob Weinholzer shared an 80-mile ride with Gail and me to the senate district 14 convention in St. Cloud. Bob was making the rounds of the local conventions telling delegates he was running for state treasurer. Even though we rode together, we had separate campaigns, so we entered the restaurant dining room where the convention was meeting a few minutes apart. At the convention both Bob and I made our pitches to the delegates. On the way home, I drove. Bob sat in the middle row of the minivan on the passenger side. I turned to him and asked what he thought about my endorsing Al Quist.

Bob responded in the measured pace that was his custom. "Well, Doug, given the results of the conventions, which as you saw, continued through today in district 14, Quist is cleaning up in the delegate count."

"Yeah, so I saw."

"Quist is a genuine hero to the party activists who are going to be the great majority of delegates to the convention in June. If you endorse their hero, you can bask in Quist's reflected glory at the convention. If you're with their man, they'll likely be with you."

"But, Bob, do you think the delegates will make the transfer?"

"These are smart people. They'll appreciate what you've done."

"What about the Carlson people? I've been telling everyone I'm neutral."

"Well, Doug, that was then, and this is now. You were telling them the truth at the time, but times have changed. You know, there just aren't going to be that many Carlson delegates."

"I still hate to go back on what I said."

"We know Bert is thinking about endorsing Quist. If Bert does it first, he'll rake in all the political capital from the move."

"Uh-huh."

"Doug, all of this adds up to the conclusion that endorsing Quist would be a smart political move. I think you should do it, and do it as soon as possible," he concluded.

My common sense still sent shivers up my spine, but my two key advisers were both recommending—urging—the move. "OK," I said, "I'll do it."

In the moment, the decision seemed to be high risk with the potential of high reward: a bold, daring, decisive gamble, one that took political courage to make. If the proper analogy were not rolling dice, then surely it was poker. Like a poker player with only a short stack of chips left, I pushed all my chips into the pot on a less than ideal hand.

Monday morning, Gail called a press conference for Tuesday afternoon. We told no one of the content, not even Quist. The word didn't leak out. We were excited. We were going to beat Bert McKasy to the punch!

Tuesday afternoon I told reporters that I had been inundated at the local conventions by questions from delegates about the gubernatorial race, and delegates had a right to know my personal position. Our press release noted "While McFarland has thrown his support to Quist, the other four Republican Senatorial candidates have all either previously expressed their support or worked for Governor Carlson." Real subtle.

The reporters were enthused at the press conference. As I walked out of the room, I said to Bill Salisbury of the *Pioneer Press* "Thanks for coming." Salisbury smiled broadly as he said "Thanks for making news." Both Twin Cities newspapers featured big stories and included a reaction from a Carlson campaign spokesman that this was "finger-in-the-wind politics." Of course, I denied that. Who could think such a thing?

I didn't feel bad about endorsing Allen Quist. He seemed to be a good man who could do the job. I did feel a little bad about endorsing someone trying to take the job from popular incumbent Arne Carlson, as he seemed to be a good man who could continue to do the job. The endorsement wasn't about the two men, their campaigns, or their political philosophies. It was about my campaign. I had pushed all my remaining chips into the pot, and soon enough I would find out whether they would produce a winner or a loser.

That same evening was my home district 53A convention in Arden Hills/Shoreview. I was standing in the aisle of the middle school auditorium when I heard one woman say "Oh, that's McFarland. He's the guy who endorsed Quist, so he must be all right." Yes! The reaction we wanted.

The next morning was a breakfast event sponsored by the Center for the American Experiment. At the end, I approached Wheelock Whitney, who had told me in our meeting a year earlier that his priority for the year was re-electing Arne Carlson. Whitney glared at me. I said "I see you've heard of my endorsement yesterday."

"Yeah."

"As I told you when we met at your office a year ago, I'm trying to bring both sides of the party together."

"Humph."

"I'm hoping to bring prolife conservatives around a little," I said as I made a circling motion with my hand.

"Hah," he snorted. "You've just joined them." No! Not the reaction we wanted. Whitney's invitation to play golf with him at Augusta National would not likely be forthcoming.

The next evening, we drove to Duluth for two senate district BPOU conventions. Time and again, Carlson people came up to me with hurt in their eyes. I tried to explain to them that my endorsement of Quist should not affect their support for me. They said they could not continue to support a Senate candidate who had endorsed Quist. No! Definitely not the reaction we wanted.

On the drive home from Duluth, Gail went out like a light as soon as we left town. She was totally worn out from her heroic efforts in the convention season over the past few weeks. After about 50 miles, I saw a highway billboard for the casino in Hinckley. Gail often talked about liking to stop by casinos, so I decided to surprise and reward her. We pulled into the parking lot of the casino, and I woke up Gail. She stumbled, half-asleep, into the casino, withdrew $20 from the cash machine, and plopped down at a blackjack table. Four straight losing hands later, she stood up and stumbled back to the car. So much for a reward.

That Saturday was the last big day of BPOU conventions around the state. Once again, three of us were on the road from before dawn until after dusk. Once again, I have almost no memory of the day. I do know that we were in greater Minnesota, and Carlson people were few and far between. These people were for Quist. That meant they should be my people too, but that remained to be seen. No one complained about the endorsement, but no one praised it either.

Of the entire day, I remember a single convention. We arrived at the Todd County convention in Long Prairie in northwest Minnesota shortly after lunchtime. After my speech, the first delegate who raised his hand asked whether I thought the country should go back on the gold standard. Now there's one you didn't hear every day—in fact, I'd never heard it. Every once in a while a candidate runs into a delegate who is off in a strange corner by himself. The best response is to answer in a few words and move on. Next question.

The second delegate asked a follow-up question about the gold standard. With commendable effort, I kept my eyes from bugging out. The third delegate wanted my opinion on whether the Internal Revenue Service was illegal. I don't know whether these activists ended up as Quist delegates or Carlson delegates, but I'm pretty sure they didn't line up behind a know-nothing who couldn't answer a few simple questions about the gold standard and related issues of prime importance to the country.

* * * * *

The election year BPOU local district convention season ended as March became April. The results of my endorsement gamble emerged slowly over the next several days.

Part of our analysis had been correct. More than two-thirds of the delegates elected to the state convention were for Quist. He was going to beat Carlson for the gubernatorial endorsement on the first ballot. The more important question to us was how many of the Quist delegates were grateful enough that I had endorsed their man to vote for me? Turned out the Quist delegates felt no reflected warmth or carryover gratitude toward me at all. On the other hand, delegates loyal to Carlson didn't necessarily know who they would endorse for Senate, but they knew damn straight who they wouldn't endorse. They were mad as hell that I had stabbed their man in the back, especially after my many claims of neutrality.

So, 30 percent of the state convention delegates—the Carlson delegates—were gone for good. That left 70 percent of the delegates—the Quist delegates. While Joanell Dyrstad wasn't going to get any, the other four of us Senate competitors—Rod Grams, Bert McKasy, Gen Olson, and I—would split them. If I took my share, 70 percent divided by four, that would give me maybe 18 percent of the total delegates at the convention. That's a mite short of the 60 percent needed to endorse. I had lost and lost big.

Looking back, I now see the decision to take the gamble was a gasp for life by a campaign suffering congestive cash failure. We had little money and therefore little choice. Also, I made the decision based on too narrow a range of political advice. Not only was Gail Sutton advising me as a committed social conservative and Quist fan, but also I thought I was getting a second, independent opinion from Bob Weinholzer, the former state party chair, and his years of Minnesota political experience. A few years later, I found out Gail and Bob really were more like two halves of one political animal when they married. My guess today is the idea had probably been Bob's in the first place. Even so, I failed to make the additional telephone calls. That was my own boneheaded fault.

My gamble to endorse Allen Quist turned out to be the big mistake of the campaign. When Gail first proposed to me the endorsement, my immediate reaction was bad idea. It turned out to be disastrous. I had no one to blame but myself; I should have stuck with my first reaction. People always say your first reaction is best.

CHAPTER NINETEEN

Dead Candidate Walking

By the first week of April, the BPOU convention season was complete. The eight congressional district conventions would begin a few weeks later, on Saturday, April 22. While my campaign never ran on even a half-full tank of gas, by this time it was not even running on fumes. The financial tank was dry.

Gail Sutton, Bob Weinholzer, and I met in the small campaign office to discuss a tentative budget forward to the state convention in June. With the congressional district conventions fast approaching, we needed to spend some money soon. Gail had prepared a budget with expenses for a new literature piece for the district conventions, hospitality suites at two of them, and travel and lodging of our teams. Even doing everything on the cheap, we were talking about thousands of dollars that we didn't have.

I shook my head as I looked at the budget. "Gail, can't we just print some more of the same literature piece we used at the BPOU conventions? That would save money."

"No" she answered. "If people see you trying to recycle the same literature piece, they'll know you don't have any money."

"Well, at least we can dump these damn hospitality suites. You know how much I hate them anyway."

"No" she repeated. "All the other candidates will have hospitality suites. If you don't have one, you'll stick out like a sore thumb."

Bob chimed in "Gail is right. You may think you're saving money, but all the delegates will think you don't have any money. You're trying to sell the same message as Bert, Rod, and Gen. Why should a delegate vote for you if you can't even afford a hospitality suite?"

"You must have a hospitality suite at the second and seventh districts," said Gail. "They're having social events on the Friday evenings before their conventions. We're lucky that the other six districts are having only the convention. You won't need a suite at those."

I kept looking at the numbers for a few more dollars to slice.

Gail said "I don't think you'll find anything. That's a bare bones budget."

As I continued to scan the figures and shake my head, Bob said "We both think this thing is still winnable."

"You do?" I said, looking up hopefully. "Do you really think so?"

Gail answered. "Yes, we do. Bob and I have talked about this a lot, and we both think that we still have a chance. All eight district conventions will have straw ballots. We won't do very well in the first or third, but we should take our share in the other six. If we can make a good showing in the straw ballots at six of the conventions, you can go into the state convention as a viable candidate, and who knows what will happen there?"

"That's right" Bob said. "Rod is probably ahead, but he doesn't have it locked up. With all four of you fighting for the endorsement, the votes could shift all kinds of ways. You wouldn't have to be the leader. If, say, Rod and Bert deadlocked, you might be everyone's compromise candidate. No one is against you; the problem is, right now, not enough delegates are for you."

Obviously, I liked what they were saying. A unanimous first ballot endorsement by acclamation would be nicer, but a late-night compromise squeaker would work. I said "So what are you telling me?"

Gail said "Bob and I have gone over the figures and decided that $6000 will get us through the district convention season. If you do well, money should come in. If you don't, well, then—."

"You want me to throw in another $6000?"

They both nodded.

"I can do that by selling a few more stocks, but I don't want to throw good money after bad. Do you both really think another $6000 gives me a realistic chance and I wouldn't just be throwing it down the toilet?"

They both nodded again. "I think if you throw in $6000, you can still win the party endorsement" said Bob.

All decisions should be so easy. My two options were to walk away from 18 months of grueling, intense, debilitating effort with empty hands, or to throw in some more of my own money and keep fighting and hoping. I sold some stocks and wrote the check. I owed the contribution to myself. More importantly, I owed it to Gail Sutton, Steve Clark, Bob Weinholzer, and all the people who had thrown their dreams and efforts in with me.

★ ★ ★ ★ ★

A few days later, I received a telephone call from Barbara Seagle-Peterson, one of the three secretaries for Chief Justice William H. Rehnquist. I knew her from my days at the Supreme Court a decade earlier; at the time she worked for my boss Chief Justice Warren E. Burger, and she had made the transition to the new Chief. She was an elegant woman, combining a soft, melodious, light southern accent with solid, competent efficiency.

Seagle-Peterson had heard about my campaign. She wanted to leave the Supreme Court and be my secretary in the Senate. What a day brightener! I wanted to jump up and down. I wanted to say "Absolutely, Barbara. I'm thrilled you're interested. You can count on it." Of course, I couldn't say that in good faith. Prospects didn't look good. I had slipped from front-runner to a hanger-on hoping to be a compromise choice at a deadlocked convention. All I could honestly say was "I have to get elected first, Barbara, and I have some competition. Let's see how the campaign goes over the next few months. You may be sure I will remember you if I can get to Washington."

Speaking of people from Washington, I attended the annual Minnesota Republican party fundraising dinner the next evening with guest speaker former Congressman Jack Kemp. I had met him when he hosted one of the White House Fellows/Supreme Court Fellows luncheons. Kemp was at that time and remained a viable future Republican presidential candidate and a national spokesman for conservatives. At the luncheon in Washington, Kemp was able to include more words per minute than any other speaker I have heard before or since. His performance was impressive. At the end of luncheon, one of the Fellows joked "I feel I've been listening to a 33 and 1/3 record being played at 78 for the past hour." Another added "I was sitting right across from him and think I have windburn."

At the Republican dinner a decade later in Minnesota, Kemp did not speak so rapidly. He must have saved that pace for small groups.

★　★　★　★　★

Friday evening, April 15, all five Republican candidates for Senate appeared together on the public television show *Almanac* hosted by Eric Eskola and Cathy Wurzer. Our segment of the hour-long show was only 15 minutes. Eskola asked each of us to identify one primary issue for the next Congress. I said we had to eliminate the federal deficit and stop passing taxes along to our children. Gen Olson said education. Rod Grams agreed the key issue was the deficit. Joanell Dyrstad said jobs. Bert McKasy said health care.

The quarter-hour was long enough for a few more questions and answers, and a couple of games of what I call campaign gotcha. Dyrstad, who was still the sitting Lieutenant Governor under Arne Carlson, attempted the first gotcha by mentioning that Allen Quist had recently been quoted to the effect that the wife should be subordinate to the husband in the household. She challenged the rest of us to disassociate ourselves from that remark. McKasy immediately said his wife Carolyn was more than his equal. Since I was the only one who had endorsed Quist, this gotcha was really targeted at me. I ended the first game by saying "I wouldn't have said it, but I'm not going to tell him what to say."

McKasy then tried for a gotcha. He reached into the inside pocket of his suit coat and pulled out a pledge he had signed not to run in the primary election if he did not receive the party endorsement at the Republican state convention in June. This game was targeted at Rod Grams. McKasy challenged him to sign the pledge right then and there. Grams bobbed and weaved as he both agreed to accept the delegates' endorsement decision and backed away from pledging to abide by it.

Who cared whether Rod Grams pledged to abide by the party endorsement? The people who cared were the delegates to the state convention. A delegate wanted to make a difference. A candidate who tried for the endorsement, was turned down, and ran in the primary anyway, would be thumbing his nose at the delegates. Many delegates would not vote for a candidate at the convention who refused to accept their decision.

The decision to abide by the party endorsement was a no-brainer for me. I had no money, so the concept of going on to the primary without party endorsement was ridiculous. A sitting Congressman like Rod Grams, or a sitting governor like Arne Carlson, could realistically raise enough money to be able to kiss off the convention delegates and go to the voters.

Soon enough, the small segment of *Almanac* was over. None of the five of us had scored or gaffed. The evening was a wash.

Watching a videotape of the show, I was struck by one thing. Four of us looked good on television; former television news anchorman Rod Grams looked great. He was good-looking; not a strand of hair was out of place. His voice was mellifluous and soothing. Grams's answers were confident, smooth, and measured. He was a comfortable, solid presence. Television was his medium. He put on a good show. The rest of us were in trouble.

The frustrating thing was that, over the months of competitive campaigning, I had come to conclude that Grams was all good show. Rod was a good guy, to be sure, but he just didn't have the substance to be a Senator. Several of us in our inside circle talked time and again about how to convey that to activists. We never thought of a way I could do that without looking like a sourpuss. I could have said to a delegate, "Think, man! For endorsement, you can choose from McKasy, a lawyer and businessman; Olson, who holds a doctorate in education; me, a lawyer with a doctorate; or Grams. A recent survey we all filled out asked, 'In a word, what is the single greatest obstacle confronting Republican candidates?' Rod answered, 'unity.' Do you really think he has the ability to carry our conservative message in Washington?" Delegates would have run for the hills from such negativity.

A few times, I did try telling delegates "Please take a close look at the credentials of all of us, and decide who will best carry the conservative message in the Senate." Too subtle. They didn't get it.

One time when a delegate praised Grams to me, I went so far as to say "Yes, he can read a script well." From the narrowed eyes of the delegate, I could tell he caught the barb, and he didn't like it. He was still voting for Grams. The only difference was that I probably dropped from second to last in his preference list.

Politics requires unnatural acts. People who run for public office are competitive. They go into battle. They are willing to lay it on the line. Yet open, no-holds-barred competition is impossible. Candidates must compete with one arm, or at times both arms, tied behind the back. When an opposing candidate makes a false claim, the acceptable response is "I believe my opponent has misstated the matter somewhat," instead of the far more personally satisfying "My opponent is either a bald-faced liar or hasn't got the brains to know truth from falsity." Of an opponent not up to snuff, an acceptable argument is "I can carry the party message better," but not the inner thought "He's a moron who couldn't argue his way out of a paper bag." The problem is especially acute in Minnesota, where people pride themselves on being Minnesota Nice. "Have a nice day!" is ubiquitous. Politicians can't really compete.

My first political encounter with the general public was a campaign for the Minnesota state house 20 years earlier. On my very first day of door-to-door campaigning, I eagerly approached the first house and rang the first bell. A woman opened the door.

"Hi, I'm Doug McFarland, and I'm running for the state house of representatives. Could I leave a piece of literature with you or answer any questions?"

"No. I don't believe in politics. I don't want your literature."

"Well, maybe I could just leave this piece and you might look at it later?"

"If you do, I'll just walk through the house with it directly to the wastebasket."

Now what? Any candidate worth his or her salt smiles a brave smile, says "Thanks anyway," and moves on to the next house. That's what I did. What did I want to do? A quick, economical flipping of the bird would have sufficed. This person would then have believed enough in politics to tell all her neighbors about the ass who came to her door. That would have been one way to ensure name recognition.

Worse was a homeowner later in the same campaign. As I stepped onto the porch—literature in hand, reaching for the doorbell—she appeared on the other side of the screen door and announced brightly "I'm voting for your opponent John." She was so cheery and so in your face. I said "Let me just leave a piece of literature for you then. You might read it over and change your mind." Yes, indeed, the temperature was dropping fast in hell. I really wanted to say "I hope you'll be happy with your vote for that incompetent boob, and by the way, you're obviously a nut case yourself." Once again that would have been satisfying to let the competitive juices flow, but it would have been neither politically astute nor Minnesota Nice.

★ ★ ★ ★ ★

By this time of the election year, the national media had taken notice of the Minnesota Senate race. We had successfully convinced the editors at *Human Events* that I was a reliable, prolife conservative. They ran a "Senate Roundup" that identified Rod Grams and me as the two contenders for the endorsement with the other three candidates as also-rans. They even called me "feisty," and said I was "a dynamo on the stump."

Candidate on the stump

Not so successful was the treatment by writers at *National Review*. They ran a "Political Notebook" in February that essentially endorsed Rod Grams and dismissed me as "only mildly active in party politics," with "no political experience to speak of." Gail and I decided that Vin Weber, who had connections at the publication, was probably behind the article. I couldn't resist firing back a letter to the editor. The problem was that I had to try to remain positive, not to criticize a fellow Republican, and not to alienate Vin Weber. With those constraints, I was able only to recount my long party experience and say that Grams was not fiscally conservative enough. The letter served only to give the writers a chance to reaffirm their endorsement of Grams in the April issue.

★ ★ ★ ★ ★

What all of this meant was that the four contenders for the party endorsement—Grams, McFarland, McKasy, and Olson (Dyrstad having no chance)—entered the eight April congressional district conventions trying to convince the delegates each was the most reliable conservative. The only things we had to differentiate ourselves from the others were nitpicks.

As to Gen Olson, Gail and I figured she was running fourth of four. We decided I didn't need to say anything about her.

As to Bert McKasy, Gail prepared talking points for me that included his vote in the state legislature for gun control, his vote in the legislature for the Democratic position on the state tax bill, and some nepotism concerns when he was a state commissioner. Not exactly hot stuff.

As to Rod Grams, Gail's talking points for me included his apparent willingness to go to the primary, his refusal to support sufficient budget cuts, his vote against boot camps for first-time criminal offenders, and his earlier endorsement of Arne Carlson for governor before he flip-flopped to neutral. Rod also had done some odd things: he told a reporter he was disappointed not to find smoke-filled rooms in the endorsement process, and he announced his candidacy and the same day flew off to New York instead of staying in Minnesota. Also, not exactly hot stuff. A delegate who looked at the four of us most likely thought "Why don't I just go with the proved commodity and vote for the sitting Congressman?" I wanted desperately to compete, to rip Rod's political guts out, to tell delegates what I really thought of his abilities, and I was able only to smile and nitpick that he might not trust the decision of the delegates.

The opening congressional district convention was in the third district, set for Friday evening at the Sheraton Park Plaza Hotel in St. Louis Park. What a bad omen. The convention season started in my weakest district, and at the hotel that was the site of the state central committee meeting debacle nearly a year earlier.

Every candidate for Senate, for governor, for secretary of state, for auditor, for treasurer, for attorney general, for Congress, for local offices, showed up to spout two cents to the delegates. So did party officials. I felt sorry for the delegates. By late Friday evening, they had listened to more than two dozen politicians each try to be memorable. Rod Grams won the straw ballot for Senate, but that wasn't a surprise. We didn't expect to do well in the third. I was satisfied with my finish, and ecstatic that the evening convention meant no hospitality suite.

The next morning, nearly all of the same candidates were on the highway north to Brainerd for the eighth district convention. As we had all done the evening before, all of us arrived early to grip and grin with as many delegates as possible. We all delivered our speeches, and we all listened politely to the others' speeches—when we were not working individual delegates in the side aisles. None of us had experienced a revelation overnight, so the Saturday speeches offered no surprises. All the candidates' speeches were not only repetitions of the evening before, but also were repetitions of each other. After all, only so many cashable, crowd-pleasing conservative buttons can be pushed.

At the end of the morning, as the delegates formed a line to the lunchroom, Gail tried to propel Mary and me toward the head of the line so we could shake the hand of every delegate. I said no. Gail and I often had the same disagreement.

Gail was convinced the candidate needed to get as close and cozy as possible with the delegates. That meant repeated telephone calls, constant schmoozing, rubbing shoulders, and shaking hands in the lunch line. I suppose if she could have figured out how to position me tastefully in the men's room, she would have pushed for that, too.

On the other hand, I believed a candidate should maintain some remoteness and mystery. I had read many political biographies in which the candidate/leader did just that. A delegate saying "Oh, look, there's McFarland," seemed to me much better than, "Oh, it's just Doug again." Of course, maintaining some distance melded with my own personality, but that was not the primary basis. I'd rather vote for a leader instead of a next-door buddy, and I think others would like to do that too.

As usual, Gail won. Mary and I marched to the head of the lunch line and started shaking hands. This spot was particularly unnerving to me. I mentally placed myself into the head of every delegate who passed by. The last thing I wanted to do before picking up my food was to shake hands with a guy who's been pressing the flesh with everyone else in the room all morning. Why doesn't he just rub his germy fingers over my silverware while he's at it?

The vote in the afternoon straw ballot for Senate was evenly divided amongst the four of us. By this time, Rod Grams had become the front-runner for the endorsement, so the other three of us were engaging in stop-Grams efforts. When no clear winner emerged from the ballot, we all went home happy.

★ ★ ★ ★ ★

Wednesday, April 27, was a big day for the campaign. Ed Meese, former Counselor to President Ronald Reagan, former Attorney General of the U.S., and national conservative icon, came to town.

The first event was a luncheon for about 25 large donors at the downtown Minneapolis Club. Ed and I sat at the head of the table side by side. When the lunches were served, Ed reached for his fork. I noticed Cary Humphries halfway down the left side of the table rustling around, so I placed my hand over Ed's arm. Sure enough, Humphries spoke up and said "Should we say grace before eating?" We all agreed, and Cary gave the blessing.

The lunch was a huge success in goodwill. I said a few words. Ed said a few words and answered questions. Everyone who attended was thrilled to meet Ed Meese, and they all had a great time.

The lunch was less than a success financially. Most of the guests had already given money. Some had even already given the federal election individual max. I hated to have people give money for "nothing," and then try to squeeze more from them for a fundraising event. So, many of the people around the table were freebies.

After lunch, I asked Ed whether any possibility existed that he could induce former President Ronald Reagan to visit Minnesota for my campaign. That would have broken loose the fundraising dam! Ed said a visit was a possibility, wrote out the president's California office address, and said to use his name. What I didn't know was that Reagan had started his long journey with Alzheimer's disease, and wouldn't be making any more political appearances for anyone.

That evening we had a reception at the suburban Bloomington hotel where Ed was staying. This event was "popular," an event for the workers, activists, and small contributors. A crowd of 200, spread eight or ten to each round table, filled the room. Outside in the hallway, we had a silent auction underway with political memorabilia, including several copies of Ed's book *With Reagan*.

Ed Meese came in and lit up the crowd. In addition to being a truly nice man and a conservative hero, he also was something people didn't expect from accounts in the national press: a highly talented man and an excellent public speaker. Ed talked about getting to know me at the Supreme Court and at our church in Washington, and then he made the pitch for money. After quoting the truism "Money is the mother's milk of politics," he added "Sad but true, so I hope you'll be generous in contributing to Doug's campaign. We need more strong, honorable, honest people like him in the Senate."

All of us had a rip-roaring good time. The Minnesota activists shook hands with a national hero in the flesh. Ed enjoyed the occasion, too. As an outside observer to fame, I thought that a famous person didn't need any reinforcement. I've found over the years—in part at the Supreme Court and in part through this campaign—that famous people enjoy attention and reinforcement just as much as the obscure person. Ed hung with us to the end of the reception, even autographing his books for those who had purchased them. The event was a huge success from the standpoint of politics.

The event was another failure from the point of view of fundraising. The price of admission for most of the people attending was their hard volunteer work for my campaign instead of a financial contribution. Others had made contributions in the past. Few people attending contributed new money.

Virtually all of the people attending were party activists who were already committed to me. Activists supporting other candidates did not attend, although we welcomed them. The real group we were after, the traditional Republican donors, also did not attend.

This event turned out to be another object lesson in the split of the Republican party between the "conservative" activist worker bees and the "moderate" financial people, each of whom pretty much considers himself or herself the queen bee. These moderate donors of the party do not choose to work campaigns; stuffing envelopes is beneath them. They also do not choose to use their primary means of influence, money, on conservative candidates— until their only choice is between a conservative Republican and a liberal Democrat, and they are forced to choose the lesser of two evils. Here was a huge opportunity for them to be heard. They could attend a candidate's event, contribute some pocket change, whisper into the candidate's ear, and meet a national hero to boot. They all stayed home and wondered why the party continued to drift to the right.

The reception emptied out around nine p.m. At that point, all I wanted to do was pile Mary and the kids into the family minivan and go home to bed. Still, we had Ed Meese with us, and no one had eaten dinner. After thanking him again profusely, I said, "Ed, we can all have dinner somewhere near here, or if you're tired, I would certainly understand it."

He answered "Sure, let's go out for dinner."

"Are you sure you're not tired?"

"No, I'm ready to go. Where do you suggest?"

I hadn't really expected him to take up my offer, so I hadn't actually thought much about where to eat. I said "Did you have any type of food in mind?"

"No, anything's fine."

"OK, well, there are plenty of restaurants right along the highway here. Or we could head over to the hotel coffee shop. That would be easy."

"That's fine. Let's go to the coffee shop."

"All right, then." I decided to try again. "Now don't feel you have to go out with us if you're tired. We'll understand."

"No, I feel good. Let's all go have dinner."

We all had dinner in the hotel coffee shop. Even though the kids were pretty well zonked out, dinner was not the extension of the workday I had feared. Ed carried the conversation nicely. Mary and I truly enjoyed relaxing and listening to him tell stories.

Campaign events were hard work for me. I'd usually finish a hospitality suite, a reception, a dinner, or a convention exhausted, my shirt soaked in sweat. All I wanted to do was go home and recharge. That apparently shows I'm an introvert, a person who needs to have time alone to recover his energy. An extrovert gains energy the opposite way, by getting into the crowd and interacting with people. Ed Meese is an extrovert.

A politician is better served by being an extrovert than an introvert, but you are who you are. Many successful politicians have been introverts. The question is whether an introvert can throw the switch to "on" for campaign events. "It's showtime!"

CHAPTER TWENTY

The Last Hurrahs

The first two congressional district conventions—the third and the eighth—had been on separate days. No problem. The next four all started at nine a.m. on the same Saturday. Problem. The fourth, fifth, and sixth districts were all in the Twin Cities. No problem. The seventh district was in Moorhead, some 250 miles distant. Problem.

The seventh district people decided to have a Friday evening Senate candidates' forum, followed by hospitality suites, before the Saturday morning convention. Together the forum and hospitality suites would run from 7:30 until nearly midnight. Nothing I liked better than the prospect of working a hospitality suite immediately after a mentally exhausting event like a candidates' forum. We had no choice. The forum was the only event in the state that Friday evening, so we wrote Moorhead in ink onto the calendar. The question was what to do after the forum?

Gail Sutton, Steve Clark, and I huddled in our small, one-room office and plotted strategy. As we had for congressional district conventions a year earlier, we again batted the options back and forth. This was one of the fun times in politics.

Option one. After the forum and hospitality suite, stay overnight in Moorhead, speak at the seventh district convention as early as possible Saturday morning, and then either drive like crazy or fly to the Twin Cities. Even with flying, we couldn't count on arrival at the fourth convention before it adjourned, and the plan also left the three Twin Cities conventions the scraps of my time. No good.

Option two. Drive home late Friday night after the hospitality suite closed, and speak to the three Twin Cities conventions on Saturday. A surrogate speaker would speak for me at the convention and remind people in the seventh I had been there the evening before. We would essentially be kissing off the seventh. No good.

Option three. Drive home late Friday night, speak to the three Twin Cities conventions on Saturday, and fly back to Moorhead. That would work, but the downside was I would be on the road until three a.m., and on Saturday I needed to be at my best. Not much good.

Option four. Stay overnight in Moorhead for a decent night's rest, fly to the Twin Cities early Saturday morning, speak at the three conventions, and fly back to Moorhead. I would be late getting back to the seventh, but I could mention the flying to impress delegates with our resources. We decided on option four.

Friday afternoon, I found myself rolling northwest on I-94 to Moorhead in a minivan crammed full of boisterous, young campaign workers. I was on the way to the evening candidates' forum. They were on the way to an evening of plastering the walls of the convention hall with posters followed by a morning of plastering every possible delegate with a red and white McFarland for Senate lapel sticker.

A half-hour before the 7:30 start of the candidate forum, I walked into the Holiday Inn ballroom to grip and grin with the delegates. Many of them were already milling about, making their own political connections. I saw Bert McKasy working a delegate. The room swam into and out of focus. Even though I'd walked into hundreds of political events over the months, the whole scene now seemed surreal. For the first time in the campaign, I felt like a disinterested, outside observer instead of a participant.

I sidled up to the first familiar face I saw and stuck out my hand. The delegate said "Oh, Doug, I'm so glad you're here. I heard that you dropped out of the race. I'm glad you didn't. You have to keep going."

"Well, I don't know where you might have heard that" I said. "I have heard that one of the campaigns is spreading false rumors to that effect here in the seventh district. That's just dirty tricks. Don't believe it for a second." I didn't mention Gail had heard the Grams people were behind the rumor.

The rumor was probably not hard for the delegates to believe. The other campaigns had been inundating them with mailings. Every week, and sometimes twice a week, the delegate found a letter or flyer in the mailbox from Joanell Dyrstad or Rod Grams or Bert McKasy or Gen Olson. The Grams campaign especially was spending a lot of money on mailings. In contrast, we mailed one lonely letter with a small piece of campaign literature enclosed. We could afford no more. Our single missive was easily lost in the tsunami of other candidates' mailings.

We probably should have acted more quickly to squash the rumor. We didn't for two reasons. First, I naively thought it was just another lowbrow political dirty trick that was too transparent to fool anybody. *Looking back, I realize now that these dirty tricks do fool even seasoned delegates. All such rumors and tricks should be addressed immediately.* Second, we didn't have the money to do much of anything about it anyway.

We could have played hardball ourselves. A tasty rumor about Rod Grams's personal life was circulating through a small group of party insiders. Gail and I discussed whether to promote it to delegates. For obvious reasons, I couldn't personally spread the rumor, but we had key people who could have done the job. I told Gail no. We weren't going to play that game.

The candidates' forum went as expected. With five of us responding and rebutting, the amount of time for each answer, and for each candidate, was not long enough to make much of an impression. A good answer didn't score many points, yet a bad answer could lose points. Consequently, the game for the candidates was to play safe. The goal was not to win; it was not to lose.

I watched the other candidates as they responded to the questions.

Joanell Dyrstad didn't really count; being prochoice, she had zero chance for the party endorsement. Bert McKasy was, as usual, earnest and serious. Bert lacked pizzazz. I wasn't that worried about Bert. Gen Olson was like the neighbor across the street: friendly and always willing to help. A super person. But that's your neighbor, not your Senator. I wasn't that worried about Gen. Rod Grams was polished and smooth. He was in control and apparently well-informed. He sounded great. Rod was killing me.

To a question about taxes, Rod delivered his standard lines on taxes. To a question about term limits, Rod delivered his lines on term limits. To a question about abortion, Rod delivered his lines on abortion. The pat answers rolled out of his mouth effortlessly. The only two times during the forum that he was thrown into brief bouts of stumbling and incoherence were when audience members asked unexpected questions. When he had no lines to roll through, Rod sounded confused and unorganized. After one delegate's subtly negative response to his answer, Rod turned to me and whispered "Was that a shot?" I allowed as how it was.

The delegates would choose among four candidates. All were conservatives. All were good people. All had little or no personal baggage. All could speak articulately. The decision would come down to which of the four candidates the delegate liked the best, or which of the four could best carry the conservative message, or which of the four was the most electable. The delegates were listening to a sitting Congressman who delivered the conservative message in a polished and smooth manner, and who had won a tough election only a year earlier. The question for the rest of us was how could we convince the delegates to reject Rod Grams and vote for one of us?

More specifically, how could I hope to beat Rod? This seventh district candidate forum was one of the last opportunities prior to the state convention to train my sights on the man. What I desperately wanted to do was set the competitive juices free. I wanted to grab Rod Grams by the rhetorical throat and throttle him out of the race. I wanted to wait until he gave one of his bumbling responses to an unanticipated question and say "You all heard that answer. Rod's a nice guy, and I like him personally, but don't you want to elect someone who can do more than read from a script, someone who can represent our state for years to come and make us proud?" Did I ever want to cut loose! Of course, I never said any such thing.

Maybe that sounds like bitterness. Maybe it is. I think the proper word is frustration. I would have taken a swipe at Rod Grams and succeeded only in clobbering myself. So, the candidates' forum came and went without any major developments, which at this stage of the campaign meant it was a failure for me.

After the candidates' forum, the hospitality suites were a complete waste of time. I could just as well have driven to the Twin Cities instead. The candidates and their workers, who outnumbered the delegates, wandered the motel hallway and visited the suites. We had little else to do. The delegates had apparently satisfied their political hunger for the evening at the forum.

★　★　★　★　★

Saturday morning Gail drove me from the motel to the Fargo/ Moorhead airport. She had decided I would arrive in the Twin Cities just as early flying on a commercial jet as on a single-prop private plane. At the airport gate, lame duck Senator Dave Durenberger was waiting for the same flight. The two of us cordially ignored each other.

In Minneapolis, I had the field to myself as I gripped and grinned with delegates as they arrived for the fifth congressional district convention; all of the other Senate candidates had stayed in Moorhead to start the day at the seventh. When the fifth district convention started, I stood in the back of the hall waiting to be introduced. A rustling of paper and flutter of air movement behind caught my attention. I turned to see one of my posters slipping from the wall to the floor. Oh, hell, I knew that meant a losing candidate. Now one of my posters was on the floor. Well, I told myself, believing in omens and signs was pretty silly anyway. At least I delivered the speech to a friendly, receptive audience.

Next stop was the fourth, my home congressional district, which was meeting at the technical college in St. Paul. After speaking, I took my seat as a delegate from my state house district 53A to hear the last speech or two and then to vote for myself in the Senate straw ballot. When the 20 or so ballots from 53A were counted, I got only half the votes. In part, that was my own fault: I had taken my friends and political neighbors for granted instead of working them. At the same time, I was completely aghast that my own state representative Phil Krinkie and people close to him had apparently voted for Gen Olson. Thanks for all your help working on my campaigns, Doug, and here's a return favor. As my dad used to say, you have to laugh to keep from crying. In the count of the overall vote in my home fourth district, I did well, but Rod Grams won there too. Another bad omen.

We finished in the Twin Cities at the sixth district, which was meeting at a hotel in Arden Hills only a mile from my home. Gail and her crew had done another fantastic job: when we rolled into the driveway, the parking lot and exterior entrances of the hotel were a sea of red, thick with McFarland signs. The convention hall was also bathed in red. We had crushed everyone else in the battle of signs. The delegates were excited. I got excited. The sixth seemed far more like home than the fourth. The speech thundered from my lips, by far my best delivery of the day. I received the reciprocal roar of the crowd, shook as many hands as I could reach, and raced for the door.

We sped the few miles to the Crystal airport where a small plane was waiting. The plane touched down in Moorhead a little after two in the afternoon.

I arrived at the hall to find the seventh district convention in a temporary recess. The delegates had already voted in the straw ballot and counting was in progress. That was a shock. The other Senate candidates had all spoken in the morning and left town; I was the only one the delegates had not heard. My people reminded convention chair Georgiann Stenerson time and again that I was on the way. She insisted on proceeding with the ballot anyway.

Why Stenerson before or then wouldn't give me the time of day was, and remains, a mystery. She might have been taking direction from a party power. Maybe she just plain didn't like me. In any event, I felt her sharp political elbows again and again.

Until the convention started up again, all I could do was prowl the rear area, accosting any delegate who might happen to wander within gripping and grinning range. I had to be careful not to step on my own posters, which littered the floor at the rear of the hall. Red omen after red sign altered my steps. Leon Oistad, Bert McKasy's campaign manager, and I chatted a bit just outside the rear door about law school. He had a sad grin on his face. We both knew what was coming.

Soon enough, Stenerson announced the results. Rod Grams won big. Bert McKasy and Gen Olson trailed. I ran a distant fourth. I was used to pulling knives out of my back but hadn't seen this shiv coming. Stenerson had committed to Grams, but I had expected minimal fair play.

While the fiasco was sinking into my head, Stenerson announced to the delegates that another candidate wanted to address them. She introduced me. Thoughts filled my head of screeching off on a diatribe about fair play in politics and politicians whose supporters engage in dirty tricks. I swallowed those words on my way to the stage, swallowed hard, and delivered my standard speech. Of course it was flat. To say my heart wasn't in it would be an understatement. I didn't care anymore.

The flight home passed in a blur of mental and physical exhaustion. Interstate highway 94 slipped slowly by below in the evening haze. I did think that I might as well enjoy the flight since I wouldn't likely be needing to fly in a private plane much longer.

* * * * *

A day or two later, Gail and I talked about the possibility of withdrawal from the race. I wanted to go down fighting. Yet we couldn't ignore reality. The prospects were bleak. We talked about whether to endorse anyone else should I withdraw. Even though it would have been the smart political move at that point, I couldn't bring myself to endorse Rod Grams. I didn't know Gen Olson well. That left Bert McKasy—and I did think Bert would be a good Senator. I authorized Gail to make an overture to his campaign manager Leon Oistad. The word came back that Bert would love to have my support.

At least I would finish out the string. Two congressional district conventions remained—one each on the following two Saturdays.

The next event was a dinner Friday evening before the second district convention. Drive 100 miles to New Ulm, meet and greet, work the crowd, eat a little, drive home. Same old, same old. No speeches. No candidates' forum. No hospitality suite!

Saturday morning, we drove back to New Ulm for the convention. Since this was the only convention for the day, every candidate for every conceivable office was there competing for hand-shaking rights with the delegates. The day's entertainment consisted of each of us listening to the others' speeches. I gave my speech somewhere in the middle; positioning didn't much matter this day.

The following Saturday in Rochester at the first district convention was a carbon copy. All the candidates were there again competing for attention, delivering their speeches, and listening to the other speeches with a show of interest. Just as a year earlier, by this last convention of the season, I was convinced that I could deliver the other candidates' speeches and other candidates could deliver mine. I suggested to Bert McKasy that we should swap speeches and guaranteed him the delegates wouldn't even notice. He didn't take me seriously. I made the same offer to Allen Quist. He didn't take me up on it either.

CHAPTER TWENTY-ONE

That's All, Folks

Gail Sutton called me at home the next day, on Sunday, and said we needed to meet to discuss withdrawing from the Senate race. We agreed to meet at the campaign office Monday afternoon after I taught my two classes for the day.

Gail and Bob Weinholzer were waiting at the office. Gail quickly sketched the facts of our situation. We had no money. I had been bombed in the straw ballots. Prospects were less than dim. The only feasible way of carrying on was another large contribution from my pocket.

"Gail," I said, "a month ago the two of you told me to put in another $6000, and I did. I thought that was supposed to carry us through to the state convention."

"No" she answered. "That got us through the congressional district conventions. It's gone. The state convention is a month from today. We'll have to spend a lot of money to get through the state convention, and we don't have it."

"How much money are we talking about for the state convention?" I asked.

Bob said "About $10,000."

I almost jumped from my chair. "$10,000? That can't be right. We must be able to do it for far less than that."

"No," Bob said, "not if you want to do it right."

"Well, who says we have to do it right? We've been getting by on a shoestring for months. Why can't we continue?"

Gail said "The delegates will see. We either need $10,000 or you should drop out now."

Bob added "We can call a press conference for tomorrow."

"Hold on a little here" I objected. "The state convention is a month from today. Why should I drop out? There's nothing happening between now and the convention that will cost money. Why can't we just keep going around to the free appearances, limp along to the convention, and wait for lightning to strike? You said before the convention might deadlock and turn to a compromise candidate. That might be me. But it's damn sure not going to be me if I'm not there."

"That's not going to happen" said Bob. "The straw ballots show that Grams is probably going to take it. Nearly a third of the delegates won't vote for you under any circumstances. Since your message is the same as the others, the delegates are not going to turn to you."

Bob didn't point out the obvious. My big gamble in endorsing Allen Quist for governor had not only lost but also blown me out of the race. Arne Carlson's 30 percent of the state convention delegates were gone for sure. I needed six out of seven of the Quist delegates for endorsement, but the fact that I had endorsed their man meant nothing to them.

The last time the three of us made a big decision for the campaign, Bob and Gail had implored me to endorse Quist. My own instincts had said no, and my instincts had been right. This time my instincts said keep fighting for another month; after running for over a year-and-a-half, why pull up with the finish line in sight? For 19 months of sweat and tears, I at least deserved to be nominated. I said "I still think we can limp into the convention and see what happens."

Gail responded "Doug, you don't want to limp into the convention.

You need money right now to send out a minimum of two mailings to delegates and alternates before the convention. At the convention, we need to have a hospitality suite—"

"Hah! We can dump that!"

"—a hospitality suite," Gail continued, "another piece of literature, and a video and big demonstration when you are nominated."

"We can get rid of that, too" I said. "Demonstrations are a waste of money."

"Maybe they are," she said, "but all the other candidates will have them. Grams will probably have indoor fireworks. That's $10,000 right there. You'll look like an idiot without a demonstration."

Bob added "Doug, you don't want to go into the state convention on the cheap and embarrass yourself. You need either to put in another $10,000 or withdraw."

"I'm not putting in another $10,000."

"Then you should withdraw now."

Over the years, I had watched political candidates withdraw from their races. Every time I wondered why they would campaign for months and then just plain give up. Why didn't they keep fighting? Now I knew. I had taken a beating financially, physically, and mentally. The money was gone—nearly $100,000 out of our family pocket. My back ached constantly. My upper right teeth throbbed on and off every day. My stomach was upset regularly. The mental strain of avoiding a gaffe, remembering names, making embarrassing fundraising calls, dealing with losses, forcing myself to wade into groups of strangers, fending off hostile questions, holding a smile, and maintaining Minnesota Nice was unrelenting.

All of this was the result of my attempt to pound the square peg of a private man into the round hole of public life. I didn't want to be a quitter, but I didn't want to be a brain-dead body kept alive on a ventilator. I was beaten and ready to let go. Gail and Bob were right. My instincts agreed this time. I had to withdraw.

On Tuesday, May 17, I held a press conference in the same room of the state office building where I had officially announced my candidacy eight months earlier. Again, Gail turned out family and friends to surround and support me.

My prepared statement may have been the best speech I wrote for the entire campaign. Running because my father had never pursued his life's dream. Running to bring a conservative message that had been picked up by other Republican candidates. Winning the off-year state convention straw ballot. Running out of money. Running out of physical and mental energy. Rich memories. Happiness in finishing with my name and integrity intact. Thankfulness to my family and supporters. Lifting of a weight. Feeling good about trying. The ability to wear bow ties again. The peroration was "During the glories and the gloom of the campaign, I always thought if God wants me to be a Senator, I will be a Senator; if not, I will not be a Senator. He has given the answer. I look forward to the next challenge."

I answered a few questions from the reporters. I endorsed Bert McKasy. There were no tears. I felt more relieved than saddened.

Nineteen months of all-out effort stopped in that half-hour. People who have never run for office—and probably also those few lucky ones who have run for office and never lost—have no conception of the utter sense of emptiness and aimlessness that follows election day, or in this case withdrawal day. Frenetic and demanding activity for months or years stops cold. After the unrelenting pressure of endless days of endless campaign events, the daily calendar is suddenly a void. The losing candidate has nothing to do. How to fill the hours of the day?

CHAPTER TWENTY-TWO

Hard Won Political Insights

The campaign reaffirmed some things and taught me many other things about politics and campaigning that I want to pass along. I can't help myself from adding this chapter. After all, I am a professor.

Politics is about people and money. Before the campaign started, I knew about the people component: activists, supporters, donors, volunteers, and voters. A politician who does not connect with the people goes nowhere. Today I remain amazed and humbled at the countless hours of volunteer work for the campaign by hundreds of people, and especially by a score of dedicated supporters. I don't delude myself into believing they volunteered just for me; they had their own motivations, including the friendship of political chains, hope for personal advancement in the party, and promotion of their political views and ideals. As the candidate, I almost became irrelevant. The campaign belonged to all of us.

While I had often heard before that money is the mother's milk of politics, I didn't entirely believe it. Now I know that grassroots efforts, volunteers,

249

and hard work can take a campaign only so far. A point arrives at which the candidate needs to reach out to large numbers of people beyond the range of personal contacts. In order to reach out, the campaign needs money; a statewide campaign needs a lot of money. In the end, the lack of money kills even highly successful grassroots efforts. Politics is perception. When lack of money makes people perceive a campaign is in trouble, it is. Napoleon Bonaparte said an army moves forward on its stomach. A political campaign moves forward on its purse.

Where is this money to be found? Traditional large donors to party candidates, and interest groups, will not contribute early in a contested race. They won't back the field. They want to back the winner. Telemarketing is iffy and expensive. That means a non-incumbent, even more so a newcomer, must rely on either personal money or money raised from family, friends, neighbors, and colleagues. Personal contacts must be made beyond the social world of the candidate. Forming a strong finance committee is just as important as putting together a kitchen cabinet.

Ironically, campaign finance reform laws are intended to lessen the influence of large donors on candidates, but the effect I saw is different. Today the individual contribution maximum to a federal candidate is $2800; when I ran, it was only $1000. We worked like dogs for a handful of $1000 checks. Even the max is a drop in the bucket in a statewide campaign. A couple of checks for $10,000, or more, might have made all the difference. The practical result of campaign finance reform law is not to take big money out of politics but rather to ensure that potential candidates who are not incumbents or personally wealthy need not apply.

Do I want to pass along political realities and nitty gritty campaign tactics? Yes, many.

- Get up close and personal when speaking to every audience; don't hide behind a rostrum, especially not on an elevated stage.
- Dress for success; think about appearance, clothing, gestures, voice, and even your name.
- Be prepared to make crucial decisions almost daily based on inadequate or wrong information.

- *Realize the driving directions to the next event are likely wrong; GPS may help or hinder.*
- *Know where the nearest restroom is.*
- *Don't travel alone with a member of the opposite sex.*
- *Work every room.*
- *Parades are hard to work; county fairs are harder.*
- *Don't be photographed with a glass in your hand; who knows what someone might think is in it.*
- *Respond to every rumor or attack immediately no matter how many times you have beaten it down.*
- *When the inevitable disaster happens, get back on the bike (the telephone, the meeting, the speech) as soon as possible and keep pedaling.*
- *Be prepared to have life as you know it stop the day after the election.*
- *Know a good campaign manager is a boon; just do what you are told.*

Someone thinking of running for office should be prepared to spend a lot of physical energy and even more mental and emotional energy. Many others told me this. I didn't fully believe this either. Now I do. No one except a candidate—and maybe the candidate's spouse—fully realizes this. Daily scrapping for a dollar or a vote here and there. Physical ailments. Absorbing disappointments. To this day, I avoid receptions and public gatherings and don't like to hear the telephone ring. The saying is all politics is local; I say all politics is retail.

Candidates always say they want to fight for something. A campaign is an opportunity to fight for a political philosophy, but fight is not the right verb. A candidate can compete only with an impenetrable veneer of pleasantry. On television and radio, commentators and journalists take nasty potshots at each other with great glee. None of these people are running for office. That's why they're free to let the competitive juices flow. Anyone whose primary goal is to advance political ideas should go into the media, not run for office.

Of course, a candidate does have the opportunity and the necessity to advance political ideas. These will be both on the issues of the day, for which the candidate has formed firm opinions, and on bizarre, oddball questions, for which the candidate hasn't the foggiest idea what the questioner is asking about.

As for the issues of the day, the candidate has to take firm positions and live with them. Flip-flopping is not an option morally. It's also not an option practically. Even though one-issue voters are the bane of the candidate's life, and they are found on various issues on all parts of the political spectrum, the candidate must answer directly even with the knowledge that a single wrong answer loses that vote. Waffling results inevitably in loss of that vote, loss of self-respect, and eventual loss of voters on both sides of the issue.

Many politicians try their best to get around this problem. When asked about a hot button issue, the candidate has three choices. Answer "right" and be thankful the position matches the voter. Answer "wrong" and lose that vote and many others. Or answer using something such as the triple-drop technique. "That's a tremendously complicated issue. You're absolutely right, we need to address it. It's especially important here in [fill in name of town]. You make me think of the school student here who asked me about helping our kids get a good education. Well, I'm in favor of kids, so my position on education is—." People bemoan crooked politicians and maintain they want honesty in their candidates. Candidates seldom give straight, honest answers because they're too dangerous.

As for answering totally unanticipated questions, the best advice is to admit ignorance on the subject and promise to study it, no matter how many times that answer must be repeated. Again, the saying is far better to be thought a fool than to open your mouth and remove all doubt.

Many candidates talk about trying to reach out to people of differing views to find common ground. I talked that way during the campaign. I really believed it. I don't believe it anymore. I haven't seen any evidence of common ground on the national or state scenes in the years since. I would like to be more optimistic about bringing the country, or even a political party, together, but I cannot.

In part, this is the natural result of politics melding diverse groups and interests: urban v. rural, consumer v. producer, liberal v. conservative. In Minnesota, for example, the Twin Cities tend to be strongly liberal; in greater Minnesota, even Democrats are fairly conservative. That's why over the years several notable Twin Cities political stars have fizzled quickly in statewide races. That also helps explain why—in my attempts to create a conservative base of support—I did well in greater Minnesota but couldn't gain much traction in the Twin Cities.

Some issues, such as taxes and spending, will always be with us. Others, such as term limits or health savings accounts, come and go. Some issues remain as powerful today as they have been for decades: both sides of the abortion issue are so afraid of the slippery slope that they still can't make the slightest concession to the other side.

In part also, we are getting exactly what we should expect from a political system that relies on party caucuses or early, small turnout primary elections. Those who care enough to show up are truer believers. They support candidates who match more closely their positions. Moderates stay home. Any candidate in this process is going to move in the direction of the political and financial support coming from the party activists or early voters. That direction is toward the ends of the political spectrum, not the middle.

That is what the party activists want. Maybe there are indeed hidden powers that be who want it too. The ideal officeholder, and so the ideal candidate, is a reliable voting machine. A Republican who cannot be counted on to achieve a 100 percent approval rating from conservatives or a Democrat who cannot be counted on to achieve a 100 percent approval rating from liberals is suspect. A moderate, a compromiser, a seeker of common ground, is not a desirable candidate. A popular incumbent can get away with acting the part of a maverick. A newcomer can get away with nothing.

Modern communication contributes. A candidate's positions on a wide range of issues become well known, and the candidate is locked into place. Any change of view, or even an attempt to compromise, on any issue is immediately known and thus is open to attack not only as flip-flopping but also as betrayal of the principles that elected the person to office. Television and radio talk shows, and internet blogs, always need fodder, the hotter the better, to fill airtime and empty pages, and what better fodder than political betrayal. Social media greatly exacerbates the divisions.

Accordingly, I don't see our political leaders finding much common ground over the foreseeable years to come. At the same time, I remain optimistic about the future of our country. Conservatives have survived liberal governments, and liberals have survived conservative governments, since 1789. Times and events have been far more severe than a failure to find common ground on certain issues of the day and a breakdown in civility. The next election is only a few years ahead.

EPILOGUE

A losing political candidate has a strong desire to reciprocate the rejection of the dumb voters. Upon losing re-election to Congress from Tennessee, Davy Crockett said "Since you have chosen to elect a man with a timber toe to succeed me, you may all go to hell and I will go to Texas." That response to the voters of the Volunteer State did not work out well for the King of the Wild Frontier when he left for the Alamo.

The sense of rejection was not as great when I dropped out of the Senate race for lack of money. While I did think a little of moving to the Big Sky of Montana or the warmer, more hospitable state of Texas, I have never left my adopted home state of Minnesota. Also, I didn't have much time to wallow.

Within the month after my withdrawal from the Senate race, Allen Quist asked me to run with him as his lieutenant governor candidate. The politically canny thing to do would have been to say no. Other elections were coming. A political appointment from a grateful party might be coming. When I said yes to Quist, all of that ended. The one thing I remember from the press conference announcing me as his running mate is a question to him from one of the female reporters that amounted to couldn't you have done any better? I had to laugh.

Why commit to joining a ticket that was perceived as hard right?

The main reason was I had campaigned constantly for 19 months with nothing to show for it. I was all dressed up with no place to go. Besides, Allan Quist was and is a good man. He did win the party nomination and he would have been a good governor. Trouble was that he scared the bejesus out of liberals, and there are a lot of liberals in Minnesota. Arne Carlson hammered him (and therefore me) in the party primary in large part because of a huge crossover of Democrats who voted in the Republican open primary. Actually, I didn't feel that bad about another loss. The pay for lieutenant governor was mighty low.

For several years, people often asked me whether I would run again for office. My answer was not likely. Why would I expect to be able to raise money next time? Sometimes, the questioner added that Abraham Lincoln lost several campaigns before he was elected President. I appreciated the thought, but never was sure whether the correct analogy for me would have been Lincoln, who eventually won through persistence, or Harold Stassen, who deteriorated into the butt of jokes by running time after time without success. Now, enough years have passed that no one asks anymore.

My campaign for the U. S. Senate was the experience of a lifetime, even though it didn't work out as hoped. I saw a real chance to win. I thought at least a political appointment would follow. I found out the telephone rings for a losing candidate even less often than for a prospective candidate. What I did receive was a life-changing experience. I have good friends, good memories, good feelings from doing my part to carry the flag for my party and my political philosophy, and satisfaction that I stepped forward and took a shot at the brass ring. An inexact analogy is going through basic training in the Army. Almost everyone says "I'm glad to have been through it but I never want to go through it again!" As for the campaign, I'll stop with the first half: I'm mighty glad I did it.

Our American system is incredibly open. A person who wants to follow a dream to run for public office can run. Political miracles do happen.

Miracles, being what they are, do not happen often. I knew the odds when I told my dying father I was running. Nearly a hundred people in Minnesota seriously and realistically considered running for the Senate seat. More than a dozen Republicans and Democrats—plus minor party candidates—pursued their dreams so far as to campaign for the seat. Two, Republican Rod Grams and Democrat Ann Wynia, gained the nominations of their parties to run in the general election. One, Rod Grams, won the election.

Six years later, Senator Grams ran for re-election and lost—in large part because he kept listening to bad political advice, such as refusing to meet with the *StarTribune* because of its liberal editorial policy. I'm not at all happy to say I told you so.

As more years have passed, some of the major figures in this story have also passed: Rod Grams, Bert McKasy, Bill Cooper. I'm sure others are also no longer with us. God rest all of their souls.

The story would be different today. Campaigning and raising many smaller contributions over the internet. LASIK surgery to ditch glasses and contacts. Cell phones for constant communication. More hostile political positions and less respectful debate. This story is set in its time. Yet, except for some details, I think it is every bit as useful and true today as then. Matthew 22:14 says "Many are called, but few are chosen."

APPENDIX

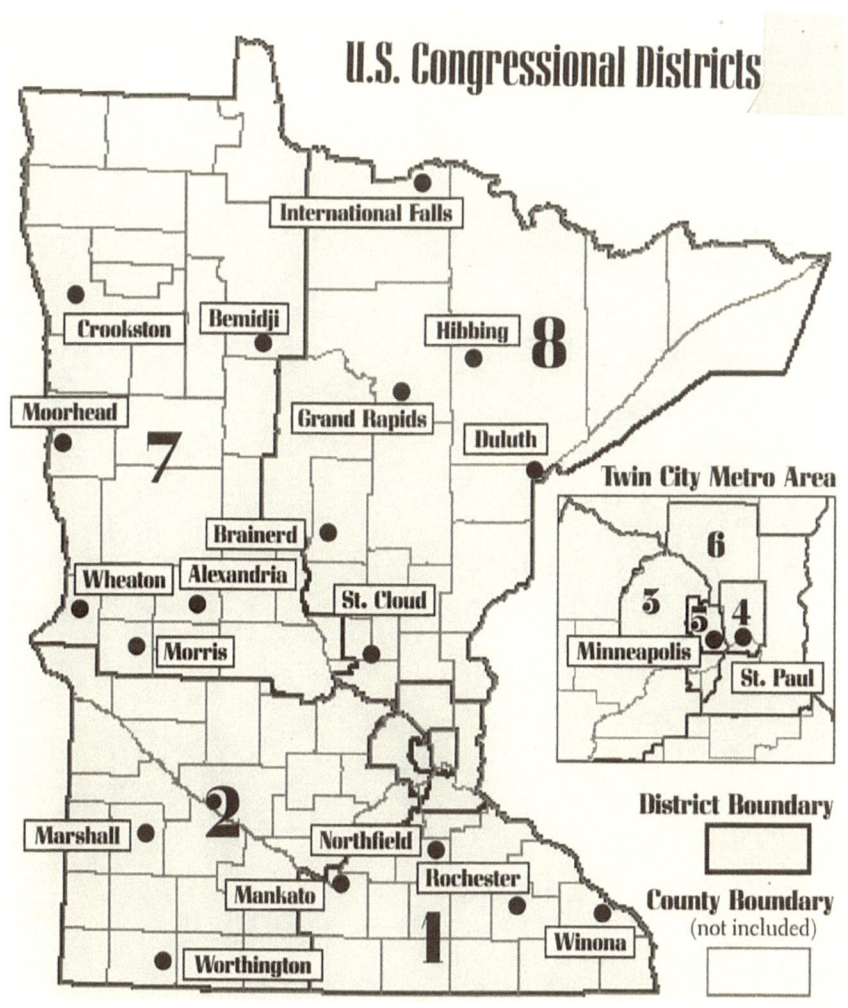

U.S. Congressional Districts

International Falls

Crookston • Bemidji •

Hibbing 8

Moorhead • Grand Rapids •

7 Duluth •

Twin City Metro Area

Brainerd •

Wheaton • Alexandria • 6

Morris • St. Cloud • 3 5 4

Minneapolis St. Paul

2

Marshall • Northfield •

Mankato Rochester

1 Winona

Worthington • District Boundary

County Boundary
(not included)

www.ingramcontent.com/pod-product-compliance
Lightning Source LLC
Chambersburg PA
CBHW030425290526
45786CB00001B/137